Keep Your Own Pony

Keep Your Own Pony

George Wheatley

Stanley Paul, London

Stanley Paul & Co. Ltd
3 Fitzroy Square, London W 1 P 6 JD

An imprint of the Hutchinson Publishing Group

London Melbourne Sydney Auckland
Wellington, Johannesburg and agencies
throughout the world

First published January 1962
Second impression November 1965
Third impression September 1966
Fourth impression October 1968
Fifth impression July 1970
Second edition October 1977

Printed in Great Britain by The Anchor Press Ltd
and bound by Wm Brendon & Son Ltd
both of Tiptree, Essex

ISBN 0 09 131271 X

To my parents

who first taught me to love horses when I
was very young. And to my beloved friends
Lassie, Pickles and Playboy, who, among
other horse friends, have assisted in their
way in the writing of this book.

Contents

Introduction

Because riding is becoming increasingly popular, this book has been written to help and encourage new recruits who are making their first acquaintance with a horse.

Today many people drive cars and understand their mechanism; yet how many know anything about a horse? Consequently, people tend to treat horses like cars – as something which, when not required, can be left out and attended to when convenient. So this book is written as much for the horse's sake as for its owner's. More suffer through ignorance, carelessness, thoughtlessness, or selfishness than through deliberate cruelty.

In keeping a horse certain fundamental principles must be observed: it must have regular daily attention at regular hours, not whenever the owner happens to think of it or it is convenient. A horse is easily kept happy and healthy if the basic rules are kept.

Because of this, owning and caring for a pony teaches youngsters self-reliance and a sense of responsibility, besides self-confidence and pluck. For these reasons it should be part of every child's education.

People may ask how they can possibly keep a pony under modern conditions, apart from the expense. Yet it is possible, even for those living in or near a town. Keeping a hardy, native British pony eliminates stabling, as it will live out quite happily throughout the year, under certain conditions. Keeping a pony does not cost as much as running a car. Most people seem able to find the money for their own particular hobby.

The joy of owning, looking after, and riding one's own pony can be fully understood only from actual experience. Also, there is no healthier pastime than riding; it provides fresh air and exercises muscles in every part of the body, including many not normally used. And, unlike many sports, there is no age-limit! One can ride at five or seventy-five! The writer started when he was two!

Those who only hire a horse miss all the fun and happiness derived from owning one. They never know their horse intimately and never experience that sense of companionship, or the pleasure of being welcomed by a friendly head over the fence and a soft nose nuzzling into their hand. A horse responds to kindness: once its confidence and affection have been won it is a lifelong, loyal friend. A horse puts up with many things and has to suffer fools gladly, so try to consider him. Also, his life is so uncertain. He is too often regarded as just a chattel, to be bought and sold with no say in the choice of home or master. A stabled horse must eat what he is given, and when, and put up uncomplainingly with his owner's moods! The wonder is that he remains so sweet-tempered, docile, and obedient. How many people would in similar circumstances?

A good horseman puts his horse before himself, even when it entails personal inconvenience or discomfort. Otherwise he should not own one!

Horses differ in mentality, temperament, character, conformation, and action. Therefore, handle and ride as many different ones as possible. Study their psychology and their varying characteristics and mannerisms. Each must be handled and ridden slightly differently, and only knowledge and experience will enable one to size up quickly and handle a strange horse.

The pleasures of owning a horse are endless, even if one only hacks. Riding enables one to see and know the country better than in almost any other way. By keeping one's eyes open and being quiet one sees many interesting things; wild creatures seem less shy of a horse. For more specialized riding there is dressage, from the most elementary to the most advanced Spanish High School or Haut École – a lifetime study in itself. There is the fun of preparing and entering for even a small horse-show or gymkhana. Or the fascination of jumping. There is the skill and craft of hunting, within the means of anyone prepared to 'do' his own horse.

Riding is also a discipline – for rider and horse. 'He who wishes to rule others must first learn to rule himself' applies especially to a horseman.

Before buying a pony do take lessons from a good instructor, who will prevent you acquiring many bad habits, and will make you a better, safer rider. If you buy a pony and then try to teach yourself you will inevitably make many mistakes. For your pony's sake have some really good lessons, including practical stablework under expert supervision, before you buy one.

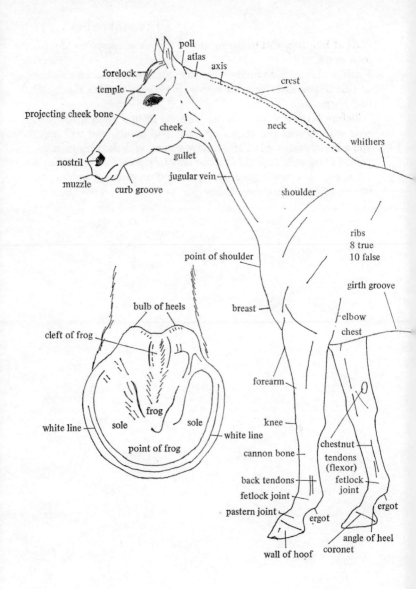

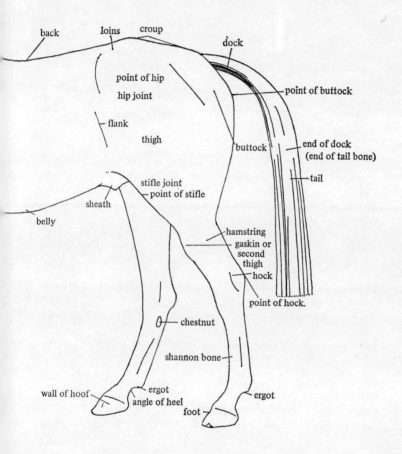

back
loins
croup
dock
point of hip
hip joint
point of buttock
flank
thigh
buttock
end of dock
(end of tail bone)
tail
stifle joint
point of stifle
sheath
belly
hamstring
gaskin or
second
thigh
hock
point of hock.
chestnut
shannon bone
wall of hoof
ergot
angle of heel
ergot
foot

1 History of the Horse

Origin

The origin of the horse dates back approximately fifty million years to the Lower Eocene period. The first prehistoric horse, known as *Hyracotherium*, was about the size of a fox terrier, with four toes on its front feet and three on its hind. Its forearm and shin each had two separate, complete bones.

Remains of the earliest prehistoric horse have been found both in Europe and the United States of America; it probably roamed in Asia even earlier.

The next type, in the Ogliocene period, was called *Mesohippus*. It was twice the size of the *Hyracotherium* and had tridactyl or three-toed feet. The ulna bone in the forearm, and the fibula in the shin were smaller.

The *Merychippus* species existed between thirty-five and fifteen million years ago in the Middle Miocene period, and was a still larger animal. The species living about fifteen million years ago was about two-and-a-half times bigger in width and height.

The *Pliohippus* lived in the next Lower Pliocene period; some species were about the height of a small pony (10–11 hands).

The first real horse, *Equus*, which had hooves instead of toes, followed next and was probably about 12 hands. It is not known exactly when *Equus* first appeared in Britain but it was almost certainly many thousands of years before man's first appearance on earth.

Some authorities believe that the modern horse migrated from

Asia in three streams: the first, westward to Europe; the second eastward to Mongolia and China. Horses from Mongolia and Tartary (China) differ greatly in appearance from those of Europe. They are small, wiry, and very hardy, averaging about 13·2 hands, and not more than about 14 hands, with coarser heads and thin tails. They can stand extreme cold and manage to exist on very little food. Climatic conditions have probably kept them small. The third migratory wave went to India, Persia, Egypt, North Africa, Asia Minor, and Greece, and from there to the northern shores of the Mediterranean. The hot-blooded Arabs, Barbs, and Thoroughbreds are descended from this third stream.

About eighty years ago bones of horses were found in a cave at Bruniquel, Tarn-et-Garonne, in France; similar collections of bones have more recently been found at La Solutré. In both cases they had been split, obviously to extract the marrow, showing that horses were eaten by prehistoric cavemen many centuries before they were first ridden or driven.

Native British ponies

The Shetland pony is believed to be the only British breed of prehistoric origin, though there is no clue as to when or how it arrived here.

Ponies of the third migration which eventually reached the British Isles developed into several individual types, with coats of different colours for camouflage according to the surrounding country in which they lived. Being a defenceless animal, the pony depends on its protective colouring, and its speed, for survival.

Scotland

Highland ponies : grey to match the snow on the hills.
Lowland : dun colour, to tone with the bracken on the lower hills and moors further south.

England

Dartmoor : brown or bay, to match the bleak moors.
Exmoor : very similar.

Fell and Dale: black to match the rocky country of the Lake District and the Pennines. Other colours, such as bay, are found as well.

New Forest: are no longer pure bred, as stallions of other breeds have been introduced into the herds from time to time. Many New Forest ponies today have Arab blood in them.

Modern history

Horses were not driven or ridden until about 4000 years ago, and probably were driven or used as pack animals before they were first ridden. They were both ridden and driven about 2500 years ago in Assyrian and Babylonian times, and a little later in Egypt. Xenophon (430–357 B C) wrote the first book on riding and horsemanship, containing rules and principles still used. Hittite clay tablets dating back to 1300 D C still exist which describe the care and treatment of horses used for war and racing chariots.

In our own history William the Conqueror introduced Spanish horses into England after the Norman Conquest. Horses were then so greatly prized that a law was passed prohibiting their use for ploughing in Wales. Oxen had to be used instead.

While men wore armour, large, heavy horses, strong enough to carry their weight, were needed. Clydesdale cart-horses are descended from these old war-horses. King John imported one hundred Flemish stallions which resembled the dray- and cart-horses of today. This was done to increase the size and weight-carrying abilities of the English horse.

Edward III imported more Spanish horses and forbade their export from England. Henry III continued this policy but allowed the export of mares over two years old.

Henry VIII tried to make the English horse larger and therefore passed a law that no horse under 15 hands should be allowed to live in 'Forests, chares, moors, or on waste land'. He disliked and despised small horses and ponies, calling them 'Little stand horses and nags of small stature', and decreed that all forests and land were to be driven and all horses and ponies killed which were unlikely to grow into 'serviceable animals or to produce them'. Fortunately, this law was not strictly enforced in all parts of

England, especially in the West Country, otherwise all the native breeds of ponies would have been exterminated.

Until Queen Elizabeth I's reign ladies rode pillion behind the rider on the horse's croup; women still ride like this today in Spain. Carriages became more generallly used in Elizabeth's reign and ladies began to ride alone, side-saddle, the Queen herself setting the example. She is usually depicted as riding a milk-white horse when reviewing her troops. Thus, pillion-riding went out of fashion.

After gunpowder came into use armour gradually ceased to give protection in war, so that mounted soldiers no longer required such large, heavy horses. A lighter, faster type of horse therefore was needed for riding; heavy horses were still used for drawing wagons and large carts. Both the Shire and Cleveland Bay trace their descent back to the old English war-horse, which in turn had descended from the chariot-horse of ancient Britain. This originally had been much smaller, but, as stated, had been interbred with foreign breeds to produce a large animal, strong enough to carry the combined weight of its own protective armour plus that of its rider.

The English Thoroughbred today traces back to the Arab blood which was imported when the lighter riding-horse became popular.

Three Arab stallions were imported in William III's reign, one being the Byerly Turk. The Darley Arabian, imported privately, was the second, the third being the Godolphin Arab, imported about twenty years later. The first English Thoroughbred was bred early in the eighteenth century.

Racing

Racing dates back some 3000 years and was practised by the Greeks. In 496 B C a race for mares was run in the Greek Games, while horses were raced even earlier in Greece. It was not started in Britain until many centuries later.

Undoubtedly the influence of racing improved the quality, speed, and endurance of horses in Britain. James I was very interested and imported the Markham Arab from Constantinople for 500 guineas. Compared with prices today this is not much, but it was a very large sum in those days. This stallion was unsuccessful, as it bred stock of very poor quality, thus giving Arab horses a bad reputation. Charles I continued trying to improve the English breed; Charles II imported more Eastern horses, chiefly Arabs and Barbs.

2 Points of a Horse

Conformation

People who have been brought up with horses develop an instinctive 'eye for a horse'. Those who have not had this advantage can cultivate it if they know the points of a horse and what constitutes the difference between a well-shaped and a badly formed animal. Good conformation is easier to recognize in a horse than a dog, as the good points are broadly the same for most breeds, especially the native British ponies; whereas each breed of dog has its own special features which fanciers require.

The salient points of a well-shaped horse are: a small, intelligent, rather lean-looking head, with eyes set well apart; a broad, soft muzzle and firm lower lip; well-shaped, rather small ears, carried alertly forward; a bold, rather large and prominent yet gentle eye. Also, it should have a graceful yet muscular neck, not too thick, with a well-laid-back shoulder (especially important for a riding-horse; a rather upright shoulder gives power and is not a disadvantage for a horse used in harness); elbow standing well out from the body; deep through the chest, broad when viewed from the front, giving plenty of heart and lung room. It should have a long forearm to the knee with good bone below it; short cannon bones with short, clean legs going straight down to the ground when viewed from the front; long pasterns, not too upright; wide-open feet of equal size, with a large, well-developed frog. The back should be short, broad and level from behind the withers, or rising very slightly to the loins; broad quarters with good thighs; well-sprung, rounded ribs; withers neither too high nor too low. There should be a good sweep from stifle to hock, which should be clean and well shaped; a broad, comfortable chest; all four legs going straight down to the ground whether viewed from in front or behind; tail well set on, high up and gaily carried. A line drawn from the point of the buttock to the ground should coincide with the back of the shannon bone, from the point of the hock to the fetlock.

Horsemen say that a good horse should have 'a head like a lady's maid's and a behind like a cook's'!

Points to avoid

Eyes too close together, indicating a poor field of vision; a pony with close-set eyes shies easily. A small pig-eye often indicates bad-temper. A wall-eye of bluish colour frequently means defective sight; also possibly a blind eye. A large, heavy head; a large fiddle head often denotes stupidity, obstinacy, and wilfulness; an abnormally large and long head is sometimes called a 'coffin-head'. A short, thick, heavy neck, though useful in a draught-horse, is bad for riding; a thick neck often means a puller, hard to control. A ewe-neck, curving the wrong way, causes a horse to 'poke its nose' and 'star-gaze', making it difficult to control and ride up to its bit; as it does not look where it is going it is apt to stumble. A 'cock-throttled' or 'swan-necked' horse, with a thin scrawny neck like a chicken's, is difficult to ride. A heavy, upright shoulder gives a jolting, uncomfortable action and ride, though useful for collar work in a draught-horse. Over at the knees: badly shaped knees. Upright, straight pasterns give a jerky, 'pottery' action. A narrow 'boxy' or 'mule' foot and shallow, brittle hoof. 'Down at heel', and heels too narrow. Leg too close to body at the elbow, affecting the horse's free action. Narrow chest and shallow girth, giving insufficient lung and heart room. 'Running up light behind' to the hindquarters; also called 'herring-gutted', 'like a greyhound', 'waspy', 'tucked up'. A large, pendulous belly, called 'cow belly', 'pot belly', or 'grass belly'. A long back from withers to croup is often weak and often found combined with shallow back ribs and weak loins. A hollow back has an exaggerated curve from withers to croup. A roach back: back and loin curve upwards. Goose-rumped: tail set on too low down. Small narrow quarters. Flat ribs and sides without much support for a saddle. High wither; low wither. Very high withers are generally too narrow and are liable to be rubbed by the saddle; the latter also slips too far back, necessitating the use of a breast plate. Low, thick withers, especially with a high croup, make the saddle slip too far forward, necessitating the use of a crupper, which is a strap passed from the saddle under the tail. Cannon (front legs) or shannon bones (back legs) too long. Spavin. Boggy, sickle, or cow-hocks.

Avoid a horse which shows the whites of its eyes, lays its ears back and carries its tail tucked between its legs! Look out for its heels!

Bad conformation may be due to accident, or injury caused by carelessness or bad horsemanship:

Broken knees: due to a fall. Curb, caused by sprained ligaments at the back of the hock. Splint: due to carrying too much weight, or to overwork when young; also a knock or jar; the splint bones alongside the cannon bones form a bony growth of lime deposit which helps to strengthen them; incurable but harmless when formed. Capped hock: probably due to a stabled horse lying down at night on a hard floor with insufficient bedding, or by getting cast. Capped elbow: due to the iron shoe on a hind foot pressing against the elbow of a foreleg when lying down. Girth galls: caused by friction of the girth; may be due to girthing up when the horse is wet and/or dirty; to girthing up too tightly, or to a hardened leather girth which has not been kept pliable; also by a horse just up from grass being in soft condition. Cracked heels: caused by wet or exposure; native British ponies accustomed to living out do not generally suffer from cracked heels.

Mouth

Most important from riding and health aspect. 'Hard' and malformed mouths both give a bad ride. A hard-mouthed pony nearly always pulls and disobeys; being insensitive it does not respond to the bit. Malformed teeth cause ill-health through digestive trouble.

Teeth

Structure

Adult horse: 40 or 42 teeth, depending on presence or absence of small 'wolf' teeth among the molars.

Adult mare: 36–38 teeth; no tushes (canine teeth).

Front teeth (incisors): used for tearing.

Back teeth (molars): grind food to pulp ready for swallowing, helped by saliva secretion which softens food, making it digestible.

Soft gums (bars of the mouth): separates both sets of teeth.

Dental arrangement

Horse: both jaws: 6 incisors, 3 each side. 2 canine teeth (tushes), 1 each side. 12 molars, 6 each side. Total: 20 in each jaw.

Mare: both jaws: the same but without tushes. Total: 18 (each jaw).

Structure

Fang: hollow root, embedded in jaw.

Fanghole: cavity in fang.

Neck: gum and tooth meet.

Crown: part visible above gum.

Table: biting surface.

Mark: blackened depression on table of incisors; gradually disappears as tooth wears, forming a guide to age.

Development: (a) temporary teeth: birth–2½ years

Birth–2 weeks: teeth rounded at gum surface: small triangle of gum between each tooth, 2 central teeth in each jaw.

4–8 weeks: 2 lateral teeth appear in each jaw.

8–10 months: 2 corner teeth appear (each jaw).

12 months: all temporary teeth present. Corner incisors only partly touching each other.

18 months: corner incisors level. Back molars appearing.

2 years: all milk teeth present and level.

Development: (b) permanent teeth: approximately 2½ years

Permanent central incisors start replacing milk teeth.

Rising 3 years: incisors, both jaws, sufficiently worn to meet at front edges in closed mouth.

3 years: permanent central incisors in full use.

3½ years: permanent lateral incisors appear.

4 years: central and lateral incisors now level; front edges in wear. Mark visible across table.

4½ years: permanent corner incisors replace temporary milk incisors.

4–5 years: horse grows tushes (canines).

5 years: all teeth present. Having shed last milk teeth, colt becomes a horse, and filly a mare. Corner incisors only wear at front edge. Teeth look neat, fitting compactly. Called a 'full mouth'.

6 years: all teeth in wear and fully grown. Upper corner incisors longer than lower at the back. Marks in central incisors less.

Rising 7: as central incisors wear down, tables start assuming fang's triangular shape. Marks on central incisors now oblong; beginning to look worn.

7 years: upper jaw's corner incisor becomes notched where it overhangs the lower jaw's corner incisor. Lateral incisors' marks start disappearing through wear.

Rising 8: central incisor's fanghole appears as a line in front of the mark. Corner incisors' marks start disappearing.

8 to 8 off: all incisors becoming triangular-shaped. From 8 onwards horse is called 'aged'; does not mean old or senile.

9 years: all teeth lengthening, gradually becoming less upright; project outwards. Jaws come closer together. From 9 onwards accurate determination of age becomes increasingly difficult.

Estimating age

Thoroughbred: reckoned from 1 January, regardless of month when born. All other horses and ponies reckoned from 1 May. 'Rising' – approaching. 'Off' – over; e.g. '5 off' – 5 years old, but not yet rising 6. 2-year-old incisors can be confused with 5-year-old unless different appearance between milk and permanent teeth is known. 3½ years is a difficult age: front gum starts receding, becoming much inflamed. Horse cannot graze properly; should be stable-fed on soft food. Temperament becomes uncertain, needing extra careful, understanding handling; becomes capricious and wayward, and suffers exactly like a teething baby!

Lower incisors' appearance shows a horse's age: (a) size and shape of mark; (b) shape of teeth; (c) length; (d) angle of teeth sloping outwards from jaw.

(a) *Size and shape of mark: 4 years:* mark fills the table. Disappears from central incisors at about 13 years. *9 years:* mark vanishes from corner incisors, about a year after disappearing from lateral incisors.

(b) *Shape of teeth:* young horse's permanent teeth are curved. At 8 curve starts altering: at about 12 it becomes triangular; increasingly pronounced until 15.

(c) *Length:* increases with age.

(d) *Angle:* from 9 years teeth slope increasingly outwards. Mouth looks more irregular and untidy.

Galvayne's mark

Famous veterinary surgeon Sydney Galvayne first noticed it; discovered how to estimate age from 10 to 20 years. At 10 a yellowish-brown groove appears on outside of upper corner incisor. Takes 11 years to reach the bottom. From 21 onwards top of corner incisor gradually becomes rounded; top of Galvayne mark becomes obliterated. Rounding continues downwards; at 30 years tooth is rounded half-way down; upper half of groove disappears, only extending down lower half.

Faking

Widely practised in the past: an old horse's mouth made to look younger, and vice-versa.

Bishoping

Crowns of corner incisors dug out and plugged with black composition, imitating the marks; thus an old horse could be sold as a 7-year-old. Named after a horse-coper who brought it to a fine art. A very old horse's long teeth were shortened, rasped and plugged; the slope, however, could not be altered.

Malformations

Undershot : lower teeth protruding beyond upper.
Parrot-mouthed : upper teeth protrude beyond lower.
Both prevent proper grazing and digestion.

Wolf-teeth

Grow in the bars before first pair of molars: between 3–6 months.
Increasing size causes pain from the bit; often cause bolting,
boring, jibbing, rearing, swerving, and head-tossing. May cause
refusal to be bridled. Sometimes permanent; usually shed between 6–8 years old. Generally small and sharp; sometimes
flattened and compressed, pointed and uneven, or round. If very
small may remain beneath gum surface.

3 Height, Colour, Markings, Sex

Measuring

A horse or pony is measured from the withers down to the ground. Height is reckoned in hands: 1 hand = 4 inches (10·2 cm); e.g. 12·2 hands = 12 hands 2 inches (50 inches – 1·27 m), probably originating from the average span of a man's hand across its palm at the widest part. A Shetland pony is always measured in inches, owing to its small size.

For show classes, half an inch either way is allowed for the difference between the wear of shoes; these can make a considerable difference whether a pony has been measured with or without them. A horse or pony can be officially measured and a life certificate of height obtained.

Show classes

Arranged according to height: 12·2 and under; 13·2, 14·2, 15·2, or over. 12·2 to 14·2 are usually children's ponies or juvenile classes. Cobs, Galloways describe horses not over 15·2 hands.

Measuring stick

A special stick is used for measuring horses. It is usually marked in hands and inches up to 18 hands, sliding up and down a hollow walking-stick. At the top a metal arm containing a spirit-level goes at right angles to the ground across the withers.

Colours

All colours and shades are found, generally classified as Bay,

Black, Brown, Chestnut (dark or bright), Cream, Dun, Grey (Flea-bitten, Iron, Dapple), Roan, Sorrel.

Bay: can vary from very dark rich mahogany, merging into brown, to light, golden or yellowish colour which is almost dun. Bright, blood bay is the colour of polished mahogany.

If in doubt whether the colour is bay or brown, look at the colour of the fine hair on the muzzle. Distinguish between bay or dun the same way.

A horse can be the same colour all over or may darken to black on the mane, tail, and feet. A bay with black mane, tail, and feet is described as a bay with black points: it is generally considered to be hardy, with a good disposition, and so a good worker. It often has white markings on its face and legs, though usually not so much as a chestnut.

Brown: can vary from almost bay to nearly black. The muzzle determines the colour in any doubtful cases. Like a bay, a brown is favoured which shades into black towards the legs and feet. Some white markings are permissible, especially on the face, and sometimes on the legs.

Black: can be very handsome and attractive, but is not so generally favoured as bay or brown. Blacks are often considered unreliable in temperament. People may be prejudiced against black horses because they were always used for funerals. Thoroughbreds and Arabs are quite often black; this colour is very common in Belgium. There can be white markings on the face and legs.

Chestnut: may vary from dark liver chestnut to a light, washy, indeterminate colour, which should be avoided. Plain chestnut without any markings is unusual, except in the Suffolk Punch cart-horse. White markings on face and legs may become exaggerated. Mane, tail, or points may be black.

A chestnut, especially a bright chestnut, is generally believed to be fiery, headstrong, and excitable, especially when considerably marked with white, just as a red-haired person is often quick-tempered.

Dun: can vary from golden dun to a rather undistinguished mouse-colour. There may be pronounced zebra markings, uncommon in England but often found in India. It is usually con-

sidered hardy and a good worker, especially if it has black points.
Cream : is uncommon and usually has a silvery mane and tail. Can
be very attractive, though not much favoured for ordinary riding.
Grey : may be almost black when young. It lightens with age until
an old horse may become almost white.
Dappled grey : circles of black hair all over the body, particularly
the hindquarters (like a child's rocking-horse).
Iron grey : has a considerable distribution of black hair all over
the body, without any definite marking.
Flea-bitten : black specks of hair give the appearance its descrip-
tive name. Points may be black or white; other markings on the
face. Mane and tail may be almost white.

A grey is handsome, but is generally reputed to be rather
uncertain in temperament, and high-spirited.
Strawberry roan : has a mixture of red, white, and yellow hairs
all over its body.
Blue roan : has a similar mixture of black, white, and yellow hair;
less common than the strawberry roan.
Sorrel : rather similar to the roan, but with a mixture of black and
reddish hairs.

Washy colours

Pale, indeterminate, washed-out colours should be avoided as
they often seem rather nondescript and lacking in character.

Markings

Piebald and skewbald

Horses with large, irregular-shaped patches of any size all over
their bodies.
Piebald : black and white patches.
Skewbald : white and bay, chestnut or brown patches.

Some colours not being favoured may be prejudice more than
actual fact that colour and temperament are closely related. Similarly, a white foot and hoof are considered less hardy than a black.

Odd-coloured

Similar to piebald and skewbald, but the patches have more than two colours. Only circuses, requiring something striking, usually favour them; they are generally considered too conspicuous for ordinary hacking.

Head markings

Star: a more or less round white mark in the centre of the forehead; can be large or small.

Stripe: a narrow white marking down the face, not necessarily in the centre. It may or may not be joined to a star. There may be a stripe without any star; can be described as broad, narrow, irregular, or short, according to shape and size.

Blaze: wider than a stripe, covering nearly all the forehead between the eyes. It may extend up into the position of a star, and down the front of the face covering nearly its whole width.

Snip: a white mark either central between the nostrils, or running into either the left or right nostril. It may be a continuation of either a stripe or blaze.

Upperlip, underlip: white markings at the edges of either lip.

White muzzle: white, covering both lips; extends to the nostrils.

Body markings

Zebra marks: stripes on withers, neck, quarters, or limbs. Fairly common on donkeys and mules but not on horses.

List, ray: dark lines on the backs of donkeys, many mules, and a few horses.

Leg markings

White feet: a light hoof, usually pinkish-yellow rather than white; also applies underneath to the sole of the foot.

White heels: white hair at the heel of an otherwise coloured leg.

White pastern: pastern joint is white.

White fetlock: white hoof (or hooves) and leg or legs as far as the top of the fetlock.

White sock: white hoof and leg up to the top of the pastern.

White stocking: white up to the top of the fetlock.

White leg: white from the hoof up to the knee joint or further.

Ermine markings: small black markings at the coronet, on an otherwise white foot.

Whole coloured

Horses without any dark or light markings are uncommon; e.g. the Suffolk Punch, black Belgian, dun, Indian Kathiarwar, and Yorkshire Cleveland Bay.

Although washy colours, mealy legs, and certain colours should be avoided, the old saying that 'a good horse is never a bad colour' can be taken in two ways: if it is a good animal its colour does not matter; or, a good horse cannot be found which has a bad colour.

Sex

Horse : used loosely in general conversation to describe the whole species without any reference to sex. Correctly used, it means a stallion, or entire.

Gelding : a male which has been 'cut', i.e. had its reproductive organs removed.

Colt : a young stallion up to 3 years old (as applied to racehorses). Used loosely for any young, usually unbroken, male.

Filly : a young female up to 3 years old (as applied to racehorses).

Foal : applied to male or female under a year old.

To describe accurately, use the terms colt foal, filly foal, yearling colt, yearling filly.

Mare : a female horse or pony over 3 years old.

Rig : a male whose reproductive organs have been imperfectly removed.

Stallion : an entire male horse.

4 How a Pony Moves

Structure of horse

To understand the correct seat and the proper application of the aids, one must know the structure of a pony and how it moves.

Examination of a horse's skeleton shows that it is strongest in front just below the withers, where it has the greatest depth of ribs. The largest ribs are in front; they gradually become smaller and taper off towards the hindquarters, ending just in front of the loins. The loins are therefore a horse's weakest part so far as carrying weight is concerned.

The rider's weight should therefore be as far forward as possible, though not so far as to impede free movement of the shoulder-blade. The shoulder-blade bone is free and unattached to the rest of the skeleton except for ligaments and muscles.

The rider's weight also should come well forward because the large muscles lie along the top of the ribs, just below the spinal-column vertebrae.

If the saddle is too far back, or the rider sits too far back, on the cantle, his weight is thrown on to the weakest part of the horse's back, near the loins, where it is unsupported. Hence the modern forward seat, so that the rider leans forward when galloping or jumping, putting his weight forward on to the strongest part of the horse's back. A jockey's racing seat throws no weight at all on the horse's back, leaving its hindquarters completely free; all his weight is taken on his knees and ankles. In the old-fashioned seat the rider leant backward as his horse landed, when jumping, thus throwing all his weight on the weakest part at the worst possible moment, when his horse was trying to collect and balance itself as it landed. Leaning back also encouraged the rider to hang on by the reins and pull on his horse's mouth, thus preventing free movement of its head and neck, just when it was essential for them to be stretched forward freely, as a horse balances itself by its neck movement.

Impulsion

The horse's skeleton also shows that its hindquarters provide all energy and impulsion. That is why it should have broad, powerful hindquarters – 'a behind like a cook's'! A rider creates energy and obtains impulsion (forward movement) from the hindquarters by his leg aids. He rides the hindquarters, using seat and back muscles to supply the power and drive to make his horse bring its haunches and hocks well under it, and to use its hindquarters properly with plenty of energy.

A horse can be compared to a motor car with its engine at the back, pushing it forward; usually it is in the front pulling it forwards. Some car designers have seen the natural advantage of the rear engine.

How a pony turns

Most beginners mistakenly try to turn a pony by using their reins to pull its head and neck round. They think that if its head is pulled round where they want to go, then its body will follow. This is a natural mistake, because one turns a bicycle or car in this way; by turning the front wheel(s), the rear wheel(s) follow in their tracks.

A horse actually turns on its centre by pushing its hindquarters round, when its forehead (head, neck, and shoulders) follow. A horse's head and neck can be twisted round while the shoulders and the rest of it continue moving forward in a straight line. This is the basis of advanced work on two tracks, i.e. shoulder-in, shoulder-out, etc., in dressage work.

To turn a horse, a rider must push its hindquarters round with his leg aids while keeping its head, neck, body, and hindquarters in a straight line; e.g. turn on the forehand, or on the haunches. A horse should always move forward with its head, neck, body, and hindquarters in a straight line, turning or doing any move-

B

ment on a single track. It should only be bent and move diagonally when working on two tracks in advanced riding. Hence the meaning of the saying that a horse is a 'straight mover'.

Application to riding

This must be understood and applied practically; it is the foundation of all riding and of schooling a young horse. The latter can quickly be ruined if these principles are not understood and applied correctly from the beginning when first schooling on the lunge-rein.

To summarize: hands control the forehead through reins and bit and regulate pace. Hindquarters provide energy and impulsion, controlled and energized by the back, seat, and leg aids.

5 Native British Breeds

Nine different breeds (ten, if Highland and Lowland are counted separately) live in the British Isles, roaming wild since time immemorial. All are hardy, living out throughout the year, doing better out than stabled. The smaller breeds make excellent children's ponies; the larger can all carry an adult, making ideal family ponies. The Dale, resembling a miniature cart-horse, is better for driving, making an excellent harness pony. Welsh Mountain, Fell, Connemara and Dartmoor and some of the world's prettiest ponies, competing successfully in the show-ring.

Until recently the various breeds were becoming rather mixed, their individual characteristics being threatened, especially the New Forest. Now societies keep each breed's strain pure; ponies of each breed are registered by their respective society.

Shetland pony

The smallest of all native ponies; the hardiest and strongest for its size. Its small stature makes it the only pony measured in inches, instead of hands. Height: up to 42 inches; smallest recorded, 21 inches.

All native breeds living out wild in winter lead a hard life, the Shetland more than any. It often exists on seaweed when the scanty grass is buried under snow.

Though small, it is not an ideal first pony and pet for very young children, being wilful if not properly broken and schooled. It is, however, lovable, friendly, and amusing, and about the only type of pony suitable for keeping solely as a pet.

Though delightful to drive, it is not good for riding, especially

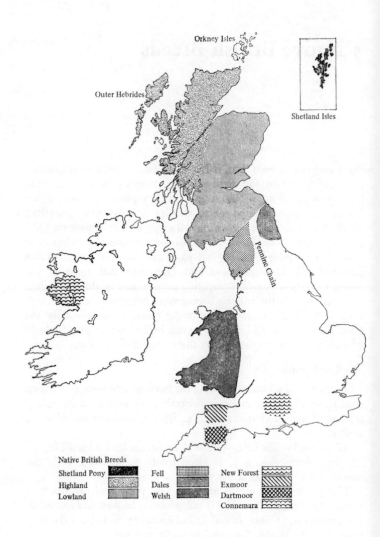

Orkney Isles

Outer Hebrides

Shetland Isles

Pennine Chain

Native British Breeds

Shetland Pony   Fell   New Forest
Highland   Dales   Exmoor
Lowland   Welsh   Dartmoor
                             Connemara

for very small children, being too wide; it is too heavy and its head and neck are insufficiently supple.

Shetland islanders use it for carrying pannier baskets of sea-weed. The USA imports many for showing in harness; the Dutch use them to draw small carts and show them.

Characteristics: heavy, rather shaggy mane; thick tail. In winter a long-haired outer coat keeps the thick woolly undercoat dry. In summer they shed both, growing one of much finer hair. Their small size and great strength used to make them in great demand as pit-ponies. They live long, many reaching forty years.

Colour: any colour, including piebald and skewbald.

Society: The Shetland Pony Stud Book Society. D. M. Patterson, 8 Whinfield Road, Montrose, Tayside.

Highland

One of the heaviest and strongest British ponies. Three types:

Mainland (Mull): massive, honest, docile. 14·2 hands. Very strong; useful for almost any farm-work. In the Highlands they carry a 20-stone deer for the deerstalkers.

Scottish Riding pony: about 13·2 hands. Not particularly fast but can go all day. Too heavily built to jump well, so it is not a good hunter.

The smallest: from Barra and the many small Hebridean islands. 12·2 to 13·2 hands – the original Highland ponies; the Mull and Garron are later types, developed by cross-breeding under the better conditions on the mainland.

All are very strong, hardy, sure-footed, and sweet-tempered. Some Arab blood gives them beautiful heads, with large, wide-set eyes. Dish-faced; strong, rather short neck. Those dun-coloured have a distinct dark eel-stripe right down their backs; dark markings below the knee.

Origin: probably Iceland and other countries inside the Arctic Circle. May have originated in Northern Asia during the Ice Age. Louis XII of France gave James IV some French horses to increase their size in 1535.

Colours: dun and cream preferred. Can be black or brown without white markings; fox, with silver mane and tail. Its size and gentleness make it an ideal child's pony, especially the small Barra; the Garron is a good adult's pony.

Society: The Highland Pony Society. J. McIldowie, Dunblane, Central.

Fell

Lives in the Lake District (Cumbria), west of the Pennine Chain.

The Dale, living east of the Pennines, is closely related; originally one breed.

Characteristics: hair ('feathers') on heels; long, thick, curly mane and tail.

Height: 13·2–14 hands. Lighter-built than the Dale; very safe and sure-footed. Has a long, swinging, easy walk and trot. Goes well in harness; a good adult's riding-pony. Has a sweet, gentle disposition.

Colour: black, dark brown, bay, grey, or dun; any except chestnut. Bay usually has black mane, tail, and points. Has a lovely, silky summer coat.

Society: The Fell Pony Society. Miss P. Crossland, 'Packway', Windermere, Cumbria.

Dales

From Northumberland and Durham; Upper Dales of Tyne, Allen, Wear, and Tees.

Bred to carry weight; large, heavier-built, and stronger than the Fell.

Height: up to 14·2 hands.

Type: like a small cart-horse, having probably some Clydesdale blood. Useful in harness for ploughing, harrowing, etc. Too thick-set and heavy for riding. Walks freely; trots well with rather high action; formerly competed in trotting matches. During the nineteenth century Dales carried lead from Northumberland and Durham mines to the docks, about 16 stone, in panniers slung each side, travelling about 240 miles a week. The tracks used still exist.

Characteristics: 'Feathers' at fetlocks down to the heels (cf. Fell).

Colours: jet black; long curling mane and tail; bay, brown, sometimes grey.

Appearance: neat, pony-like head; small, neat ears; well-shaped jaw and throat; short, rather thick-set neck; upright shoulders; short back, loins, and hindquarters; well-sprung ribs. Tail set on rather lower than the Fell's. Short, sturdy legs; good bone. Very hardy and docile.

Society: The Dales Pony Society. G. H. Hudgson, Ivy House Farm, Yarm-on-Tees, Cleveland.

Welsh Cob

Originally descended from the Welsh Mountain: now completely different in height and build.

Height: 14–15·1 hands.

Appearance: big-bodied; short, strong legs; small head; small, alertly carried ears; arched neck. Broad, powerful quarters; tail set on high, gaily carried. Shoulders well laid back; short back. Makes a good adult's pony; a good hunter, being a bold, natural jumper. Hard feet; fetlocks have a little silky hair.

Used in various countries to breed trotting ponies and in Britain to develop the Hackney horse and pony. Many years ago was interbred with the Fell to develop the latter's trotting action. Useful for harness, farm-work, or riding. Its strength and docility also made it useful for haulage at Welsh coal-mine pit-heads.

Colours: bay, brown, black, grey, roan, chestnut, dun, cream; no piebalds, skewbalds, or nondescript colours.

Welsh Mountain

Height: about 12·2 hands. Strong; tough; good in harness.

Appearance: concave or 'dished', Arab-like profile. Beautiful head; large, deep-set eyes; small, alert ears; broad quarters; tail carried high. Often crossed with an Arab, which it resembles. Docile temperament; a good ride and outstanding child's pony.

Colour: any except piebald or skewbald.

Society: The Welsh Pony and Cob Society. T. E. Roberts, 32 North Parade, Aberystwyth, Dyfed.

New Forest

Since Canute's reign, or earlier, ponies have inhabited the 60000 acres of the New Forest, north of Southampton, in

Hampshire. Used to be called a wild horse, differing considerably in type. Arabs and Thoroughbreds were introduced at different times to improve the breed. Type is now well established.

Height: 12–14·2 hands. Makes an excellent riding-pony. Being used to motorists it is traffic-proof. Friendly, docile, and sociable. Suitable for adults or children; goes well in harness.

Colour: any colour, usually bay or brown.

Appearance: a rather large head; fairly short neck; good shoulders; good, deep girth, giving ample heart room; drooping, rather narrow quarters. Many, broken and unbroken, are sold annually at Beaulieu Road.

Society: The New Forest Pony and Cattle Breeding Society. Miss D. Macnair, Beacon Corner, Burley, Ringwood, Hants.

Exmoor

Characteristics: mealy nose; mealy rimmed eyes; similar colouring between legs and underneath body. Winter coat usually harsh; springy, almost nylon-like bristles. Beautiful, soft, shining summer coat.

Height: stallions: to 12·3 hands. Mares: to 12·2 hands. Though small, are exceptionally strong; can carry abnormally heavy burdens. Farmers hunt them with the Devon and Somerset Staghounds.

Not easy to handle, but can be broken in, given time and patience. Difficult to keep fenced-in; will escape from almost any enclosure if they want to.

Appearance: small head, nostrils, ears. No feathering on fetlocks.

Colours: all bay, brown, or dun; no white hairs; no black or grey.

Society: The Exmoor Pony Society. Mrs J. Watts, Quarry Cottage, Sampford Brett, Williton, Somerset.

Dartmoor

Has inhabited the moors from time immemorial; very hardy, having to scratch through snow for food and battle against gales.

Appearance: a very pretty pony. Beautiful head; small ears, good shoulders; full, well-set-on tail. An equally good harness or child's riding-pony. Small, very active, honest, and very strong for its size; once much used in mines and as a pack-pony.

Height : not over 12·2 hh. for a stallion, 12 hh. for a mare.

Colours : any except piebald and skewbald. Bay, black, or brown most favoured.

Society : The Dartmoor Pony Society. D. W. J. O'Brien, Chelwood Farm, Nutley, Uckfield, East Sussex.

Connemara

Ireland's mild, moist climate and rich limestone soil are noted for horse-breeding. Native breed: Connemara (West Coast). Galway traders and breeders introduced Arab blood.

One of the best adult's native riding-ponies; hardy, good-looking, and very tough.

Height : 13–14 hands. Useful general-purpose pony.

Colours : bay, black, brown, dun, grey (the most popular). Chestnut or roan are rare.

Society : The Connemara Pony Breeders' Society. J. Killeen, 4 Nuns' Island, Galway, Eire.

One is well advised to buy a native pony, the breed depending on the work for which it is required (child, adult, general utility). But, many good ponies of no special breed, best described as nondescript, will give good, faithful service. Pure-bred, registered ponies will cost more than one of no particular breed.

6 Other Breeds of Horse

Besides native British breeds of pony, other breeds and types of horse exist, as distinct from ponies, suitable for riding, e.g. the pure-bred Arab, Anglo-Arab, Cleveland Bay, and English Thoroughbred.

Arab

Originated in the Arabian deserts; was first introduced into Britain in William III's reign (see page 18) and since then crossed with the native breeds, being the English Thoroughbred's ancestor.

It is noted for its intelligence, speed, endurance, and docility, largely due to its native environment, as the Arabs treated their horses as one of their family; good treatment of their horses is part of their religion.

Size : between 13·2–14·2 hands up to 15 hands; it is always called a horse, never a pony. It is noted for its grace, being one of the most beautiful breeds in the world.

Appearance : distinguished by its small head and ears on a graceful neck; has a 'dished' (concave) profile tapering to a small muzzle, large eyes and nostrils, and a fine mane. Legs are delicately formed; its tail is graceful, silky, and gaily carried. It is noted for its graceful carriage and movement.

Colour : bay, chestnut, grey, and white are most usual; brown is often found; black is rare. Head and/or legs may have white markings.

Society : The Arab Horse Society. Lt.-Col. J. Denney, Sackville Lodge, Lye Green, Crowborough, Sussex.

Anglo-Arab

Originally a cross, it is now so thoroughly established that it can be recognized as two definite and distinct French and English breeds. It is a cross between an Arab and a Thoroughbred, with no other mixed blood. Usually breeding is by Arab stallion out of a Thoroughbred mare, though sometimes it is a Thoroughbred stallion and an Arab mare.

It makes a good hunter and show-ring hack.

Appearance : it derives its points from both parent breeds.

Colour : bay, chestnut, or grey are most usual. The head may have white markings such as a star or blaze, though rarely a white face; legs may have a white stocking or sock.

Society : The Arab Horse Society. (Address at foot of p. 42.)

Both Arab and Anglo-Arab are registered in the Arab Horse Society's Stud Books.

Cleveland Bay

A large, powerful type of horse between 15·3–16 hands, originating from the fifteenth-century War- (or Great) Horse; when no longer used for that purpose it was long regarded as a general-purpose horse for drawing stage coaches, carriages, and vans for farms, and under saddle. It was developed by interbreeding with Arabs and Thoroughbreds. It is now favoured for breeding hunters and hacks.

Appearance : height: 15·3–16 hands; short legs, wide, deep, rather short body with strong, muscular loins. Quarters are strong and powerful, running level from the back. A large head, carried well on a rather long, thin neck. Tail is gaily carried standing well out from the body. Strong, muscular legs, with not less than nine inches of bone below the knee. There should be no superfluous hair and the pasterns are sloping.

Colour : bay to bay-brown. Only markings favoured are a small white star, and a few grey hairs on heels and coronet.

Society : The Cleveland Bay Horse Society. J. F. Stephenson, York Live Stock Centre, Murton, Yorks.

English Thoroughbred

The word 'Thoroughbred' originated from the Arabic *Kehilan*, being a literal translation, the English Thoroughbred having descended from the Arab. Mainly used today for racing, it is most carefully bred for speed from parents proved to possess that quality. A young stallion Thoroughbred is raced until he is rising four years, and if successful is then put to stud. As stated (page 18) the English Thoroughbred is descended from three Arab stallions, the Byerly Turk, Darley Arabian and Godolphin Arabian. Both English and Arab mares were used for breeding. As time passed, increasingly less Arab blood was used; as racing became more popular the Thoroughbred was increasingly bred for more speed until today it is much faster than the pure Arab. Today a Thoroughbred unsuccessful at racing has comparatively little value, unless it has some particularly sought-after blood and is sold as a hack or hunter. Some have become show-jumpers after re-schooling; others, if not too big, have become polo-ponies. Unsuccessful stallions are gelded. Some mares are put to Arab stallions to breed Anglo-Arabs for hacks, as Anglo-Arabs are much more reliable and docile than Thoroughbreds.

Unlike a native pony, a Thoroughbred is not hardy. Being thin-skinned, it usually cannot winter out but must be stabled and rugged-up. It is also liable to become unsound in wind and/or limb.

Appearance: having a large proportion of Arab blood it has some of the best characteristics of Arab conformation; e.g. the small well-shaped head and ears, well set on to a graceful arched neck. Withers are fairly high with a very sloping shoulder, giving it a superb action for riding. Ribs are deep and well sprung, giving ample heart room; the back is short with a high croup. Legs are hard, clean, and well shaped, with plenty of bone and good strong tendons. Tail is well set on, high up, and well carried.

Height: usually 16–17 hands: some may be under 16 hands.

Colour: any sound colour: e.g. bay, chestnut, or grey; black seems fairly prevalent. May have face and/or leg markings.

Society: The Thoroughbred Breeders' Association; The Thoroughbred Owners' Association (two different bodies). General Stud Book, Weatherby & Sons, 41 Portman Square, London W3.

The Jockey Club controls all flat racing in this country.

Besides definite breeds there are also various types of horses and ponies: the Hackney Horse and Pony, Hacks, Polo-Ponies, and Cobs. Their actual breeding can vary.

Hackney horse

Its ability to keep going indefinitely at its natural pace, the trot, created a big demand for the Hackney horse for riding, in the past, though its high leg-action made it somewhat uncomfortable. *Appearance:* characteristics: high leg-action, great speed and endurance in trotting, and arched neck. Now used in harness in the show-ring it is the most brilliant and showy of all harness horses. The action has been developed so that the forelegs are extended moving well forward before its feet touch the ground with an exaggerated shoulder and hock action: short, powerful legs with strong quarters. Haunches and hind legs moving well underneath are lifted high and bent. Tail was usually docked short. Docking is now illegal.
Height: 15–16 hands.
Colours: all except grey, which is uncommon.

Hackney pony

A harness pony, now used for showing like the Hackney horse, having the same high, showy action.
Height: up to 14·2 hands.
Colours: most usual: bay, brown, chestnut.
Society: The Hackney Horse Society. Includes both Hackney Horse and Pony.

Hack

Merely a general term used for any horse or pony suitable for hacking or general riding for pleasure.

The word 'hack' is quite distinct from 'hackney' which comes from the old Norman French *hacquenée*.

The hack is frequently shown today in special riding classes; to win it must not only have well-nigh perfect conformation, but must also be highly schooled; it must stand perfectly, absolutely motionless when mounted or dismounted, walk freely, move straight, and be collected or extended at the different paces at its rider's wish. It must also perform such dressage movements as the passage, rein back, changing legs at the canter, etc., as the judge requires, and must have perfect manners.

Height : should not exceed 15·3 hands for most hack classes.

A good hack can be of any breed, but usually has a good deal of Arab, Anglo-Arab, or Thoroughbred blood as perfect conformation is essential.

Appearance : It must possess all the points of a good riding-horse; good head; light graceful neck; sloping shoulders with good withers; deep girth, well-sprung ribs, and generous, strong quarters; strong, clean legs moving straight and level, close to the ground without any knee action – just the opposite of a Hackney horse's action.

Colour : any colour, either whole or with black points; some white markings on head or legs, without any exaggeration. Bay, chestnut, or grey are probably most usual.

Society : The Show Hack and Cob Society.

Cob

Any sturdily built, rather thick-set type, 14–15 hh.; between a horse and pony in size. It can carry considerable weight, thus making a good hunter or hack. Cobs always used to be docked.

Polo-Pony

Any breed can make a good Polo-Pony; some have Welsh blood; many first-class ponies come from the Argentine. Originally height was limited to 14·2 hh. Although there is now no upper limit, they are always called ponies, not horses.

This list is not complete and includes some types rather than breeds. Heavy (shire) horses have been omitted, being solely draught animals. Only riding-horses have been included. Ponies and horses from other countries have been excluded.

7 Keeping a Pony at Grass

Catching

Always take some tit-bit. Approach from in front, never from behind. Call; speak while approaching. Walk quietly. Never shout, never run. Do not walk right up; let pony come to you, holding food out at arm's length. As it nibbles draw back your arm slowly until close to its head or shoulder. Let it eat for a few moments. Have the head-collar ready; while eating slip it gently over its head. If always fed and gently approached, a pony will usually come to call and let you catch it.

If there is a shelter always feed in it. The pony learns to follow one inside, where, while eating, its head-collar can be put on at leisure.

Never run after a pony. Chasing only excites and makes it increasingly difficult to catch. Never shout at it. Never walk quickly. Ponies hate being hurried. They become nervous, excited, and difficult to catch and handle.

Turning out

Never let a pony fling up its heels and gallop off. It is dangerous and makes it difficult to catch. Lead it into the field; shut the gate; then, leading it slowly forward some ten yards, turn it round facing the gate. Make it stand still while you fondle it for a few minutes and give it a tit-bit. Then, speaking quietly, unfasten the head-collar; pat it and walk away quietly and decisively. While it turns you can move a safe distance away should it fling up its heels and gallop off.

Water

Have clean water always available in a properly constructed trough with mains water on tap. An old bath is dangerous as a pony may injure its leg on the turned-over rim. A wooden tub can be used. Clean rainwater collected from a roof is good. If neither is available use a large zinc cistern. Buckets, especially zinc ones, are bad, being so easily upset; heavy wooden or rubber stable buckets can be used. Place a large bucket in one corner of the shelter so that it cannot be knocked over. Water must always be available during the night. Break the ice during frosty weather! Stagnant, muddy ponds are bad. A swift stream running over a gravelly bed is quite good. If the field has a slow-moving stream or ditch, see that it is not a drain or open sewer.

Food

More needed when living out in winter than if stabled. Use haynets; loose hay is very wasteful, getting scattered, trampled on, or blown away. Never hang a haynet high so that the pony must look up when eating and get seeds into its eyes. Do not tie it so low that it can catch its feet in the meshes. Use a quick-release knot to tie it.

Amount : haynets: pony, cob, full-size. 10-hh. pony: about 3 lb. hay; three, preferably four feeds. 10–12 hh. – 5–7 lb.; 12–13 hh. – 7–8 lb.; 14 hh. – 8–10 lb.; 14–15 hh. – 10–14 lb.; over 15 hh. – 14–20 lb. Exact amount depends on individual appetite; also amount and nature of work. A hungry pony is a cold pony.

Supplement with bran. Warm bran mash is slightly laxative. Dry bran has the opposite effect. Only give oats if a pony is working hard; otherwise it becomes too excitable and difficult to handle and ride. Only give children's ponies an occasional handful as a treat.

Feed hay from about the end of October to mid-May; exact dates depend on weather conditions and amount of nourishment in the grass. In summer good pasture provides all nourishment. Give some bran to counteract the laxative effects of grass. Never turn straight out into very lush, rich pasture; upsets digestion and can cause laminitis.

Care of feet

If living out and unused, remove pony's shoes and fit grass tips; or leave unshod. Have its feet trimmed every 4 or 5 weeks to prevent overgrowth of hoof, especially the toe.

Catch pony daily, examining its feet for any possible injury; pick out with a hoof-pick. Daily handling also helps to make a pony easy to catch. Always tie pony up before examining, grooming, tacking up, or doing anything to it.

Grooming

Do not clip a pony which lives out; its thick, winter coat protects it. If it sweats after fast, strenuous work, always dry thoroughly before turning out, to avoid the risk of a severe chill, or even pneumonia. Leave saddled but ungirthed, for about ten minutes to cool off while rubbing down. Pay special attention to the breast and neck, between fore and hind legs and elbows, and under the saddle and girth, where a horse sweats most.

A pony living out and doing strenuous work can be trace-clipped, to avoid excessive sweating, provided it wears a New Zealand rug in winter.

A pony living out loves to roll and plaster itself in mud. The mud, long hair, and natural oil and grease in the skin protect it from cold and wet. It should only be lightly groomed to make it look presentable before riding, to remove mud, burrs, and tangles; never use a comb. If not ridden daily examine its coat frequently for lice. After a ride, having dried the pony, brush it thoroughly. Gently slap or briskly massage and then brush vigorously where the saddle has rested with the dandy-brush, to restore circulation.

Actual cold does not harm a well-fed pony which can exercise itself freely. A hardy pony, living out and cared for in a common-sense way, keeps healthier and freer from coughs and colds than a thin-skinned, clipped, and stabled Thoroughbred. A stabled horse is more prone to illness through insufficient fresh air and exercise.

General care

Give protection, trees, a thick, fairly high hedge, or a shelter, from cold winds, etc., in winter, and sun and flies in summer. The shelter should have a wide opening. Cleanliness is important. The ground in the shelter should be dry; remove droppings. Encourage the pony to sleep in its shelter in bad weather by putting down a thick bed of straw. Damp, dirty ground underfoot can cause foot-rot, cracked heels, and thrush.

Poisonous plants

Yew, deadly nightshade, ragwort, laurel, wild arum, privet, autumn crocus, bracken, acorns and laburnum should be removed. Ragwort is more poisonous after being cut down, when dead; should not be left lying on the field after being uprooted.

Fencing

Keep properly repaired; gates should have effective hinges and latches. A post-and-rail fence is best and most enduring, though expensive. Barbed wire is dangerous; avoid it if possible. Pull plain wire taut; have at least three strands, about 18 inches apart. Have fences about 5 feet high. If poles instead of a gate are used across the entrance they must be firm, so that the pony cannot push them out of their sockets. A horse straying on to the road can be badly injured or cause a serious accident. Its owner can be fined and the horse impounded, or even sold. You are also liable for any damage or accidents.

Remove all rubbish, anything that could injure the pony in any way. Fill in all holes; a galloping pony could break its leg through putting its foot in a hole.

Never turn a pony out in a head-collar, unless particularly difficult to catch. If a pony can get into trouble, it will! Leave nothing to chance and remove any source of injury.

Giving lump-sugar teaches a pony to nip. Never let it feed from your pockets or beg for food; this also makes it nip. It should not expect food every time you appear. Some show temper if not given something and try to bite. If it does, rap it sharply on the nose and scold it. Never allow visitors to feed it at all hours. Only give a tit-bit when catching, before turning loose, or as a reward after grooming or after a ride.

A shy pony may prefer being gently scratched under its jowl, on its shoulder or neck, to being patted. Some like their ears gently pulled; this also warms a cold pony.

A horse grazes irregularly, leaving the coarser grass. A field becomes 'horse sick' if not rested periodically; droppings sour the ground, killing the grass. Turn cattle or sheep on to an over-grazed field to rest it.

Strip-grazing is best; one part can re-grow while the next is being grazed. Allow 1 acre per pony; a 4-acre field divided into 1-acre strips is the ideal. An electric fence would divide the strips.

If only one field is available and strip-grazing is impossible, remove the droppings, daily if possible, or scatter them. Chain-harrowing is a useful method. If alternative grazing is available, plough in winter; in spring, top-dress with lime and re-sow.

Always tie up a pony with a quick-release knot.

See that only ponies which agree well are turned out together. Friends are company and in summer give mutual protection against flies by standing head to tail and whisking them off each other. Leaving a docked pony out in summer when flies are bad is sheer cruelty.

A strange pony may be resented and attacked, so turn it out first in late evening. Keep haynets well apart. Ponies get very jealous, especially when fed.

When catching one of several ponies, first try to separate it. If one gallops off they all go. Give the others some food and while they are busy, catch your pony. You may be kicked or bitten if you try to catch it while among a group of others.

Never give a hot, sweating pony a large drink of cold water; it may cause colic. Never exercise strenuously immediately after a big meal or a long drink. Both upset its wind and digestion.

8 The Stabled Horse

A horse or pony stabled or 'kept up' needs more care, attention, and time than one living out because conditions are entirely artificial. A stabled horse must be mucked out, watered, fed three or four times, groomed and exercised regularly, preferably twice daily. It cannot be left standing all day in the stable and cannot exercise itself like one that lives out. A stabled horse should be kept clipped, necessitating rugging up at night in cold weather. Few people today can afford a groom; even if they can, they miss the pleasure which comes from 'doing' one's own horse. A stabled horse is not recommended for anyone who can only look after it in their spare time. To do it properly is really a full-time job for the professional making his living out of horses; e.g. a riding-school proprietor, professional groom, racehorse trainer, or professional show-jumping rider, and so on.

Routine

Hours of work

Regularity is essential. Horses like a regular routine with everything done always in the same order, even picking up feet in the same order. Regular feeding hours are essential for health. Exercise a stabled horse daily, morning and afternoon (or early evening when sufficiently light). Let it have two hours' rest, absolutely quiet, at midday or early afternoon. Many horses sleep then; during the night they feed at any rate for part of the time. Exercise varies from a half to four hours depending on how strenuous it is and upon the horse or pony's size.

	Summer	Winter
Morning stables	6–7 a.m.	7–8 a.m.
Exercise	9–11 a.m.	
	4–6 p.m.	2–4 p.m.
Midday stables	11–12	
Evening stables	6–7 p.m.	3–5 p.m.*

*depending on light and artificial lighting facilities in stable and yard

Morning stables

Water. Straighten night rugs. Give a 'crow's nest' of hay. Muck out. Feed.

After breakfast

Remove night rugs. Pick out feet. Groom lightly (quarter or 'knock over'). Set box fair (put down straw). Saddle up. Exercise.

Midday stables

11 a.m. Water. Hay. Unsaddle. Groom thoroughly (strapping). Feed. Rug-up (day rugs).
12–2 p.m.: rest. Keep stable and yard absolutely quiet so that horse can sleep.
2 p.m.: afternoon exercise (winter) 4 p.m. in summer.

Evening stables

Remove droppings: replace soiled bedding with fresh straw; bed down for the night. Water. Feed (the largest). Pick out feet. Groom lightly. Put on night rug. Leave clean water and full haynet for the night.

Besides stable routine, tack must also be cleaned; few things are more frequently neglected. A bad, slovenly horseman keeps his tack dirty, and nothing looks worse than dirty tack on a well-groomed horse. It should be cleaned daily after riding: take it to pieces and clean thoroughly at least every fortnight (preferably once a week). Good tack is very expensive and nothing wears it out so quickly as dirt. Wet leather hardens as it dries and then cracks. Regular cleaning should also mean regular inspection for wear. Neglected tack causes many accidents; e.g. broken stirrup leather, girth strap, or rein. Keep the yard swept and tidy, free from mud, litter, straw, droppings, etc.

Watering

A horse drinks between 8–15 gallons a day, according to its size, the time of year, and other conditions. Water is almost more important than food. A horse can fast for a considerable time, but soon dies without water. Use only clean, fresh water: clean rainwater is good. Keep buckets or receptacles clean. Tap water is satisfactory. A heavy, wooden stable bucket is better than a zinc pail, being less easily upset. Empty, rinse out and refill buckets before each feed; i.e. at least thrice daily. Always water before feeding. Allow at least 45 minutes after a large drink before exercising. Take the chill off water in very cold weather.

Times for watering

1 After mucking out and bedding down: before first morning feed.

2 Before midday feed.

3 Before evening feed.

4 Last thing at night (8–9 p.m.).

Some people remove the bucket after watering, but it can be left for the horse to drink at intervals whenever it wants during the day. This is a more natural way. If left while feeding, a horse may take a few sips while eating; this is quite harmless. Never give a large drink of cold water immediately after a heavy meal; it washes food out of the stomach, upsets digestion, possibly causing colic.

General principles

1 Never water after a full meal. Can cause colic.

2 Never give a heated, sweating horse a large drink of cold

water after exercise. A small drink of tepid water can be given to quench thirst, provided the horse is afterwards walked about for 10–15 minutes. Never give icy cold water in winter, especially to a stabled horse: give tepid water (with chill off). Both the above may cause colic.

3 Leave water in the stable in some heavy utensil. Do not leave zinc pails as a horse can knock these over and seriously injure itself. Plastic or rubber buckets can be used.

4 Use clean, fresh water, preferably rainwater if obtainable. Tap water is permissible if not too hard. Keep all buckets clean and exclusively for drinking.

5 Water at least three times daily if there is no constant supply.

6 Never give a long drink immediately before hard exercise. A horse may have a short drink from a clean pool or stream (be careful the latter is not open sewage!) while out, even if heated, provided it keeps moving and does not gallop or exercise hard immediately afterwards. A short drink while jogging home after hunting or a long hack does no harm.

When watering, especially from an outside trough, do not take the horse away directly it lifts its head; it often pauses, raises its head, and then drinks again. It may first play with the water, blowing bubbles before settling down to drink.

Feeding

When first opening up stables give a crow's nest, or small haynet, of hay to keep each horse or pony amused. After watering, mucking out and bedding down give the first main feed.

Feed

The amount depends on the nature of work and the animal's size. A pony on light work needs much less than one doing heavy work. Also more is needed in winter when much is used up in supplying warmth. A horse doing strenuous work needs corn. Do not give a pony corn, especially if ridden by children. Is it too stimulating, making it too excitable and difficult to handle.

The following is an approximate guide:

Size	Light work	Medium work	Heavy work
11–12 h.	7 lb.		
13·2–14 h.	10 lb.	15 lb.	17 lb.
Over 14·2 h.	15 lb.	20 lb.	25 lb.
(hunters, etc.)			

A proportion must be hay to provide bulk (roughage). Haynets are in three sizes: small; cob or pony; hunter.

> Small (very small ponies): 3 lb. stuffed full.
> Medium (cob or pony): 7–8 lb. stuffed full.
> Large (hunter): 10–12 lb. stuffed full.

The rest ('short feed') can be horse-nuts, Silcocks, bruised or whole oats. Chaff (chopped straw or hay) mixed with oats is useful, especially for a greedy horse which bolts its food, to make it eat slowly.

Several well-known firms now market special horse or pony cubes which they claim form a completely balanced food, eliminating hay in some cases.

Food constituents

All natural or manufactured food must contain proteins, carbo-hydrates, mineral salts, and vitamins. As proteins help bone formation they are particularly necessary for young, growing colts: they also form flesh and muscle. Digestion breaks down carbohydrates into fats, starches, and sugars, producing fat, heat, and energy. Foods rich in carbohydrates are especially important in winter when much energy is absorbed in keeping warm. Mineral salts keep the blood pure and healthy; a prolonged deficiency can cause death. Bones, hair, horn, muscle, sweat, and some fats also contain them. Those chiefly needed are lime, soda, and potash compounds. Natural foods contain minute quantities of vitamins, influencing nutrition out of all proportion to the amounts present. Their absence can cause bone degeneration, nervous diseases, scurvy, rickets, and sterility. Young growing colts especially need them. Prolonged heating destroys them, so they may be absent in boiled foods.

Fibrous, woody material is also needed to provide bulk (roughage), helping the stomach and intestines to digest. It helps, mechanically, to split up other food constituents during digestion so that the blood stream ultimately absorbs and carries them where needed in other parts of the body.

Grass ('green meat'), containing all the different constituents is the best and most balanced of all foods. Good hay, particularly lucerne and sanfoin, is rich in mineral salts. Maize alone is an unsatisfactory diet, being deficient in salts. Pulped sugar beet forms a valuable additional ingredient to the diet. Natural foods contain the different constituents in varying quantities. Some, like beans, are rich in carbohydrates (very fattening and heating). Others are rich in proteins but lack carbohydrates. So a balanced diet must contain different foods. Plenty of water is also essential.

Give only fresh, scrupulously clean food. Hay must not be dusty, musty, or mowburnt.

The nitrogenous ratio is the proportion of proteins required to carbohydrates (nitrogenous foods: fats, starches, sugars). This varies from 1:5 for horses doing very hard work to 1:10 for resting horses. Thus, hunters, racehorses, show-jumpers, or any others doing hard work are corn fed, while ponies or horses only doing light work, must not have oats. Young colts should have a 1:3 nitrogenous ratio, as in milk.

The fatty-ratio is the proportion of fats to proteins: fat 1 part, proteins $2\frac{1}{2}$ parts. Excessive starch or sugar makes proteins harder to digest. If proteins are absent, fats, starches, and sugars cannot produce energy. Fat produces $2\frac{1}{2}$ times heat and energy than starch or sugar.

A diet containing excessive carbohydrates merely produces fat. If the body has more proteins than it needs over a prolonged period, digestion is upset causing swollen legs, diarrhoea, liver disorders, and overheating with skin eruptions.

Kinds of food

1 *Grains*: **Oats**, Maize, Barley, Wheat, Rye, Millets, Rice,

Beans, Peas, Linseed. May be used in winter when the grass has no nourishment.

2 *By-products:* Bran; Brewers' Grains (wet); Linseed Cake, Seeds, or Oil.

3 *'Green meat':* various grasses; Vetches; Lucerne (Alfalfa Grass); Sanfoin.

4 *Hay:* Meadow; Mixture Clover; Lucerne; Sanfoin.

5 *Straw (used as chaff):* Wheat; Oat; Barley straw should never be used; its awns may irritate the throat and/or cause colic.

6 *Roots:* Carrots; Swedes; Sugar Beet (fresh or dry). Do not give potatoes; some authorities say that their raw skins are poisonous. They are used in some parts of Ireland.

Grains

Oats: the best grain for horses. Being very stimulating they excite a horse, so should only be given to one in hard condition, doing hard work and never to an excitable animal doing light work, or to children's ponies. Mature them for twelve months before using. Do not give new oats. Good oats are plump, having little or no beard. Colour: black or deep brown to almost white. Oats heated in store have a peculiar acrid smell, and are termed 'foxy'. Oats stored while damp become musty or mouldy.

Maize: lacks mineral salts. Use with nitrogenous diet; e.g. clover hay; alfalfa; beans. Unsuitable for young stock. Easily becomes heated, musty, or mouldy. Rich in carbohydrates.

Barley: grains are good food. Do not use barley straw.

Rye: used in Belgium, Denmark, Sweden. Much inferior to oats in food value.

Rice: unhusked rice (paddy) is used in Burma and Indian rice-growing districts. Can be very indigestible if a horse is unused to it.

Wheat: unsuitable; almost unobtainable in England because used for human consumption.

Beans: nutritious; rich in proteins; valuable when great speed or hard work is required, for a horse in poor condition, or, being heating, in severe weather. Varieties: Soya and field beans. Should be a year old: split their skins before feeding to make them digestible. Give only 2–3 lb. daily, and not in summer.

Peas: white, grey, or blue; dried. Should be a year old.

By-products

Bran: a by-product of wheat after extracting the flour by milling. The amount of flour and the presence of vitamins B and E determine its food value. Grades: broad, flaked, medium, fine, and No. 2 Bran. Broad bran is most nutritious. Good bran is quite dry, sweet, flaky, free from lumps, and varies slightly in colour, according to the wheat from which it is milled. A hand plunged in should be floury when withdrawn. Given as bran mash it is mildly laxative, and is often given in large stables on Saturday night when horses are rested on Sunday. It has the opposite effect when dry so is good for a horse at grass. It can replace chaff to make a horse chew its food thoroughly, or to make very heating foods more digestible. Prepare a mash by scalding 2–3 lb. with boiling water; cover the bucket and leave until cool enough to eat. Most horses relish a pinch of salt which improves the flavour.

Brewers' grains: obtained wet or dry from malt refuse; dried grains are disliked. Use fresh wet grains as they soon turn sour; mix with other food. They are a useful change of diet, or for a horse off its feed to tempt its appetite, but are useless for strenuous or fast work.

Linseed: seed of the flax plant. Useful for fattening a horse and improving the appearance of its coat; when preparing a horse for show give it linseed for about a month beforehand. Sometimes given when the coat is being changed. Valuable during illness for tempting the appetite or when the digestive tract is inflamed, and during convalescence for a horse in poor condition. Obtainable as whole seeds, cake, meal, and oil. Cake is crushed and fed dry; add $\frac{1}{2}$ lb. to a bad doer's daily ration. It is also made into linseed tea; or give $\frac{1}{2}$ lb. to 1 lb. of seeds or meal as a mash. Never given unboiled seeds as they contain prussic acid when moist and warm. Linseed oil is not so easily digested and is sometimes disliked. One or two table-spoonfuls mixed daily with other food helps to improve condition. In cases of slight colic it forms a mild laxative.

'Green meat'

Fescues: Meadow Fescue is one of the best. Timothy (Meadow Cat's Tail); Meadow Fox Tail; Cocksfoot (quickly becomes coarse and does not make good hay).

Meadow grasses: smooth stalked; rough stalked; evergreen and annual Meadow grasses.

Rye grasses: many known varieties. Perennial and Italian are two of the best, most often found in hay.

Yellow Oat Grass: grows especially well in the Thames valley and southern England.

Tall Oat Grass: much larger; has a rather bitter taste.

Sweet Vernal: smells very pleasant, largely giving hay its 'nose' (smell).

Vetches: Kidney Vetch (found only in Hampshire).

Lucerne: a tall green plant bearing a purple flower; originates in warm countries; known as Alfalfa (Spanish name of Arabic origin).

Sanfoin: a large fine-leafed plant bearing pinkish flowers; two kinds, Common and Giant.

Hay

Characteristics: colour: greenish or brownish; not yellow; crisp in feel; sweet taste; pleasant aroma, called its 'nose'.

Faults: dust in old hay; also when the crop was cut too late and so was extra dry, having been exposed too long to the sun; stems may have become brittle through being weathered too long.

Mowburnt: hay carried before it is dry enough ferments in the stack, causing great heat which chars it; the rick may even catch fire. Slightly mowburnt hay is tinged brown, having a sweet, rather pungent smell. Its quality is unaffected and horses like it. Badly burnt hay is useless.

Musty, mouldy hay: stacked damp or subsequently wetted causes mould. Musty hay is dark brown or bright yellow with a characteristic unpleasant smell and bitter taste. Mould causes light or white patches, surrounded by deep brown or black hay.

Meadow: should be well saved and free from weeds: rather soft.

Clover: excellent and palatable, but difficult to save well. Becomes brittle and rather dusty, and therefore somewhat wasteful. Susceptible to mould. Kinds: red and white and Dutch; Alsicke (originally from Sweden); Valerian (crimson Italian clover).

Lucerne: (alfalfa); rare in England. Considered wasteful because dusty and very brittle; an excellent food.

Sanfoin: good when cut at the right age and well saved. Though coarse, bulky, woody, and rather rough looking it is very nutritious.

Straw

Generally used for bedding unless chopped up for chaff and used to slow up a greedy feeder. Wheat and oat straw make the best chaff.

Roots

Carrots: the most valuable; a few horses refuse them. Do not dice, but cut lengthways; the former may stick in a horse's throat.

Swedes, mangolds: most appetizing, especially after Christmas. Chop into fairly small, long strips.

Sugar beet: good winter feed. Well chopped up can be used fresh or dry. Soak overnight before feeding as it swells.

Bedding

Kinds of bedding

Wheat, oat, and rye straw; Peat moss; Sawdust; Wood shavings; Bracken; Sand.

A stabled horse needs a good thick bed to encourage it to lie down and rest for long periods of the day and night, saving wear and tear of the feet, and preventing filled legs, caused by too much standing; also prevents capped hocks and other injuries caused by lying on a hard floor: in the long run it is more economical in use than a thin bed. Bedding should be elastic and level, warm and dry, absorb urine and be deodorant, or alternatively, let it drain away immediately. A dirty, wet, soggy bed is bad for the feet and may cause disease, such as thrush.

A horse stands so many hours that it should have every encouragement to lie down: it rests, and even sleeps standing. A horse usually sleeps about four hours out of the twenty-four.

It grazes most of the night when living out (in summer) but sleeps during the early part of the morning, about 2 or 3 a.m.

Wheat straw: the best of all bedding, being more waterproof and not so easily sodden. Stalks should be long with their varnish unbroken, dry, free from mould, clean, and brightly coloured. Wheat straw looks better than anything else and is readily sold as manure.

Oat straw: not so good; being softer it becomes sodden more easily. Horses like the taste and are inclined to eat it.

Rye straw: one of the best beddings if obtainable; very expensive and difficult to buy, the supply being more limited; what is available is used for stuffing harness. Is the toughest straw and lasts longest.

Peat moss: quite a good bed but is apt to clog and cake; digging out soiled parts is very hard work. Remove all droppings and dig out wet parts. If neglected it clogs the horse's feet, causing disease. Is apt to block drains if allowed to get into them. Is valueless as manure.

Sawdust: a bad bedding which gets hot, overheating the horse's feet. It easily becomes fly-blown and full of maggots. Only use sawdust from well-seasoned wood; green sawdust ferments and heats quickly as soon as it becomes bedded down and damp. Remove soiled parts very frequently; turn and air the bed daily. Valueless as manure: like peat moss it blocks drains easily.

Shavings: the same drawbacks as sawdust. Also sharp splinters may cause injury; remove all small wooden blocks and chips before putting down the bed. Less absorbent than sawdust but does not become so heated.

Bracken: bracken and leaves are used in some parts of the country, especially in the Scottish Highlands. Not being very absorbent, only use it if nothing else is available. Do not use stored, dry bracken as it soon powders into dust.

Barley straw: should never be used. The awns irritate a horse's skin, while if eaten they may cause colic.

Sand: in hot countries it can make quite a good bed. It must not be used in cold, damp climates. If not absolutely free from salt, a horse will eat it in large quantities and get sand colic. It could be used in cold weather if covered with a fairly thick layer of straw but it causes much work removing the straw daily; air the sand well after digging out all damp patches.

Laying a bed

When laying a straw bed, spread evenly, tossing with a hay fork so that the stalks do not all lie in the same direction but criss-cross each other. Have about 4–6 inches deep, piled up about a foot high round the sides of the loose-box so that the horse can lean against something soft when lying down.

Mucking out

If possible first remove the horse. If there is no other available stall or loose-box, tie it up. A horse is an inquisitive, wrong-headed creature which invariably gets in the way if possible; also, if allowed to remain free while one is trying to muck-out, there is the danger of getting kicked. If it must remain, short-rack to keep it out of the way.

With a two-pronged stable fork separate clean straw from droppings and wet, dirty bedding, spreading it round the sides of the loose-box. If mucking out a stall put clean bedding at the manger end and where it cannot be trodden on. Next separate out any not too soiled straw, putting it with the clean for economy's sake. Collect droppings in a skep or spread-out sack, which is then gathered up corner-ways. Remove wet, dirty straw and droppings to the manure heap, using a wheelbarrow if available. Sweep the floor thoroughly with a hard-bristled broom; when clean replace the less-clean bedding. Spread the clean straw, with fresh added, round the walls to protect and prevent the horse getting cast when lying down.

If the horse is out of its box, put the less-clean bedding outside in fine weather for the sun and air to dry and sweeten. In wet weather spread it out in any open shed or spare loose-box. This is important as soiled bedding gives off unpleasant, unhealthy ammonia fumes. Dirty bedding attracts flies and midges in summer. Wash the floor fairly frequently with strong disinfectant, leaving the box open to dry and sweeten.

Remove droppings and any wet, soiled patches of bedding at least thrice daily, and at evening stables before the last feed.

Spread fresh straw fairly thickly to form a comfortable bed, inviting the horse to lie down at night. A thick bed also provides warmth in winter. Thin bedding is false economy; a hard stone floor may cause capped elbows and hocks and is cold in winter.

Keep the manger, water trough, or bucket scrupulously clean, scrubbing them out at least once a week. Sluice drains out with disinfectant. Leave doors and windows wide open while the horse is out.

Since manure breeds flies and midges keep the heap well away from the stable, preferably, for tidiness' sake, in a bricked-in enclosure: the retaining front wall should be about 30 inches high, with, ideally, another brick wall 5–6 feet high at the back.

When several horses are kept, manure can provide a useful source of revenue, helping towards their upkeep. Firms advertise regularly in *Horse and Hound* for it, or a local nurseryman might be glad to buy and collect regularly. Fresh manure is hot, so it should be at least six months old before being used in the soil.

Picking out feet

Do this daily before quartering; also after a ride to see that no nails or broken glass have been picked up, or stones wedged in the hoof. When picking out feet before quartering see that shoes are not worn or loose and that no clenches have risen; also examine for injuries and chapped or sore heels. Dirt can cause thrush so pick out the feet daily. To pick up a foot: speak to the horse and run your hand with a semi-circular movement from its wither down to its fetlock, so that it is not startled by a sudden, unexpected movement. Grasp the fetlock and say: 'Foot'. Stand with your shoulder against its body, facing the tail. Pick up the foot by grasping the hair (if any) at the fetlock. If the horse refuses to lift its foot, pinch the tendons just above the fetlock between finger and thumb, lean your weight with your shoulder against its shoulder, again saying 'foot', or 'up'. When the foot is lifted slide your hand gently under its hoof, resting it in the palm of your hand. Use the hoof-pick in the other hand. Do not lift, especially a hind leg, too high. Always work away from you, downwards from frog to toe. Pick up the dirt from the floor and do not leave it to be trodden in.

Grooming kit

1 *Hoof-pick :* cleans out feet, removes stones, etc.

2 *Dandy brush :* removes heavy dirt, caked mud and dust: especially useful for a horse living out. Do not attempt to brush off wet mud. Also useful for the clipped legs of a hunter.

3 *Body brush :* removes body scurf and dirt; acts as a massage when used with a rotary movement.

4 *Curry comb :* a rubber and a metal type. Use the rubber type on the coat, especially when moulting, for removing loose hairs. Only use a metal curry comb for cleaning the dandy or body brush, and never on a horse. Two kinds: with a handle; (cavalry type) with a leather strap across the back, going across the knuckles. This type is better because one's hand can be rested on the pony while grooming, without fear of knocking the curry comb against it.

5 *Water brush :* use damp on mane, tail, and feet.

6 *Sponges :* two: one for cleaning eyes and muzzle: one for cleaning the dock. Always use separate sponges.

7 *Whisp :* promotes circulation and massages (known as 'strapping'); 18 in. to 2 ft long, made of twisted hay, woven tightly into a rope.

8 *Mane and tail comb :* never comb out tangles with it as it breaks, or tears out the hair, thus spoiling a mane or tail. Chiefly used for pulling and trimming a mane or tail.

9 *Scraper :* used on a sweating horse, or for scraping off surplus water after washing.

10 *Stable rubber :* gives a final polish after grooming.

Grooming

Quartering

A quick brush over to tidy a horse and remove night stains before exercising; the early morning grooming. Also called 'knocking over'.

Strapping

Thorough grooming on returning from work. Is best given when

c

warm and the pores of the skin are open, as scurf and dust brush away more freely.

How to groom

Short rack, i.e. tie the horse's head fairly tightly and high up to a ring in the wall so that it cannot move or turn its head to bite, using a quick-release knot.

The aim of grooming a grass-kept horse is simply to remove mud, dust, and sweat, to make it presentable before riding, and not to remove grease from its coat. A stabled horse is groomed to remove all dust, scurf, and grease, thus thoroughly cleaning its coat. Hard grooming acts as massage and stimulates the oil glands at the roots of the hair. A horse breathes through the pores of its skin so they must be kept open and free from dirt.

Work methodically and deliberately; poise your body correctly with the correct leg stance, with your body weight behind your arm movements, which should be rhythmical. Press very firmly without banging down the brush; drive it through the coat with long, even strokes.

A professional groom hisses as he works to soothe the horse and prevent dust entering his mouth. Grooming a clipped horse thoroughly takes about 45 minutes.

Start on the near side, working from the neck to shoulder. Then work downwards, outside and inside the front leg. Some like doing the inside of the opposite leg at the same time. Next groom from the withers, along the back to the loins. Then to the elbows and ribs, working down and along them to the flank and belly, and then underneath. Many horses are ticklish on the flank and belly, and may try to kick; so be careful. Work gently and quietly. Hold the hind leg at the hock and speak soothingly to the horse. It is dangerous to kneel or squat when grooming a horse's legs.

First, run quickly over with the rubber curry comb to remove surface dust or dirt. Tap the curry comb on the ground fairly frequently to rid it of dust. Next, holding body brush in the right and curry comb in the left hand, work on the near side, brushing with a rotary movement, in the order given, in the direction of the hair. Clean the brush fairly frequently on the curry comb, then tap the latter, edgeways on, on the ground or against the wall.

When grooming the leg, brush around the coronet; see that the heels are free from mud. Use the right hand to brush the underside of the body, using the same rotary movement. Hold the hock when brushing a hind leg to prevent the horse kicking. Use a body brush for mane and tail, never a comb or dandy brush as both split and pull out the hair.

Work in the same sequence on the off side, holding brush in the left hand and metal curry comb in the right.

After brushing use the whisp to strap, hitting the horse lightly with it on shoulders, flanks, and quarters; avoid any tender or ticklish spots.

Strapping tones up circulation and muscles and stimulates a healthy coat, making it shine. Finally go over the coat with a clean stable rubber.

Sponge the eyes, and nostrils after thoroughly rinsing the sponge. Clean the dock with another sponge.

Instead of strapping with the whisp, use the palms of the hands.

Mane and tail

Docking is now mercifully illegal in England, though still allowed in Ireland. Only horses docked before the Act may now be exhibited at the leading British shows. Apart from depriving a horse of its natural beauty (a long tail), docking was also extremely cruel; besides the pain of the operation through sawing off the actual tail bone, docking deprives a horse of its natural protection against flies in summer. Native British ponies especially look far more beautiful with natural long tails. Cobs and Hackneys were the most usual victims. A horse with a natural mane and tail is described as 'with mane and tail on'.

Hogging means clipping the mane. It looks all right on some types of show horses but seems now to be going out of fashion, fortunately, as the mane is another natural protection against flies.

Trimming and pulling

Trimming: shaping a tail to look narrow between the dock and then flow out lower down to the end. Show ponies' tails are usually trimmed and pulled. It is almost a fetish with some grooms, but the writer feels that native British ponies looks better with their tails growing naturally; especially a Fell or Dales pony with its full, flowing, and naturally wavy tail.

Always pull and never cut a tail near its root as the hairs become bristly. Pulling is a difficult job, best left to an expert if done at all. Only pull out a few hairs at a time as otherwise the tail becomes sore; take great care only to pull out long hairs in the right place; otherwise it will soon look a terrible mess, as if the rats had been gnawing it! Hair takes a long time to re-grow and a mistake once made cannot be rectified.

If shaping the tail is considered essential, first brush it out thoroughly with a body or dry water-brush. Never use a comb or dandy brush. When free from tangles take the hair to be pulled out, twist round the finger as near its root as possible and pull sharply. Horse hair being tough, one's finger may soon become sore or even cut. Alternatively, twist the hair round a tooth of the mane comb and then pull out. Only pull out single hairs. Starting just above the point of the buttock, work downwards to the end of the dock. Pull out the underneath hairs. To avoid being kicked, never stand directly behind the pony. If restive let someone stand at its head; hold up a foreleg if necessary, which effectively stops it kicking. Be patient; work gently, talking soothingly to the pony. Always short-rack it.

Brushing the tail

Start from the top and work downwards, separating the strands of hair. Brush underneath first and then the top. This is the only time when one should stand directly behind a pony.

Plaiting

Plaiting the tail is done on van and cart-horses, particularly Shires and Percherons, to show off their hindquarters; also when showing.

Brush the hair out thoroughly and then damp. Divide it just below the end of the dock and plait. The plait is then turned upwards and fastened with some form of straw and/or ribbon decoration on top of the tail. Examples can be seen at an agricultural show of heavy horses. Gipsies also decorate their horses' tails like this. To plait a riding-pony's tail (for showing) start at the dock: take the long hair from underneath on each side and plait it in front down the middle.

How to plait

Plaiting neatly is an art needing considerable practice. Practise first with three fairly thick pieces of cord, joined together at one end.

1 Fold the outside right cord over the middle one.

2 Take the outside left cord and fold over the right-hand one.

3 Continue folding alternate outside cords over the middle, down the entire length. Knot at the end. Start with either the left or right outside cord.

Length of tail

A matter of opinion as some like to see it long, others shorter. Within reason, so long as it does not drag in the mud, the longer the better as a protection against flies. A good length is 4–6 inches below the hocks, depending on the pony's size and type: a very small pony with a very long tail looks rather overweighted.

'Banged' tail

Is pulled at the top of the dock and thinned out gradually a short way down. The rest falls naturally, the end being cut square about 6 inches below the hocks.

To bang a tail let an assistant hold it out in the position the pony holds it in when moving. Decide on the length; the assistant holds it in both hands, on either side of the place where the hair is cut, keeping it taut. Cut across, slanting slightly upwards so that the tail is square to the ground when hanging naturally.

Swish tail

Also pulled at the top but goes to a long, thin point, instead of being cut square at the end.

Mane

Is either left long or 'hogged' – i.e. clipped short. Again, a question of personal taste; a pony living out should have its mane and forelock left long for protection against flies and the sun.

Groom the mane daily with a body brush. Never comb or cut it. It usually falls on the right (off) side though it sometimes falls on the near side. Occasionally it divides, falling on both sides. One can usually train it to lie flat by daily grooming. Damp an obstinate mane with the water-brush (but not in winter!). Very stubborn manes may need a mane-board which is clipped along to hold it down. Native ponies generally look better with their natural mane.

Trimming and pulling

If too thick and bushy, a mane is troublesome to groom and too heavy and hot in summer; it is then trimmed and pulled like the tail. Brush well and then pull out the long, underneath hairs. Start from the withers, working forward and keeping the ends level; pull out only a few hairs each time. Let it slope gently upwards, becoming slightly shorter towards the head.

Hogging

Run the clippers along both sides of the neck, bringing the mane to a point in the middle and following the curve of the neck. Do not have a hard dividing line along the neck. Leave the fore-lock for handling the pony and as protection against sun and flies in summer. Leave a lock of hair on the withers for mounting. A hogged mane takes nine months to a year, or even longer, to re-grow and may be rather coarse and thick. While re-growing it looks very ragged and untidy. It needs trimming once a fort-night with clippers.

Plaiting

It is a convention that manes are plaited for hunting and showing There are usually seven plaits. It keeps a mane tidy and helps to train it. Do not leave plaited for more than a day; twisting tends to split the hair.

How to plait

Brush thoroughly, removing all scurf, dust, dirt, and tangles. Then damp with the water-brush. Divide the mane into seven sections beginning from the head. Separate each section into three strands and plait them as already explained. Turn the ends under and sew with a coarse, blunt-ended needle, using brown, black, or white cotton according to the pony's colour; do not twist elastic bands round them.

Mane plaiting is a lengthy, rather tedious process. The writer feels that native ponies look better with unplaited manes even for showing and hunting.

Brush out the plaits thoroughly after undoing. Then damp and brush the mane with the water-brush.

Clipping

A stabled horse, 'kept up', exercised daily, and hunted or doing other strenuous work, should be clipped. This needs doing three times at least in winter.

The first clip is usually about the end of October, the second in early December and the third in January. A final clip in February would remove the long 'cat' hairs. Some believe that a horse should not be clipped while moulting because it ruins the summer coat; this is now disputed as it does not appear to affect it. A clipped horse must be stabled and rugged-up at night; it cannot live out. Two rugs may be necessary in cold winter weather. Clip after exercise while skin is warm and pores of skin are open.

Types of clip

Clipped right out

Clipped all over. The saddle mark is sometimes left on a tender-skinned horse. Those who favour doing this claim that (a) it prevents galling; (b) short hairs, when clipped right out, may irritate through being forced into the horse's back by the rider's weight; (c) a cold saddle on a clipped back may cause bucking and restiveness.

Arguments against: (a) a saddle mark causes considerable sweating and may cause chills if the back is not thoroughly dried. Clipping eliminates the extra work of drying a wet back; (b) a cold saddle should be left loosely girthed for a few minutes before mounting. Always do this whether the horse is clipped or un-clipped; (c) its rider's weight does not appear to irritate a clipped horse.

Hunter clipped

Clipped all over except for saddle mark and legs which are left as protection against thorns, knocks, etc. If a thorn does penetrate it is much harder to find in the long hair; cleaning and drying the legs is also harder.

Trace clipped

Used for a horse living out yet doing strenuous work (e.g. hunting). The underside of the neck, belly (trace high), and a line up the quarters are clipped. A trace-clipped horse living out wears a New Zealand rug. A stabled horse only doing light work may be trace clipped; it only needs one night blanket.

Shoeing

Reasons for shoeing

The wall of the hoof is always growing in two ways: downwards from the coronet and outwards from the 'white line', rather like the branch of a tree.

Inside the hard, protecting outer wall of horn, the hoof consists of innumerable vertical hollow tubes filled with fluid, keeping the hoof lubricated and preventing it cracking and breaking. Many tiny blood vessels penetrate the bones of the foot; a wound in the foot bleeds so profusely because it is kept literally bathed in blood. There are many nerves in the foot although the hoof itself is insensitive. At the back of the hoof (the heel), is the triangular, tough, leathery 'frog'. Round the hoof wall is the 'white line' where growth occurs, like the cambium ring in a tree branch; the horn grows outwards from this and downwards from the coronet. The sole should be hard and usually bluish white. A horse with a white hoof has a yellowish-pink sole.

Horn takes about nine months to grow downwards from coronet to toe. The frog is very important, acting as a shock-absorber and taking all the impact, especially when galloping or jumping. It also gives a firm grip which prevents slipping.

When roaming about wild, wear and tear prevents excessive growth of the hoof. The domesticated horse needs shoeing because (1) if not periodically trimmed and shod the toe grows too long, the wall tends to crack, and the hoof grows soft; (2) if much used on hard roads the horse gets sore feet because the horn wears away faster than it grows. In hot, dry countries horses go unshod on unmade, sandy roads; in this country, wet ground in winter keeps the foot too soft, and hard, made roads wear the horn too quickly. A few people ride and even hunt unshod, but shoeing is generally considered necessary in Britain. Also, good shoeing protects the feet, helping to avoid and cure corns, brushing, over-reaching and other results of bad foot conformation.

Fitting a shoe

It should fit so that the foot is level at all points with the ground. The frog should touch the ground, acting as a cushion and shock absorber. *The shoe must be made to fit the hoof, not the hoof to fit the shoe.* Hence, hot shoeing is better than cold. The frog should not be cut away but left as large as possible; the wall should not be rasped away too much and should never be dumped.

Nails holding the shoe are driven in between the 'white line' and outer edge of the hoof. A horse is 'pricked' and goes lame if a nail is carelessly driven into the 'white line'.

The sole should never be thinned in any circumstances. Years ago, some blacksmiths used to pare it away until thin enough to be springy when pushed by the thumb. This is entirely contrary to nature as the sole should be so hard and tough that nothing can possibly penetrate it.

Conformation of foot

A well-shaped foot is round and open, touching the ground evenly all round. Viewed sideways the hoof should slope at almost 50° with the ground. Both feet should be the same size and shape. Avoid narrow or upright, 'boxy' feet like a mule's; ponies with narrow feet may stumble; those with upright, 'boxy' feet are uncomfortable to ride. The frog should be large and firm, resting squarely on the ground; the sole should be hard. Heels should be wide.

Abnormalities

1 'Flat' feet, very sloping and abnormally large in circumference.

2 Narrow, 'boxy', 'mule' feet; small and too upright, making a pony potter along with a stilted action.

Both are abnormal and weaknesses, liable to cause various ailments.

Viewed directly from in front a horse should walk and trot level, with even steps. Both feet move straight forward; when trotting it should not 'dish' or throw either one or both legs outwards. 'Plaiting' means that a horse throws one foreleg inwards in front of the other; this can be dangerous.

A horse should not 'go close' in front; the feet should not pass too close to one another. This frequently causes trouble through one hoof brushing against the fetlock of the other leg. It can be alleviated by fitting a specially shaped shoe.

Types of shoes

Grass tips

Remove its shoes if a horse is turned out and is not being ridden for some time, especially if with others, to lessen risk of injury from kicking. To prevent the wall of the foot splitting at the toe fit grass tips, half-length shoes which allow the frog to press on the ground, thus keeping it healthy.

Plain stamped

A plain, suitably thick iron bar, shaped, stamped with nail-holes, and provided with a toe-clip. Usually used for heavy draught animals (e.g. cart-horses), doing only slow work; they do not protect against slipping.

Hunter shoe

Fitted for riding, whether ordinary hacking, hunting, or show-jumping, and especially designed for galloping on grass and pulling up short. To reduce suction in mud it is made of concave iron and fullered, i.e. grooved. Both help to provide more secure foothold.

The fore-shoe heels are pencilled (narrowed) to prevent the hind shoe catching and pulling them off. There is generally a single toe-clip.

The hind shoe usually has a rolled toe and quarter clips (one on each side) instead of a single toe-clip to help prevent over-reaching when moving fast. The outer heel has a calkin to increase grip while the inner heel had a wedge for the same purpose. On the inner heel a wedge is less likely to cause brushing than a calkin.

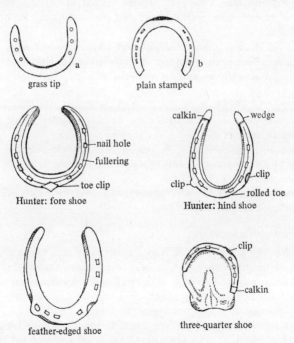

grass tip

plain stamped

Hunter: fore shoe

—nail hole
—fullering
—toe clip

calkin— —wedge

clip—
clip—
—clip
—rolled toe

Hunter: hind shoe

feather-edged shoe

three-quarter shoe

—clip
—calkin

Types of shoe

Special types

For certain abnormalities certain types of shoes are fitted.

1 *Feather edged:* to prevent brushing when a horse moves too close behind. The shoe's inner branch is narrowed (feathered); fits close in under the wall to reduce risk of a horse knocking its fetlock with the other foot.

2 *Three-quarter:* fitted if a horse is going lame from a corn; takes pressure off the seat of corn.

3 *Racing plates:* very light, usually made of aluminium alloy: fitted to racehorses, they are fitted before, and removed after the race.

4 *Rodway shoes:* formerly, usually fitted to carriage horses; not often seen now. Fairly heavy and plain, with calkins on the hind shoes.

5 *Seated shoes:* used for flat feet or a dropped sole. The bearing surface against the foot is hollowed and at the inner edge, making practically no contact with the sole.

Weights of shoes

Plain stamped: for draught-horses, anything up to 20 lb. a set according to size.

Hunter shoes: horses – 4–5 lb. per set, according to size. Ponies – from $2\frac{1}{2}$ lb. per set. 12 hands upwards – according to size.

Racing plates: $\frac{1}{2}$–1 lb. per set.

Training shoes: $1\frac{1}{2}$ lb. per set (approx.). Weight differs slightly according to size.

Blacksmith's tools

1 *Shoeing hammer:* a claw at the opposite end twists off the ends of the nails after having been driven into the foot. These ends are hammered down into the wall and are called clenches.

2 *Buffer:* for removing shoes.

3 *Drawing knife:* for trimming the foot.

4 *Rasp:* filing down the foot where necessary to ensure a good fit before shoeing; after shoeing, to finish off and prevent sharp edges of the clenches sticking out.

5 *Pincers:* removing shoe; helping to embed the clenches.

Besides the anvil, other tools used in forging a shoe are: fire-tongs; shoe tongs; turning hammer (approx. 4 lb.); sledge-hammer (9 lb.); swedge; crease or concave tool, usually just called 'the tool', fuller, stamp; pritchel.

Method of shoeing

Preparation

Old shoes are removed. Foot is rasped to level its surface to fit the new shoe. Overgrowth is removed with the drawing knife. Sole and frog are cleaned out, ragged pieces being trimmed up.

Shoeing

The hot shoe is carried on the pritchel to the foot and placed on, slightly scorching the horn. The scorched part, showing imperfect contact between foot and shoe, is rasped away. The shoe's shape and length of heel are then adjusted to fit the foot accurately. After cooling in water the shoe is usually first nailed on at the toe. The correct size nail is important; if too large the head projects above the hold and wears away too quickly; if too small it will not fit the nail-hole. The nail must be driven in very accurately; it must not go near or penetrate the sensitive 'white line'. The former causes nail binding, the latter a pricked foot, both causing lameness.

Finishing

After embedding in the wall the clenches are filed level. The toe-clip is tapped lightly into position; part of the wall where horn and shoe meet is rasped down to reduce risk of cracking.

Inspecting a newly shod foot

After the horse is shod inspect the following:

1 The right kind of shoe, suitable for the type of work done; e.g. a plain stamped shoe is useless for hacking, hunting, or jumping.

2 The shoe was made to fit the foot; not the foot to fit the shoe. The wall must not be rasped away to meet the iron because the shoe is too small and the toe must not be dumped.

3 Correct weight of shoes according to the horse or pony's size.

4 Neither frog nor sole must be cut away; only ragged pieces removed.

5 The frog must touch the ground; i.e. shoes of correct thickness.

6 Foot properly trimmed to reduce overgrowth at both toe and heel; it must be level with the ground, even on both sides.

7 The correct number of nails, four outside, three inside, are present, and of the correct size.

8 Clenches even, well formed, in line, neither too high nor low down the wall.

9 Perfectly even contact between foot and shoe, especially at the heel.

10 Clip must be well drawn and well fitted into a neatly cut hollow.

11 Correct length of shoe heels, neither too long nor too short.

Faults in shoeing

1 *Over-lowering the wall:* too much rasped away; most liable with flat, spreading feet.

2 *Uneven bearing surface:* one side of foot lowered more than the other.

3 *Dumping:* a serious fault. It often used to be done to make the foot look smaller. If the toe needs shortening it should be done at ground surface and not the front of the wall. Rasping away the hard outer horn exposes the soft moist horn underneath, making the hoof brittle and liable to crack, also narrowing the surface which bears on the ground. Flat feet sometimes need dumping so that nails can be driven in high enough up the wall to secure a firm hold.

4 *Paring the sole:* is very bad; a thick sole is nature's protection against injury. In olden days it was thought that paring the sole thin enough to yield to pressure of the thumb made the foot more elastic. The thin sole became dry and brittle, giving no protection against stones or other sharp objects on the road.

5 *Paring the frog:* it should never be cut away, as the larger it is the better. Only loose pieces should be trimmed off. In times

past it used to be cut away so that it should not touch the ground lest it should be injured. This caused a shrivelled frog, which was liable to thrush, was no longer a natural shock-absorber, and was liable to injury from the road.

6 *Opening the heels:* cutting away the bars to make the heels look wider weakens the heels, eventually making them contract.

7 *Too wide a shoe:* a shoe which projects anywhere beyond the foot is liable to cause brushing.

8 *Too long a shoe:* a shoe projecting beyond the heels may be torn off if struck by the toe of the hind foot. It should reach the end of the heel and be bevelled off in line with it.

9 *Too short a shoe:* may cause corns through not resting on the bars; it may therefore bruise the heels.

Remove

Whether stabled or living out have the feet trimmed regularly every four weeks. If the old shoes are used again instead of fitting new ones, this is called a remove.

When to re-shoe

When inspecting the feet daily look for the following signs that re-shoeing is necessary:

1 Shoe has worn thin. Some horses habitually drag one toe, especially when tired, thus wearing it away.

2 A loose shoe.

3 Clenches risen and standing out from the wall.

4 Foot growing too long especially at the toe, and getting out of shape.

5 Shoe has been cast (lost).

Duration of shoes

There is no hard and fast rule. A horse doing much strenuous work (e.g. hard hunting), or much road work, may need re-shoeing in a fortnight. Some wear out shoes less quickly than others. The animal's size and weight also affects wear; a pony will not wear its shoes as quickly as a 17-hand heavy hunter. Average wear varies between 100–350 miles. If a horse wears its shoes very quickly, shoe it with a convex shoe, having a thicker inner than an outer edge of the ground surface of the web. If a horse drags its hind toe use a single thickened toe-clip, instead of the two side clips normally used on a hind shoe.

Shoeing too frequently is as bad as not shoeing often enough as constant nailing breaks the wall, making it difficult to find enough room for the new nails.

Prevention of slipping

Normally, native British ponies are naturally sure-footed on any ordinary surface, but roads in some parts of the country have particularly slippery surfaces: so-called non-skid surfaces for motorists are the worst for horses. Also take extra precautions on icy winter roads.

Calkins : give extra grip under most normal conditions by digging into the ground.

Mordax studs : two types, nail in or screw in. If not too worn, the latter can be re-fitted to new shoes. They are made in three sizes.

Roughing : sharpening the calkins to a chisel edge; that at the outer heel lies across the shoe; the other points forward. The toe can also have sharp wedges.

Frost nails : sharp, specially hard-headed nails replace ordinary nails at the heels, and sometimes at the toes.

Screw cogs : are easily removed at night with special keys or taps. Screw cogs fit into special holes in the shoes at each heel, and also at the toe. When removed, they are replaced by blunt cogs to preserve the screw threads.

Rubber shoes : special rubber shoes are also obtainable. The makers claim they are absolutely skid-proof on any road surface and can be cold-fitted by the owner.

There is also a special method of shoeing called the 'Gragrip'.

Exercise

A stabled horse requires daily exercise as it cannot exercise itself like one at grass. It needs $1\frac{1}{2}$–2 hours in the morning and the same in the afternoon, if possible. Walk most of the time, alternating with short periods of trotting. A horse should only gallop occasionally as too much will break its wind. Even racehorses

The rider adjusts her stirrup leathers whilst in the saddle.

Holding a pair of single (snaffle) reins, the rider's forearm is in the correct position with the hands just above, but not resting on, the horse's withers.

Exercise for developing grip and balance. Standing in stirrups. Good leg position.

Exercise, bending forward and lying back on pony's croup, with knees firmly pressed against saddle. Good leg position from knee downwards.

Connemara – lovely riding pony for adult or youngster.

The Fell, a good 'ride and drive' family pony.

The Shetland is tough and hardy and very strong for its size. Sometimes too strong and self-willed for a small child's first pony.

The Exmoor, a good child's pony.

The Highland pony.

when training are only galloped once or twice a week, and then only for short distances. An occasional fairly slow canter does no harm. A certain amount of road-work, walking, does no harm and helps harden the feet. Do not trot long distances, and never canter, on a hard road; it ruins a horse's legs. Do not trot downhill on a hard road. Some trotting up- and downhill on a soft, even surface is good exercise and develops the muscles. Walk the last mile, bringing the horse in cool and not sweating; run up the irons and loosen the girths.

Dressage (schooling) and occasional jumping are good exercise and excellent training if not overdone, and the horse is not sickened by them. A dressage 'lesson' should last only 30–40 minutes; afterwards go for a hack to keep the horse interested. Only attempt about six jumps, always ending with a good one, never with a bad jump or a refusal. Do not discourage by over-facing with too high or difficult a jump; about 3 feet is quite high enough, and 2 ft 6 in. for a pony. After the jumping lesson go for a short hack.

Lungeing

Excellent exercise for a stabled horse which cannot be ridden for any reason. If a horse is too fresh lunge it for about 15 minutes before riding. Keep it going steadily on a long rein in a fairly big circle. First walk, then trot, and finally canter slowly. Always insist that it leads with the correct leg when cantering; never let it canter false. Lunge the same number of times in each direction. If it bucks or otherwise plays up pull it in and restart. Hold a long lungeing whip in one hand, trailing it behind the horse. Direct and encourage with your voice, rewarding with a tit-bit at the end if it has done well. Do not feed during the lesson or it will form a habit of stopping and wander into the middle, expecting food. Lungeing forms good action and carriage and supples a horse.

Free jumping down a Weedon Lane is also good exercise which a horse enjoys. It is an excellent way of teaching a young horse to jump and balance itself. Reward with a tit-bit at the end of the lane.

Stable vices

A stabled horse learns some tricks and vices like crib-biting, kicking and weaving through sheer boredom, and often by imitation. Satan finds mischief for idle hooves, as well as hands! Some horses behave well outside but are devils to handle in the stable. They seem to resent a human being; they will attack anyone entering their loose-box, with ears back, open-mouthed, teeth bared, and the whites of their eyes showing. Or they may turn and kick. Sometimes this is simply bluff: if spoken to firmly and fearlessly handled, nothing happens. Bad handling when young may frequently be the cause, or bad breaking-in: a rough, loud-voiced, bullying, heavy-handed, and impatient groom, too free with his fist or a stick. Horses are naturally timid and easily startled – and have very long memories. In such cases, firm but gentle handling often changes the horse's outlook and mentality by overcoming its fear. Some, however, are naturally bad-tempered and 'killers' and little can be done with them; fortunately they are rare.

Many confirmed biters and/or kickers in the stable have been cured by remaining in their box for several hours daily. Having made it harmless, by short-racking, sit down on a camp stool by its head and read. Talk to it occasionally, perhaps patting and offering it a tit-bit. Thus gradually wear down its suspicion and resentment. It needs much time, perhaps several weeks or even months, and infinite patience. Let it realize from the start that you intend to be master and enter its box, and are *not* afraid! Also, that you are friendly and kindly disposed towards it, whatever its feelings towards you. Let it become so accustomed to your presence that it takes no notice. Always feed it yourself until you become regarded as the bringer of pleasant things.

Crib-biting

A fairly common stable vice. The delinquent leans on or bites the manger, sucking in air with a grunt as it is gulped down. An incurable habit once acquired; one horse may imitate another or boredom and idleness may cause it. It wears down the teeth and may cause colic and indigestion. Minimize the effect by giving the horse as little opportunity as possible to indulge in this vice. Exercise regularly, keeping it out of the stable as much as possible. When stabled provide a haynet to amuse and occupy it. Never give it a salt-lick, which may encourage and has even been known to cause it. Isolate so that others cannot imitate. Cover a wooden manger with a sheet of tin; remove any fittings which could be bitten. Smear any immovable fittings with something unpleasant-tasting; e.g. mustard, soap, bitter aloes and treacle. Keep a bad case muzzled between meals.

Wind-sucking

Akin to crib-biting. Instead of biting anything the horse arches its neck, draws its head in towards its chest and gulps down air. It is incurable, originating through boredom or by imitation. Isolate and try to prevent it arching its neck and swallowing air; use a gullet plate and cribbing-strap.

The wood or metal gullet plate is stitched into a broad strap fitting tightly round the head and projecting on each side so that it sticks into its throat when its head is bent. A 'flute-bit', a hollow perforated snaffle, is even more effective as the horse cannot suck in air through the tube, or close its mouth. Keep well exercised and out of the stable as long as possible.

Biting

Giving too many tit-bits, or, especially, letting a horse nibble at your pockets for food, can start the habit, beginning as a playful nip, or show of temper and disappointment when not given an expected treat. Check the first time it happens with a hard rap on the nose and a scolding tone of voice. Only treat as a definite reward for some good behaviour. Short-rack when grooming so that the horse cannot turn its head round and nip. The first time it tries, scold and rap smartly on the nose. A confirmed biter may be cured eventually by spending hours in the stable. Make a really vicious biter, dangerous to handle, temporarily safe by using a side-stick – a short stick, reaching from the head-collar cheek-piece to the roller or surcingle and tied to each; it allows an up-and-down, but no sideways, movement. Alternatively, use a thick wooden bit to stop the teeth closing. Bad handling when young is usually the cause. Stallions and mares are more prone to bite than geldings.

Kicking

May start either through boredom, or fear due to rough handling at some time. Bored horses seem to like noise, the more monotonous the better; having nothing better to do they start kicking their loose-box door or stall partition because the sound amuses them. Some kick at night from dislike of the dark; a small safety light, however dim, well out of reach, may provide the remedy. Rats or mice may start a horse kicking. Itchy heels may also cause it, starting first as stamping. This type of kicking is not actually dangerous, apart from damaging wood-work, wearing hooves, or possible injury to legs or feet. Padding the door or stall partition, and any posts, with straw may prevent it; this stops the noise and lessens risk of injury. Or hang gorse or any other prickly plant where the horse kicks so that it pricks itself. Watch the effect carefully, as panic may make it kick even more.

Kicking caused by nervousness or fear is far more dangerous; mares kick more often than geldings. Spending hours in the stable may cure her. Always speak before approaching, move slowly, and handle gently. Be extra careful when grooming any known ticklish places. Hold the tail when grooming the hindquarters or hind legs, or hold the hock or hamstring firmly with your free hand. Any leg movement will be instantly felt and adequate advance warning given. Speak soothingly if you feel any movement and temporarily stop grooming that particular part.

If your pony kicks despite these precautions, scold sharply, giving a smart slap on the hindquarters, to make it realize its attentions are not appreciated! Short-rack to prevent movement while grooming. Give some hay to occupy its attention.

Strap up, or ask another person to hold up, the foreleg of a confirmed and really dangerous kicker while grooming. Since a horse can only stand on three legs for a short time, allow it intervals of rest. Have a thick straw bed lest it loses its balance and falls while standing on three legs. The nearer one stands the safer one is because the kick has less force. Laid-back ears and swishing tail are warnings of imminent trouble.

A kicking block, consisting of a shackle with a few links of heavy chain and a smooth wooden ball attached, is another preventative. If the horse kicks, the chain and ball hit its legs. Another is to tie heavy weights (e.g. sandbags) to the legs; or hang these behind so that they swing back when struck.

Weaving

Another nervous habit generally caused by boredom and idleness. Keep well exercised and out of the stable as much as possible. Wild animals in captivity often develop this habit; elephants in a zoo seem especially prone to it.

Symptoms: incessant swinging of head, neck, and forehand from side to side, sometimes lifting each forefoot in turn as the body sways to the opposite side.

Isolate a confirmed weaver as others will imitate. It gives itself no rest, prolonged waste of energy making it thin and lose condition.

A weaver is considered unsound and the vice may be hereditary. Prevention: divide feeds into small portions given frequently; in the stable keep constantly occupied with a haynet. Whenever possible keep out at grass. When stabled prevent its head moving laterally by tying to pillar-reins on both sides.

Gnawing the walls

Licking or gnawing at the whitewashed stable walls may be due to a craving for lime, owing to insufficient minerals in its diet; also to insufficient food (plain starvation) or insufficient bulk. Also caused by sheer boredom! Some internal parasite may also cause it.

Gnawing or licking through idleness sometimes leads to wind-sucking and crib-biting, so try to stop it. Tar that part of the wall with tar varnish: 1 part tar to 3 parts naphtha.

Eating dung

A depraved appetite, eating its own droppings but not those of other horses. Indigestion may cause this, so call in a vet; study the diet carefully to see that it is sufficient and properly balanced.

Stop the horse eating off the ground by passing a strap behind its poll to hang down just below the throat lash; loop it to another strap over the nostrils like a noseband. When it tries to lower its head the straps press on its nostrils and neck muscles, thus preventing extension of its neck.

Stabling

Portable stables

Most people probably do not live in a house having proper stabling. The answer is one of the portable units made by several firms, most of which advertise. They are wooden buildings, made in sections which can be assembled by anyone. You must get planning permission for it. An added advantage is that if one moves they can be dismantled and reassembled. They are made in units of various designs, say a tack-room and stall or loose-box, etc. A stable need take up no more space than a garage for a medium-sized car, and the horse being a clean animal, it can be fairly near the house. There is no smell if the horse is properly looked after, and the stable mucked out and kept clean. One of the signs of good horsemanship is that stable and yard are kept clean and tidy!

Aspect

Choose a south or south-west aspect, keeping the entrance away from north or east winds.

Size

Stall: about 12 × 6 feet.
Loose-box: horse – 14 × 12 feet; pony – 12 × 10 feet.

Ventilation

Plenty of light and fresh air are necessary, but keep the stable free from draughts. Have the windows fairly high, opening inwards from the bottom. The Sheringham type is the best. At floor level have a ventilator brick with a grating, and a roof ventilator to allow warm, foul air to escape.

Doors

Should open outwards, never inwards in case the horse gets cast near the door. Have it divided into two parts, each hinged so that both open or close independently. Always keep the top half open, except in very cold or bad weather.

Drainage

Floor should slope slightly down towards the front, with a channel and drain with a grating for the urine. It should only slope sufficiently for liquid to flow, as a horse gets no proper rest and it is very bad for its legs to stand on a slanting surface.

Fittings

Have one ring fairly high for short-racking, with a second for tying the horse with its head at its normal height, alongside the manger. Also have some place and means of tying a haynet, not too high. Hay racks high up are bad as seeds and dust may get into the horse's eyes.

Manger

About 2 ft 6 in. high, made of some easily cleaned material, preferably in a corner; do not have it directly underneath a window because of draught. Avoid sharp, protruding edges and board the underneath in level so that the horse cannot knock its leg against it. If possible, have a water-trough alongside the manger, made of easily cleaned material, with running water and a tap. Troughs are obtainable which automatically refill as the horse drinks, thus keeping permanently full of fresh, clean water.

Floor

Roughened tiles, placed edgeways, are best. Concrete can become very slippery if wet as it wears; if used, roughen the surface before it sets while being laid. Brick flooring may wear unevenly. Wooden flooring is bad: it is difficult to clean and becomes sodden and slippery.

Food storage

For convenience, store bedding straw, hay, and other food as near as possible. To avoid encouraging rats store grain and bran in bins. Corn bins are expensive, but dustbins are excellent for small quantities (e.g. 1 cwt. corn or bran). Their lids should fit tightly. Hay stored in quantity is bulky, but when bales are piled on top of each other a ton, neatly stacked, takes up astonishingly little space. Keep in a dry, waterproof place, and being so inflammable, preferably in a stone building or somewhere where there is no risk from fire if it did catch alight. Hay can catch alight through spontaneous combustion if damp and under pressure – i.e. too tightly stacked.

General lay-out

In a large stable stalls and/or loose-boxes are usually on three sides of a square round a central yard, sometimes large enough to form a show- or exercise-ring.

If no good stabling is available, a hardy horse or pony is better off living out with some sort of shelter. Stables must be dry, light, airy, and well ventilated yet free from draughts. Low, damp, dark, draughty, fusty stables are worse than none at all, a breeding ground for diseases, coughs, cold, and rheumatism!

9 Stable Equipment

There are two kinds of equipment: (a) that required for the horse's comfort and well-being; (b) articles needed for cleaning stable and yard.

Horse clothing

A stabled, clipped horse needs day and night rugs; stable (rest) bandages; exercise bandages; Yorkshire boot (if a horse knocks its fetlock, going too close behind); hock boots; boots (schooling, jumping); knee caps; tail bandages and tail guard (for travelling); New Zealand rug (for a trace-clipped horse/pony turned out in winter).

Rugs

Day rugs

In winter, for keeping a stabled, clipped horse warm. In summer: cotton rugs, for warm weather to keep clean after grooming and to keep away flies. Use woollen rugs for cooler weather, even in summer.

Rugs have braid binding of another colour, often with their owner's initials in the corner, with a roller to match, to prevent the rug slipping when the horse lies down or rolls. The roller is made of leather, well padded where it rests each side of the spine.

Between the pads is a fairly high, leather-covered metal arch which prevents the horse becoming cast when rolling. The rug should fit round the neck like a loose collar; if the head-opening is too large it may work back over the shoulders until the top is drawn tightly across the withers, causing a sore place through pressure.

Winter day rugs

Use a pure wool blanket under the rug, kept in place by the roller, providing extra warmth for a clipped horse.

Night rugs

Jute or hemp, lined with woollen material. Used for keeping day rugs clean as they become very soiled when a horse lies down. If a night rug is unavailable for economy reasons, use the day rug turned inside out.

In cold weather do not strip the night rug or rugs right off before grooming. Turn them back neatly over the loins while grooming the forehand. Then pull up again, laying them over the shoulders while grooming the hindquarters.

Rugging up

Gather up and throw the rug well forward over the horse's back; straighten the front part and fasten the buckle. Next pull it back into its correct position, standing behind the horse, using both hands. This is one of the few occasions when one stands directly behind a horse. After putting the surcingle in its right position buckle firmly but not too tightly. There must be no wrinkles underneath it on the near side; the rug must not press or drag on the neck and/or shoulder, and must be the right size, neither too small nor too large; either may rub, causing sore withers.

In winter put the blanket on first in the same way as the rug, when using, taking care to pull it high enough up on the neck; it should not hang down below the root of the tail. Do not wrinkle or disturb the blanket when placing the rug on top. After fastening the rug turn back the protruding portion of blanket lying on the neck, as an extra precaution against slipping.

Off rugging

Unbuckle the surcingle on the near side; after folding lay it down in a corner of the stall or loose-box. Undo the breast buckle of the rug, fold back rug (and blanket, if any) over the horse's back, using both hands. Holding the centre of the rug in front with the left hand, and the centre of the back with the right, pull rug and blanket off together in one gentle backward movement, in the direction of the hair. The rugs automatically fold into four as they come off.

Care of rugs

Brush night rugs carefully: keep folded when not used. Brush daily after use; air outside once a week in fine weather, especially when sunny. Also brush day rugs well daily, and air weekly. Have two of each if possible.

When winter ends, send heavy woollen rugs to the cleaners and when returned store with some moth-protecting powder (e.g. naphtha) or in moth-proof bags. Wash cotton rugs and air thoroughly before storing for the winter; also scrub jute rugs.

Stable (rest) bandages

Obtained in sets of four. Used (a) for warmth and comfort; (b) to prevent a stabled horse's legs filling (i.e. swelling) when standing unused; (c) with straw underneath to dry legs on returning from work in wet weather; (d) protection against injury especially if a horse habitually kicks: *see* Stable Vices). They should cover as much of the leg as possible from the knee (front leg), or hock (hind leg), downwards.

Exercise bandages

Use at work to protect legs from thorns or brambles, strengthen and support weak or strained tendons, and/or support back tendons. Put a thick cotton-wool or gamgee layer smoothly next to the skin underneath bandages, to allow for shrinkage if wetted. Bandage firmly from just below the knee to just above the fetlock without hindering the action of either joint; they give support when jumping, hunting, or racing, etc.

Bandaging

Stable and exercise bandages are both put on alike, except for their position on the leg.

To bandage so that it cannot slip, unroll about 10 inches, holding across the outside of the leg, close to the knee. Keep the rolled bandage close to the leg. The other hand holds the spare end, extending beyond the leg. Wind once around, letting the spare end fall over, down the inside of the leg. Wind over the spare end and then neatly down to the fetlock joint. A rest bandage covers the fetlock, continuing down to the pastern joint; an exercise bandage only goes down to the fetlock joint. On reaching the lowest point to be bandaged, turn up the remainder of the spare end, bandaging upwards towards the starting point. Fold over the end of the banadge neatly; tie on the outside of the leg – never on the inside, or at the front or back.

Unbandaging

Never roll up while removing a bandage. Untie the tapes and unwind quickly, passing it from hand to hand. After unbandaging rub back tendons and fetlocks briskly with the palms of the hands. Never kneel while bandaging or unbandaging, as it is dangerous; always bend forward or crouch.

To wind a bandage turn the tying tapes neatly over the back, on the side on which sewn, and wind over them. Keep bandage tight, holding it between your knees to make it taut.

Hock boots

Prevent injury to hocks when lying down at night. Injury causes a swollen ('capped') hock. Hock boots are not essential; a capped hock rarely occurs if the straw bedding is sufficiently thick; it usually happens through lying on insufficient bedding.

Knee caps

Worn as protection when travelling.

Boots

Worn on front legs for schooling and jumping as protection

against knocks. They should not be worn out hunting, or where it is muddy; mud may get inside, causing a rub.

Yorkshire boot

Only required when a horse knocks its fetlock through going too close behind. It is made of felt with a tape sewn across the middle. It is tied round just above the fetlock joint and folded over.

Tail bandage

Keeps tail in shape after pulling and trimming it. Damp hair with a water-brush and brush flat. Bandage from the root to below the end of the dock. Never damp the bandage as it shrinks while drying, causing acute pain. If knotted tightly on the dock it stops the circulation, causing white hairs. Do not keep it on for longer than necessary. To remove, slide bandage down the tail with both hands without untying the tapes.

Tail guard

Used over a tail bandage while travelling to prevent possible injury by rubbing. Made of wool or leather with a strap at one end fastening it to the arch of the roller to keep it in positon.

New Zealand rug

Enables a clipped pony to be turned out to graze and exercise itself by day in mild winter weather. A trace-clipped pony can live out in one, except in very severe winter weather.

Made of waterproof canvas, wool lined; leg-straps pass under the hind legs to keep it in place. So designed that even if a horse rolls, it returns to its correct position. To keep it clean and the straps free from mud, it is advisable to have two. Examine and adjust the rug daily. The 'Emston' rug is the best, and original, type.

Stable implements

Include all grooming kit; also accessories like clippers, tooth rasp, twitch; cleaning tools such as straw or hay fork, yard brooms and brushes, skep (manure basket). A list of grooming kit has already been given (page 65). A sack, cut open, can be used instead of a skep for collecting droppings.

Clippers

Hand clippers

Like the ordinary barber's clippers, only larger: used for hogging manes and trimming heels.

Clipping machine

For clipping out.

1 *Hand-operated:* needing an assistant who turns the handle to work the blades. Being noisy and cumbersome, they are now only used where electricity is unavailable.

2 *Electrically operated:* fast and silent, one can clip out a horse single-handed. The blades rotate at very high speed, making it much quicker, more efficient, and less likely to pull the hairs and cause discomfort. Resembles a modern electric dry shaver, or a barber's electric clippers.

Keep the blades of hand-operated and electric clippers razor sharp, well oiled, and free from hair. Stop frequently when clipping to empty out hairs. As the fine hairs are messy and difficult to pick up, clip outside in the stable yard. Choose a fine, mild day without any wind.

Tooth rasp

Should only be used by a vet, not by an amateur. If a horse fusses with its bit, its teeth may be causing pain. Quidding is another sign, when food drops out of its mouth while eating. Thirdly, where food (e.g. corn) passes through whole and undigested and can be seen in the droppings. These signs show that one or more teeth have sharp points which need filing down. Sharp, rough teeth can cause indigestion, and make a horse irritable. Have blades sharpened frequently.

Twitch

Sometimes used to keep a troublesome horse quiet if it will not stand still for clipping, trimming, or dressing a wound. Only use as a last resort after trying everything else possible.

Although now illegal, the ordinary twitch is still used. A piece of cord attached to a stick is looped round the sensitive upperlip just below the nostrils and then tightened by twisting the stick. Any jerk by the person holding the stick, or by the horse, is painful.

A Comanche twitch is less painful. Pass a cord over the poll, down the side of the face and under the muzzle over the gums. Then pass it up the head-collar through the 'D'.

It remains slack without causing pain until used.

Cleaning tools

Two-pronged hay fork: for bedding down and carrying hay. An ordinary garden fork; a large shovel (e.g. snow shovel). Hard-bristle brooms: for sweeping stable and yard. Skep (or manure basket), or sacks cut open: for collecting droppings. Also useful when picking-out feet. Place it underneath for dirt to fall into it instead of on the ground. A bushel potato basket makes an excellent skep.

Miscellaneous equipment

Useful accessories: saddle horse and bridle hook for cleaning; zinc bins for food; saddle and bridle racks; pails (feeding; tack-cleaning); arrange all these in the tack-room.

Saddle brackets

An inverted 'Vee'-shape, about 18 inches long; attached to the tack-room wall at a convenient height.

Bridle brackets

Half-moon shaped with a curved front. Hang bridles either below each saddle or together.

Girth-straps, stirrup-leathers

Also hung on hooks, either below each saddle or together.

First aid equipment

Three- and four-inch calico bandages. Small packet of surgical lint; 1 lb. of cotton-wool. Pair blunt-nosed surgical scissors; clinical thermometer. Bottle of some mild disinfectant (e.g. Dettol, permanganate of potash). One pint bottle lead lotion. Colic drink (vet's prescription), jar cough electuary, tin boracic powder. Tin kaolin or antiphlogistin paste. Packet of assorted safety pins. Small saucepan. Packet of fairly large darning needles (large eyes). Reel of strong thread. Drenching bottle for giving medicine. Old kitchen knife. Tablespoon. Sulphanilamide powder in plastic bottle.

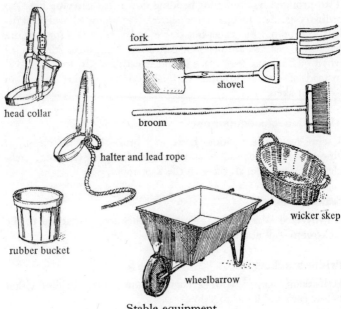

head collar

fork

shovel

broom

halter and lead rope

wicker skep

rubber bucket

wheelbarrow

Stable equipment

10 Tack

Tack

Head-collars, bridles, saddles, stirrup-leathers and irons; collectively known as tack (short for tackle) by horsemen, never saddlery. Harness applies only to a horse that is driven.

Head-collar

Leather, consisting of a headband across the poll, browband, noseband, and throat-lash; metal 'D's where the straps join, and for the leading rope. Fastens with an adjustable buckle on the near side. Primarily for the stable but often used for catching a horse; sometimes left on a difficult horse to catch when out at grass (see page 47). This is not recommended as a pony may get hooked up.

Halter

Simply two straps, one passing over the head behind the ears, the other over the nose. Made of rope or hemp and used for catching and leading.

Do not use for tethering, or racking-up in the stable as a pony can slip out of it too easily.

Bridles

Single bridle

One pair of reins: used with a snaffle bit.

Parts of single bridle

Headband : fitting behind the ears, over the poll.

D

Browband: across the forehead, in front of and just below the ears.

Cheek-pieces: on each side, buckling on to headband and adjustable in length. The lower ends fix on to the cheek-rings of the bit. Cheek-pieces or cheek-straps fasten to the cheek-pieces with billets or buckles, or are sewn on. The last is unsatisfactory as the bridle cannot be taken to pieces for cleaning; billets are better, looking neater than buckles.

Throat-lash: also buckles on to the headband; goes under the throat, preventing the bridle slipping off over the horse's ears. It is also adjustable in length.

Reins: are also stitched or fastened with billets or buckles to the cheek-rings; again, billets are best. Never have reins stitched to the cheek-pieces so that they cannot be unfastened for cleaning. Cheek-piece straps, and throat-lash, pass through fixed leather loops (keepers) and movable leather loops (runners). A broad leather strap (noseband) encircles the nose, buckling under the chin. It fastens to another cheek-strap also going over the poll, and adjustable in length. It, too, passes through the headband loop, going underneath the other headband. Always use a dropped noseband, passing below the bit, with a snaffle bridle. Some snaffle bridles have side pieces and a keeper to prevent the bit moving sideways in the horse's mouth.

Double Bridle

Really two bridles with the bits, a curb and snaffle, with a pair of reins for each.

Parts for double bridle

Two headbands (crown pieces) fitting over the poll behind the ears. Each fastens to a cheek-piece, one for the curb bit, the other for the snaffle. A third headband fastens to the noseband. Each adjusts in length with buckles. Always use a cavesson noseband, fitting above, not below, the bits as in the case of a dropped noseband, with a double bridle. The headbands pass through loops on the browband. The throat-lash buckles to the headband, as in a single bridle. The curb chain belonging to the curb bit is thick and flat, fitting *across* in the chin groove. There is also a lip-strap made in two parts, each fastened to the curb bit cheeks.

It passes through the spare curb chain link and fits loosely. The Snaffle (bridoon) rein is usually slightly wider.

Bits

Three main types, snaffle, curb, and Pelham, with a numerous variety of each.

Types of snaffle

1 *Half-moon and straight bar:* metal, vulcanite, or rubber. Both are very mild and can be used to remake a pony's mouth which has become hard.

2 *Plain ring (smooth-jointed snaffle):* a 'broken' bit, with the advantage that, being jointed, it can act on one side of the mouth without affecting the other. Should be fairly thick and free from wear or rough edges, especially at the joint; a mild bit, one of the

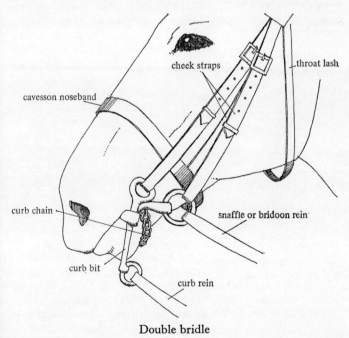

Double bridle

most suitable for a beginner or for hacking, especially for a pony with a soft mouth.

3 *Egg-butt snaffle :* fairly thick and also jointed in the middle. Also mild and one of the best for general use or a beginner.

4 *Gag snaffle :* a powerful bit, only suitable for very experienced riders; acts on the corners of the lips.

Types of curb

The bridoon (snaffle) of a double bridle has a thinner mouthpiece than any of the above snaffles. The curb bit has a fixed or movable mouthpiece and a curb chain, with or without a lip strap. The Bridoon (snaffle) raises a horse's head, making it flex or give to the bit. With a double bridle ride on the bridoon rein, only using the curb for control and for special purposes. A curb bit lowers a horse's head, arching its neck so that its muzzle is held inwards towards its chest. It stops it raising its head or 'stargazing', and prevents it trying to get its head up preparatory to bolting. The

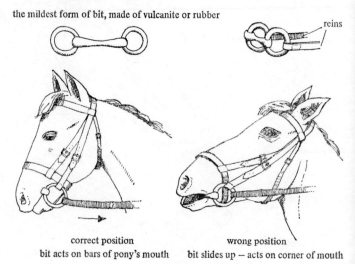

straight barred snaffle

the mildest form of bit, made of vulcanite or rubber

reins

correct position
bit acts on bars of pony's mouth

wrong position
bit slides up – acts on corner of mouth

Snaffle bit

mouthpiece bears on the mouth and tongue; the cheeks of the bit form a lever, giving increased pressure on the bars. The curb chain acts as a fulcrum, but without causing any pain. A high port (arch) on the mouthpiece presses against the roof of the mouth, adding to the bit's severity. Do not use a curb bit along without a bridoon as continual pressure on the lower jaw eventually deadens all feeling.

1 *Long-cheeked curb bit:* straight mouthpiece. The long cheeks increase severity because of greater leverage. The longer the cheeks, the more severe the bit.

2 *Short-cheeked curb bit:* a central port (arch) fits over the tongue, pressing on the roof of the mouth; the higher the port, the more severe the bit.

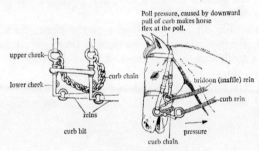

Curb bit

Pelham bit

Attempts to make one bit do the work of both snaffle and curb. Though theoretically unsound in principle, in practice some horses go better in a Pelham than in anything else. Bridoon and curb reins are used on the one bit. Occasionally there is only one rein, fastened to a leather strap which is buckled to the bridoon and curb rings on the cheeks of the bit.

1 *Half-moon Pelham:* an unbroken, slightly curved mouth-piece.

2 *Jointed Pelham:* a 'broken' mouthpiece with central joint.

3 *Scamperdale:* a variety of Pelham.

There are also a number of other types.

A frequent mistake is to use a more severe bit when a horse pulls, whereas a milder bit is often the cure; a horse often pulls through fear of pain, or from actual pain, from the bit. It often throws its head about, invents all sorts of evasions and pulls, through pain from a too severe bit. Its jaw becomes numbed and the bars of its mouth may be injured, thus ruining its mouth through becoming hard and insensitive. Pain from the bit may cause a swallowed tongue, a tongue over the bit, or a dry mouth, caused by drawing the tongue back and keeping its mouth slightly open. Air entering the mouth rapidly dries it up so that the bars easily bruise or lacerate.

A double bridle's severity or mildness depends on the rider's hands, seat, and experience, length of the cheek-pieces (the longer they are, the greater the bit's severity), height of the port, and tightness of the curb chain.

Use a snaffle bit for schooling a young horse, hacking and jumping, for beginners, and for novice dressage; also for re-making a spoilt mouth, to persuade a horse to accept the bit and lower its head.

An experienced rider should use a double bridle on a well-schooled horse, for advanced training and dressage, and for showing.

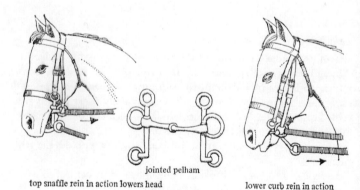

jointed pelham

top snaffle rein in action lowers head   lower curb rein in action

Pelham bit

Action of bit

A straight-barred and half-moon Pelham acts on the bars; a jointed snaffle acts on the sides of the mouth and corners of the lips with a nutcracker action. A double bridle acts with a pincer movement, the bit squeezing the bars while the curb chain squeezes in the curb-groove. The curb pulling downwards presses on the poll making the horse flex and arch its neck inwards.

Fitting a bridle

Conformation of the horse's head and neck is important when fitting a bridle. It is difficult to make a horse flex or carry its head correctly if its lower jaw branches are too close together, or if its neck is too short. If one tries to make a badly shaped horse carry its head correctly it will pull because it is in pain.

When bridling with a snaffle, the bit must lie correctly on the bars of the mouth. It must not be high enough to wrinkle the lips, nor low enough down to allow the horse to get its tongue over the bit. Adjust the length of the cheek-straps. The strap of the dropped noseband should be below the bit. Its upper part should not be so low down as to press on the nostrils or interfere with the horse's breathing. Only fasten the strap tightly enough to prevent the horse opening its mouth wide or crossing its jaw. It should be possible to insert two fingers together on edge between the strap and the jaw.

Have the throat-lash loose enough to insert three fingers between the strap and the horse; it is often fastened too tightly, which interferes with breathing.

The browband should not be too tight; it should fit well clear below the ears.

Fit a double bridle so that its snaffle bit is as high as possible without wrinkling the lips. Use a thick, curb chain, lying flat in the chin-groove. Do not have it too tight, but just tight enough to draw back the cheek-pieces to 45° with the horse's mouth. Fasten the lip-strap loosely, passing it through the loose link of the curb chain.

Adjust a cavesson noseband's cheek-straps in length so

that it is above the snaffle bit; not below, unlike a dropped noseband.

Saddle

Parts of saddle

Tree : the steel or wood frame on which the saddle is built.

Pommel : covers the front arch of the tree.

Skirt : protects the legs from the stirrup-bar.

Waist : narrowest part of saddle.

Seat, cantle : covers the back arch of the tree.

Saddle-flap : protects the leg from the girth straps and point pocket.

Panel : the stuffed portion underneath the flap.

Sweat flap : usually stitched to saddle to keep it in position; protects panel from becoming sweat-stained.

Gullet : groove down the centre of saddle to prevent it resting on or injuring the horse's spine.

Lining : leather, linen or felt.

Point-pocket : for the point of the tree.

Girth straps : two or three straps for fastening the girth; resting on the sweat flap.

Types of saddles

1 *Hunting saddle :* most often seen and the most useful general-purpose saddle for hacking, apart from hunting. Its panel is the same length as the flap, which extends slightly forward. The panel has a slight roll giving extra grip for the rider's knees when jumping or galloping. Modern saddles are cut with what is called the 'forward seat'.

2 *Jumping saddle :* especially for show-jumping, having the flaps cut much more forward to enable the rider's knees to grip when leaning forward to jump. The panel has a much thicker roll to give the maximum grip. It is not an all-round general-purpose saddle and not so comfortable for ordinary hacking.

3 *Dressage saddle :* the panel is short so that only the flap intervenes between the rider's legs and his horse, giving him as

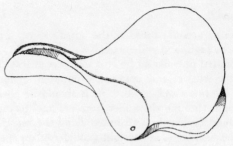

Jumping saddle

close contact as possible. The flap is cut much straighter and the panel has much less roll.

4 *Racing saddle :* very small and light, with weight pockets. Panels are much more forward and higher than the jumping saddle because a jockey's racing seat has very short stirrup-leathers.

5 *Military saddle :* high pommel and cantle with a deep seat; the flap goes straight down, more like a Western (American), or a Colonial saddle. The rider sits deep in the saddle, riding with very long stirrup-leathers and legs stretched straight down. The official *Military Handbook on Animal Management* specifies that a blanket should be used underneath.

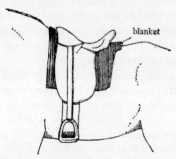

Military saddle (note the high pommel and cantle, and long stirrup-leather)

Fitting a saddle

It must on no account press on the horse's spine. The pommel arch must be high, and wide enough not to press on the withers. When mounted one should be able to insert at least two fingers between the withers and pommel, even when leaning forward and throwing one's weight on to it. It should be possible to see daylight right through the gullet from pommel to cantle. One's weight should be evenly distributed along the muscles on both sides of the backbone. No weight should rest on the loins; the shoulders must also be free.

A saddle must be the correct size and shape to suit the horse. If the arch is too broad, it presses on the withers and spine, causing a sore back and/or withers. If the arch is too narrow, it pinches the withers. Too large a saddle will roll about, again causing a sore back. A saddle must also be the right size to fit the rider. Riding on too small a saddle is most uncomfortable as one is not sitting on the correct part but is thrown too far back; one's legs also have insufficient flap to give a good grip. Conversely, if too large, the rider tends to roll about, causing saddle sores.

The panel stuffing must be thick enough and correctly shaped. If too thin or if it has become spread about and thin through use, the pommel will press down on the withers. Have the saddle restuffed; until this can be done use a wither pad, which is usually a knitted woollen, oval-shaped bag, stuffed with some soft material; alternatively use a felt or foam rubber numnah, or a folded blanket, as used in the Army. Pull the wither pad well up under the arch when putting on the saddle. It is only useful when the arch is too wide; only use it as a temporary expedient until the saddle can be made to fit properly.

When fitting a new saddle place a fairly thick folded blanket beneath it and girth up. Ride for about thirty minutes. The saddle makes an impression on the blanket where the rider's weight presses it down, making it easy to see whether it fits correctly with the weight resting on the muscles on each side of the back-bone. Look for pressure at the top edges of the tree's side bar, behind the front arch; also the bottom edge in front of the rear arch.

Change in a horse's condition may alter the fit of a saddle, and it may vary between summer and winter.

Always stand a saddle on its pommel if placing it on the ground. Never lay it flat on the ground with panels and flaps pressing outwards; this may break the tree or widen the arch. To protect the leather place the girth under the pommel.

Girths

Leather : the strongest, but may gall unless kept throughly soft and pliable, well cleaned, with saddle soap rubbed well in. Or keep a strip of woollen rest bandage soaked in neatsfoot oil, between the folds. A three-fold girth is the best type, or a Balding.

Web : does not wear very well and may snap without warning. Always use two girths. Using a single web girth is dangerous as the strain may break it. Have them wide to prevent galling. Keep soft and clean by frequent washing with warm soap and water. Web girths are also inclined to slip.

String : less liable to gall as air circulates freely, preventing sweating. Like web girths they may break suddenly, so always use two together. They last longer and slip less on an unclipped pony than web girths.

Nylon : probably the best. Being very strong they are unlikely to break suddenly. Free air circulates, preventing galling and sweating. They clean easily with soap and water and dry quickly. New nylon girths may stretch at first.

Leathers and irons

Irons should be about $1\frac{1}{2}$ inches wider than the widest part of one's shoe so that it slips out easily if one falls. Irons fitting tightly are dangerous, as if one comes off one is liable to be dragged. They are made of polished steel, nickel or stainless steel. Nickel may break; polished steel will rust and needs a lot of cleaning. Stainless steel are best; they do not break easily and are easier to keep polished. Stirrup-leathers are always called leathers and stirrup-irons are simply irons, in the riding world.

Martingales

Three types: standing, running, Irish. It prevents a horse,

especially a young one, throwing its head up: it is not meant to keep it down: the rider should learn how to do this. A young horse which throws up its head is inclined to bolt.

Standing martingale : a neck strap supports a strap, fastened at one end to the cavesson or noseband, and at the other between the pony's legs, to the girth. Only use it with a double bridle, not with a snaffle bridle and dropped noseband.

When fitting have it long enough not to come into use until the horse raises its head higher than the correct position.

Running martingale : used on the curb it makes a horse flex its jaws. The martingale rings must be smaller than those on the curb bit so that they cannot slip over the latter and cause a bad accident.

One end fastens between the legs to the girth, like a standing martingale; the other divides into two straps each having a ring at the end through which the reins pass. A neck strap supports it.

Can be used on the bridoon reins (double bridle) or with a snaffle (single) bridle.

Irish martingale : a strap 4–6 inches long, with two rings attached. Used with a snaffle bridle, the reins pass through the rings below the horse's neck. It makes it flex its jaw and stops the reins being thrown over its head if the rider comes off over its head.

Fitting

Standing martingale : when the horse holds its head correctly the martingale, fastened at both ends, should reach the horse's gullet when pushed up from below.

Running martingale : when fastened to the girth with both rings up one side, they should reach up to the withers.

On both types of martingale the neck straps should so fit that there is a hand's width at the withers. They buckle on the near side.

Whips

There are various kinds for different purposes: hunting crop, schooling whip, cutting whip (racing), cutting whip (hacking), leather-covered riding cane (hacking), plain riding cane, and ordinary blackthorn riding cane, beloved by real horsemen.

Hunting crop : should only be carried out hunting. Head is made of horn, hooked in shape especially for opening gates. Its stock is bamboo or leather-covered. It has a thong or lash with a leather keeper. Always carry with its handle pointing downwards, and never uppermost or without the thong. Only those who want to look 'horsy', but know little about horses, do this.

Schooling whip: is longer than an ordinary hacking whip: used for guiding a young pony when training and schooling.

Cutting (racing) whip: has a large leather keeper at the end; makes a resounding smack when the horse is hit, without cutting or marking it.

Cutting (hacking) whip: about 2 feet long, with a leather keeper and wrist strap (most useful). Should not be too short. The best are whalebone, while cheaper ones are wire, covered over; they can be leather-covered or plain.

Riding canes: slightly shorter than a hacking whip. Hold them balanced in the middle, head pointing towards the pony's near-side ear. They are leather-covered, plain, or made of blackthorn. Ladies generally carry a hacking whip; men prefer a riding cane though they may carry a whip if they like.

Use of the whip

It should seldom be necessary to use it seriously for punishment. Its constant use generally denotes a bad rider, who does not know how to use the aids (hands and legs) properly. A horse should not fear the whip. Never hit a horse on the head; always apply it behind the girths. A light tap is sometimes better than constant drumming with the heels to urge on a sluggish horse. Constant heel drumming soon makes a horse's sides insensitive ('dead on the leg'). Never use it on a shying or frightened horse as it will only become more afraid and restive. If one must hit a horse for something really wrong, hit it hard, once, and immediately, so that it understands why it is being punished. It is most harmful to hit it some time after it has done wrong: better forget the whole incident, as it does not understand why it is suddenly being punished. Never hit a horse when in a bad temper!

Care of tack

Good tack is very expensive, but well cared for and cleaned lasts for years. Carelessness and neglect cause many accidents. Frequently examine girths, girth straps, stirrup-leathers, bridles and reins for wear, especially at the stitching, buckles, and strap holes, and repair immediately. Clean and saddle-soap tack and polish bits and irons every ride. Periodically strip saddles, take bridles completely to pieces, and thoroughly clean. Dirty tack is bad horsemanship; nothing looks worse, however well groomed the horse, or well dressed its rider.

Occasionally shorten stirrup-leathers from their buckle end, bringing wear into fresh holes and on to another part of the leather.

Hanging up bridle

Hang on bridle brackets in the tack-room. To 'put up' a single bridle, fasten the noseband right round the outside of the cheek-straps. Hang it by its headband with the browband round the curved part of the bracket; loop reins over the top, with the buckle joining both reins in the centre.

To put up a double bridle run the throat-lash through the ends of the reins and, as before, put the noseband round outside the cheek-straps. Hook the curb chain in front of the bit.

Storing a saddle

If not being frequently used, strip the saddle before putting on its bracket. Hang up girths and leathers beside it. Do not strip a saddle in daily use; run up irons on the leathers, cover saddle with a cloth and loop girth across the seat. Before storing a saddle, rub it over with castor oil. Soak a cloth in neatsfoot oil and place between the folds of a leather girth, before storing for any length of time.

Cleaning

Keep all leather pliable with oil or fat; otherwise it dries, cracks, and hardens, causing sores.

Cleaning materials

Castor oil, dubbin, neatsfoot oil, olive oil, glycerine: all good for leather, especially when not being used. Do not use linseed or mineral oil as they harden. For bits, stirrup-irons, etc., use metal polish: those having some kind of soft material impregnated with metal polish (e.g. Duraglit) are good and save labour. Steel wool can be used but is inclined to scratch. When steel bits, irons and curb chains need burnishing, silver sand and jeweller's rouge are often used. To burnish curb chains shake them together in a cloth, or rub between the hands. Brown shoe polish makes saddles slippery and comes off on one's clothes.

Equipment

Saddle horse (cleaning saddles): a double hook, adjustable in length, suspended from the ceiling or a beam (cleaning bridles).

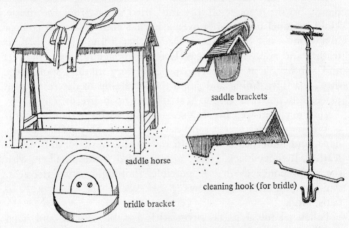

saddle brackets

saddle horse

cleaning hook (for bridle)

bridle bracket

Miscellaneous equipment

Cleaning a bridle

Hang up on the hook. Remove curb chain of a double bridle, or a Pelham, putting it in a bucket of water; remove bridoon, cavesson noseband, and lip-strap; undo all buckles, putting them into the lowest holes. Wash with warm (not hot) water, drying all leather-work with a leather. Clean and polish all metal (bits, buckles, etc.). Soap all leather, especially the undersides, keeping the soap-sponge almost dry. Wet and apply soap to sponge; do not wet the sponge and apply it to the soap. Use glycerine saddle soap, e.g. Propert's, for keeping clean leather supple. While cleaning look for enlarged buckle holes or other signs of wear. Having thoroughly dried and polished the curb chain reassemble the bridle with all buckles in correct holes and strap-ends in their keepers and runners.

Cleaning a saddle

Place on the saddle horse and strip, removing girths, stirrup-leathers and irons. Clean leather, linen, or serge linings. Wash leather lining with a sponge and warm water. Wait until mud is thoroughly dry and brush linen or serge lining well with a dandy brush. Remove all dirt and dried sweat from the inside. Hold pommel downwards over a bucket and wash with cold or lukewarm – not hot – water. Dry leather lining with a chamois leather and apply saddle soap. Use one sponge for removing dirt and another, kept dry, for soaping. If very muddy, sponge the dirt off a linen lining and stand the saddle up to dry in a warm place, but not near direct heat like an open fire or a radiator. Scrub, dry, and well brush a serge lining with the dandy brush.

When dry place on the saddle horse; thoroughly wash the seat, flaps, and underneath with cold water, afterwards drying with a leather. Remove black, greasy marks, called 'jockeys'. Then, with the soap-sponge as dry as possible, thoroughly soap the seat, flaps, and all underneath parts (panel, sweat flaps, underneath of flaps, etc.).

Polish all metal parts, cover with a stable rubber and hang saddle on its bracket.

Similarly, clean leather girths, stirrup-leathers, and reins. If the soap-sponge is too wet, lather appears in the buckle holes and should be removed with a matchstick, or by blowing through the holes, to prevent dirt accumulating.

Keep a folded leather girth soft and pliable by placing a flannel strip soaked in neatsfoot oil between the folds.

Brush daily and occasionally wash string, nylon, and web girths with soap and warm water.

Keep cleaning materials tidily in pigeon-holes or a cupboard; also grooming kit, or keep them in a large canvas bag like a shopping bag.

Carrying tack

Carry a bridle by the headband, the browband facing outwards and reins looped up by the buckle. Leave noseband and throat-lash buckles unfastened, ready to slip on the bridle. Carry in the left or right hand.

Carry a saddle (a) on the left arm, pommel facing the elbow, girth folded across over the top, irons run up on leathers; the orthodox and probably best way; (b) on the shoulder; (c) on the head; these are both unusual. By adopting the orthodox method one can carry whip, bridle, and saddle (in that order) on one arm, leaving the other free to cope with doors, gates, etc., or for carrying a pail of oats.

11 Hiring or Buying

Hiring

Has several disadvantages. The hirer has little opportunity of getting to know his pony, or of learning horse mastership and stable-management. Some stables may allow one to groom and saddle-up, and have a day at the stables each week, though many dislike having an amateur messing about. This will not suit the real enthusiast. Another disadvantage is that one only has an hour's ride and cannot go out whenever one wants. One can probably only afford one or two, or three rides at the most, per week. Riding more often would cost as much as, or more than, keeping one's own pony, having once met the initial capital outlay.

One possibility is to be a working pupil. Some stables charge a premium; others are quite glad as it helps reduce their labour costs.

If one lacks facilities for keeping a pony, a stable will sometimes keep it in return for using it. Disadvantages: one does not know how it will be handled or who will ride it. Many riding-school ponies become hard-mouthed through being badly ridden. Also, one's pony will be most needed at the week-end and during holidays, just when one wants to ride oneself.

A good arrangement is to work for an hour or two daily, or for two or three days a week, in return for stabling, even if one contributes towards the cost of the pony's keep. Thus one constantly supervises one's pony, and nobody else rides it. One also learns much about stable-management generally, acquiring many useful hints.

If one hires, in a year or two one may spend enough to cover the initial cost of buying both horse and tack, with nothing to show and less general experience and knowledge gained, than if one had originally bought.

Keeping a horse at livery is expensive, so is really only for the wealthy, and lacks the pleasure found in 'doing' one's own horse!

Buying

Has many pitfalls and the inexperienced can be so easily 'had.' A horse may look beautiful yet be an utter fraud. It may kick, be difficult to catch, or handle when stabled, a puller, or inclined to nip, shy, or bolt. Being a case of *caveat emptor*, always take a knowledgeable friend along when inspecting a horse.

Unlike a car a horse has no definite market value. This depends on age, soundness, conformation, temperament, manners, schooling, jumping ability, and breeding, etc.

Various sources for buying are: advertisements in the various papers and magazines devoted to horses and riding, or an advertisement in the local paper. Genuine sales by reputable people are usually advertised as 'open to vet's inspection', 'vet's certificate', or 'any trial'. Buying by hire-purchase is an additional safeguard.

Most riding-schools have ponies for sale. It pays them to buy new ones to keep their clients' interest. They often reduce numbers in winter when business is slacker, to reduce running costs. January and February are probably the cheapest months to buy, and April or May onwards the dearest. Hunters are cheapest in summer, and dearest from September onwards when people are buying for the coming hunting season.

There are sales in or near many large towns. Monthly sales occur at Gateshead, Reading, Leicester, London, etc. Twice-yearly sales occur at Keswick. There are three sales of New Forest ponies annually at Beaulieu Road, Hampshire. There are also sales at Hereford, Kelso, etc. At such auctions one must have knowledge, experience, and an 'eye' for a horse, and rely on one's own judgement. Sometimes ponies are sold without a vet's certificate or a written warranty. At large sales horses have a vet's certificate and written warranty, but prices are high.

The local Pony Club may know of a good pony for sale by a member for a genuine reason.

There are also dealers who in bygone days of the 'mustard brigade' and horse-copers were often dishonest. Today there are fewer dealers, mostly reputable, because satisfied clients are their best advertisement. If you go to a good local dealer, say what you can afford and leave it to him. Do not pretend to know more than you do!

A horse is sold 'as it stands', without any tack or accessories, or with saddle, bridle, and rope halter (not a leather head-collar).

Some dealers only allow trial on their own premises. Others allow a horse to go on trial for a period, from a few days up to a month, saving him its keep for that time. Having it on trial is an additional guarantee. Any vices or tricks soon appear; one can try the horse in traffic, in the stable, etc. One buys with one's eyes open, and if the horse then proves unsuitable or unsound one can only blame oneself.

Finally one can advertise in one of the riding journals, or even the local paper. State the district to save replies from too far away.

Trying a pony

Trying new ponies is great fun and valuable experience.

If one knows enough, first examine it thoroughly and methodically, bearing in mind the good and bad points given in Chapter 2 on Conformation.

Approach the pony, watching its reactions, whether it shows the whites of its eyes, lays back its ears or tucks in its tail. A gentle pony will probably turn its head, giving one a long, friendly stare, or even whicker gently, nuzzling towards one to be petted.

Does it allow you to pick up its fore and hind feet easily? Or does it plant them firmly on the ground, refusing to move?

After warning, hold the pony's tail, walking slowly and deliberately round its hindquarters, as close as possible. Watch its reactions. Did its ears go back? Did it stand quite unconcerned, or move forward uneasily? Did it tentatively lift its hind leg?

If you feel incompetent to judge, pay a vet to examine the pony and report on its age, conformation and soundness. Have an independent vet, not the vendor's. Even if sold with a vet's certificate, let your own vet examine it. If possible have a written warranty: a verbal warranty is worthless even if given in presence of a witness. A written warranty covers soundness in wind, limb, freedom from vice, and suitability for the purpose for which bought. A guarantee applies only to anything following the word 'warranted', and not before it.

After through examination, have the pony trotted away from you and back. Watch carefully for any lameness. Watch its action, how it lifts and moves its legs and puts its feet down. It should move straight, hind feet following in the tracks of the forefeet.

Lead the pony, noting if it follows immediately and easily. Does it turn easily and trot if asked? Does it lead equally well from the near and off side?

Ask to see the pony caught in a field. Try catching it yourself.

When satisfied, ride the pony. Note its reactions while mounting.

Does it stand still or fidget and try to move off before you are on?

Does it turn its head while you gather the reins before mounting?

Some ponies turn their heads and try to nip. Others try to be off directly one's foot is in the iron.

Having mounted, note if the pony stands quietly until told to move.

Look down to see what is before you. Is there plenty of room in front, or do you feel you are sitting on top of its head?

From above, the neck should look quite thick where it joins the body. Notice the head-carriage. Does it look alert, head held with neck slightly arched, or does it hang down listlessly? Does it toss or throw its head about? Does it play with and seem interested in its bit, or does this lie dead in its mouth? If so it is probably hard-mouthed.

Next look behind you. Hindquarters should look round, broad, and generous. Tail should be visible, high, sticking out, and gaily carried. Drop the reins and make some loud, sudden noise. The pony should stand still, quite unmoved. Wave a whip; it should not be whip-shy.

Test if its mouth is soft on either side, or both, by gently tightening the near- and off-side rein in turn. If the pony responds by moving its head slightly it shows that its mouth is soft on that side.

Does it understand neck-reining on both sides? Does it understand and respond immediately to the aids? When asked to walk does it respond at once or have to be kicked on? Note if it walks quickly and effortlessly with a long, easy swing, or has it to be kicked along, tending to slow up or even stop, directly you cease kicking? Does it pull? How does it carry its head and ears while walking? Are they pricked forward alertly or laid back?

Next give the aid to trot, noting how much urging is needed. It should move easily, almost lazily, with long free strides. Hind legs should move straight, following the tracks of the forelegs.

Collect the pony and start cantering. Note how quickly it responded. Did it move smoothly into a slow canter or rush off uncollected into a fast one? Did it lead with the correct leg? Legs should move smoothly, just clear of the ground. Does the pony hot up and get excited? Does it pull up easily from a canter to a trot, or a walk?

When halting notice whether it stands still, correctly balanced on all four legs.

Next try elementary aids like a rein-back, and turns on the forehand and haunches. See if you can open a gate without dismounting. Then dismount and lead it through the gate to see if it knows how to turn and stand while you shut it. Will it stand quietly for you to remount?

Try it over a few easy jumps of different kinds. Does it jump willingly and seem to enjoy it? Does it rush the jumps or approach calmly? How does it approach and take off? Does it jump too soon, too near, or too wide?

Finally test its stable manners. Groom, saddle, and unsaddle it. Does it stand quietly or fidget? Does it try to kick or cow-kick? Has it any ticklish spots? What is its reactions when you touch them?

Anyone selling a genuine pony should not mind a thorough examination and trial. Do not be hurried, but take your time. You must feel that you know, like, and trust your pony. Do not buy the first pony you see. Try several. Choosing a pony is ultimately a personal matter. What suits one may not suit another. Much also depends on the purpose for which one wants a pony. Is it for hacking, showing, hunting, or show-jumping? Is it for riding and driving? Is it a family pony, or for one person only? Some are advertised as 'patent safety', others as 'not a novice ride'. A quiet, sensible pony is essential for children or beginners. A bit of age will not matter as it will be experienced. An experienced rider may prefer a green, unmade, or even unbroken, pony which he can make and school himself, for the fun of it.

Finally, when trying a pony, take it on to a road with plenty of traffic to see its reactions!

If buying for a child and the pony is too small or not up to your weight, take a competent child rider to try it. Never buy without seeing a child ride it. Do not rely on the child's judgement for whom you are buying it. In any case they will probably 'fall' for it, saying it is perfectly sweet. After it has shown its paces let its prospective rider try it. A good child rider may manage it easily, but yours may not be so experienced. Nothing so disheartens or disappoints a child than a pony it cannot handle or ride, and on which it is just a passenger. Be certain that child and pony like each other and get on well together and that the child, on or off, is safe with it. Also that it is the right size, neither too big, wide, nor strong.

Unfortunately the type of pony required is just what everyone else wants! If found, it is worth its weight in gold. Aim at perfection; then decide the absolutely essential qualities, and what defects one can accept if necessary. If one is wealthy one can probably insist on perfection. Essentials are good manners, in and outside the stable, sound wind, limb, and sight, and quiet to ride.

12 Handling, Saddling Up

Leading in hand

Always lead a strange pony from the near side as most are accustomed to this. It is useful to train your own to lead from either side. To lead, place your right-hand palm downwards on the rope or reins about 10 inches from the head-collar or bridle. Never hold the head-collar or bridle, too close to its head; many horses, especially Thoroughbreds, hate this. Hold the slack of the reins or rope in the left hand about a foot away from the right. When leading from the off side, the left hand holds rope or reins and the right the slack.

To move, speak to the pony and walk forward; if properly trained it will follow immediately. Train it to obedience when led, accustoming it to turn right or left, to trot, or stand still. This is important for gymkhana events like musical sacks, and for showing. It must follow easily and be handy. Never look round at it as many refuse to move if stared at.

When turning always push its head round away; never pull it towards you. So to turn left, change hands, leading from the off side. Before turning slow down and speak to the pony.

When leading out of its stable always look or even walk backwards, especially at a low or narrow entrance, or a sharp turn. Hitting its poll against the doorway may seriously injure it, causing poll-evil as a result; or bumping its hip on a sharp corner, which can easily happen through carelessness, coming out hurriedly without looking where one is going.

Saddling

Short-rack so that it cannot turn its head and nip while being saddled. Always saddle before bridling so that the horse is fastened and cannot move away.

If used, put on the numnah of felt, foam rubber, leather, or sheepskin. It prevents any risk of the saddle rubbing, protecting the horse's back and withers. With a badly stuffed or badly fitting saddle use a felt numnah of half-inch thickness, as a temporary expedient until it can be restuffed and made to fit properly. Pull it well up under the pommel, off the withers. Use a foam numnah for a thin-skinned horse; it is very soft and allows air to circulate, preventing sweating. When show-jumping a sheepskin numnah prevents the saddle seat touching the horse's spine while its back is arched going over a jump; it is hot and heavy, and unless frequently cleaned can smell horrible. A thin, pliable leather numnah protects against rubbing when a horse's back is soft through not being ridden, or if already slightly rubbed. If the horse's back is sore, cut a hole in a felt or leather numnah to fit over the sore place.

The orthodox way of saddling is from the near side, but it is more convenient from the off. This saves time going round to the off side after putting on the saddle to see that the panel is not turned under.

Holding the saddle fairly high, place it on the withers, sliding it down in the direction of the hair to its correct position. Do not have it too far up on the withers so that it interferes with the shoulder's free movement. If too far back the girths will not lie in the girth-groove but slip forward and loosen. If it slips down too far back, never pull it up against the hair; it brushes the hair the wrong way and is uncomfortable. It not only irritates but may cause a sore back. Lift the saddle and replace it correctly.

Having straightened the panel, with girth straps hanging down freely on the off side, go round to the near side. Ducking under the horse's neck is better, quicker, and safer than continuously going round its hindquarters. From the near side catch hold of the girth under the belly with the right hand. See that it is not twisted and lies smoothly in the girth-groove. Fasten girth straps of saddle in the bottom or second hole on to the girth buckles. Never girth tightly immediately. Some horses have a cold back: a cold saddle pressing down may cause kicking or rearing. A horse may blow itself out with air. Girth loosely at first; then gradually tighten each girth strap alternately a hole at a time, as the saddle warms. This is another advantage of using a numnah. A numnah or a stable rubber also helps to keep the saddle lining clean; the latter may ruck up and cause a rub.

Bridling

Snaffle bridle

Having saddled up, take the bridle by headband and reins in the left hand and shake it out so that nothing is twisted. Unfasten the noseband, seeing that all straps are in their correct holes, with cheek-strap ends in their keepers and runners. With the bridle over the left forearm undo the head-collar strap, holding strap and buckles together with your left hand, putting your right arm over the horse's head, just behind its ears, thus preventing it getting free and moving away. Alternatively, slip your right hand under its throat and hold its nose if it is too tall to put your arm over its head. Let go the strap and buckle and slip off the head-collar while holding its head with your right arm. With your left fingers hold its nose just above the nostrils. While holding, take your right arm off its neck (or from underneath its throat) slipping the reins over its neck on to the withers with your right hand. Rest the bit in your left palm; while pressing it against its mouth, gently draw the bridle up its forehead. Directly it opens its mouth slip in the bit, at the same time drawing the headband over its ears, with the browband across its forehead just below them. The left hand is now free; the reins are looped over the right arm, forming an anchor. If the horse refuses the bit insert the left-hand fingers behind the front teeth, squeezing gently.

Straighten the forelock over the browband, seeing that browband and headband both fit properly in their correct positions; the headband rests on the poll; the browband lies across the forehead about an inch below the ears.

Fasten the throat-lash. Its object is to prevent the bridle getting dragged off over the horse's ears: only fasten it tightly enough to prevent this. Many make the mistake of fastening it too tightly. Insertion of a clenched fist, or full hand's breadth, between the side of the horse's jaw and the throat-lash strap should be possible.

Put the noseband round inside and below the bit cheek-rings. Fasten tightly enough to prevent the horse opening its mouth or crossing its jaw, but not tight enough to interfere with breathing or to prevent it eating. The noseband strap lies in the chin-groove; one should be able to insert two fingers between chin-groove and strap.

Next see that cheek-straps are the correct length so that the bit lies in its right place in the horse's mouth. If too low the horse can get its tongue over, and it may come out: if too high it wrinkles the corners of the mouth and presses too tightly, making it sore.

Finally, check carefully that all strap-ends pass neatly through their keepers and runners on both sides. Standing in front, see that the bridle is straight with the browband level.

If used, put on the martingale, fastening first to the noseband and then looping the girths through underneath the belly. It necessitates ungirthing – another reason for only girthing loosely when saddling. After putting through the martingale, tighten the girth. The martingale strap going over the horse's neck buckles on the near side.

Some advocate turning the horse round before bridling. This is correct if in a stall with pillar reins to which it can be fastened, but is inadvisable in a loose-box or an outside shelter where there is nothing to prevent it moving about and getting out of control.

Double bridle

Having a curb and bridoon (snaffle) bit, there are really two bridles to put on and fasten. Proceed as for a snaffle bridle with the following exceptions and additions:

1 The snaffle bit is above and the curb below it in the pony's mouth.

2 Use a cavesson instead of a dropped noseband, fitting higher up round the nose, above the cheek-rings of the snaffle bit instead of below.

3 If using a standing martingale put it on before fastening the curb chain and rest of the bridle.

4 Adjust each bit from both sides making certain that each is

level. Adjust the bridoon from the off side, easing up or down on its own headpiece.

5 The curb chain should fit snugly in the chin-groove. From the near side twist it towards the horse's body until flat, then hooking it on to the end link. Do not have it too tight. Always hook on the end links; never let them dangle.

6 The strap-end of the lip-strap passes through the lip-strap link of the curb chain and buckles.

Leave irons run up on the leathers until outside and ready to mount. Never lead out a horse with irons dangling; they may knock against something, frightening it and causing it to bolt if fresh. After saddling pull each front leg towards you to stretch the skin under the girth, easing out any wrinkles or crumpled hair which might cause a girth-gall.

Unsaddling

Slip reins over the horse's head on to the left arm. Run up irons, loosen the girth; leave the saddle on for a few minutes to let the horse cool down. Never unsaddle immediately on returning from a ride especially if the horse is warm, or on a cold day.

Having run up the irons and loosened the girth, straighten out the head-collar and hold over the left forearm ready to put on. If it is a double bridle undo curb chain and lip-strap. Then unbuckle the noseband and finally the throat-lash. Unfasten the martingale if worn.

Hold the head-collar ready over your left arm. Put your right arm under the pony's throat. Then with your left hand pick up the headband and reins and slip the bridle over the pony's head. Ease the bit gently out of its mouth; never let it fall out suddenly with a bump as this may bruise its mouth. Some horses try to hold the bit. As you bring the reins and bridle over the pony's head slip them on to your right forearm. Both hands are thus left free to put on the head-collar, and the pony cannot move away.

To unsaddle, hold up the flap with your head, unbuckle the girth from the near side and put it down gently, letting it hang down from the off side. Never let it drop down as the buckles may hit against its leg, hurting or frightening the horse. Having ungirthed go round to the off side and lay it across the saddle seat, behind the stirrup-leather. Lay the inside, not the muddy outside of the girth, next to the saddle.

Remove the saddle from either the near or the off side, lifting it up fairly high, clear of the back and withers; never drag it off.

When putting a saddle on the ground always stand it on its pommel, folding the girth neatly underneath to prevent the pommel getting scratched or dirty.

Having removed it, pat the horse smartly where it rested, down its sides and underneath where the girth has been, to restore circulation. On a cold day, pull the horse's ears gently to help warm them, especially if they feel cold. Most horses love it.

13 Psychology of the Horse and Rider

Psychology of the horse

Most authorities agree that a horse's intelligence is fairly low compared with other domestic animals; a dog has more. Its reasoning powers are not great, its thinking being mostly instinctive, governed by such fundamentals as hunger and fear. These appear to be the most important instincts in its life. Hunger, because a horse eats for about twenty out of every twenty-four hours; hence its life is largely controlled by the search for food: fear, because it is mainly a defenceless animal. When cornered, it can kick and bite; when fighting, a stallion rears up and strikes with its front feet; but horses chiefly rely on speed to escape from danger. They are timid animals, easily startled by any sudden noise or movement. Anyone handling horses must always remember this. Always speak, warning a horse of your presence, when approaching and always move quietly and gently. A rough, loud-mouthed groom has no place in a stable!

A horse is very sensitive to one's mood; a nervous, excitable rider makes a nervous, excitable horse. Quietness and confidence will produce a calm, confident, quiet horse. It very quickly senses fear; if one shows any sign of timidity when handling a horse it immediately plays up and probably tries to nip or kick. Therefore always approach it boldly with a cheerful, calm, self-confident attitude.

A horse, apparently, has not as deep a sense of affection or loyalty as a dog. It may seem to show affection for its owner or groom, whinnying at his approach, but mainly because it associates him with good things, such as food. This does not mean that it will not become attached to the person who looks after it, especially if cared for by only one person. But it will not pine for its owner like a dog and soon transfers its affection to a new master if kindly treated and well fed.

Like an elephant a horse has a retentive memory; it never forgets, especially bad treatment. Hence the importance of proper handling when breaking, making, and schooling a colt. Its handling when young can make or ruin it for life. A horse never forgets a groom who has knocked it about, and at his approach will give warning signs of impending trouble, caused by fear. A horse may be called bad tempered and difficult to handle, when really it is afraid. Shouting at or punishing a horse for shying is useless as the cause is fear. It it shies, turn its head away and try to distract its attention, or persuade it to go up to the object of fear; having had a good look and smelt it, a horse usually moves on quite happily. It often senses something ahead, or senses danger, long before its rider. It appears to have a keen sense of smell.

Most horses are only too anxious to obey and please. Win your horse's respect, and such affection as it can give. Treat it kindly but very firmly. Use the same psychological approach as you would towards a willing, but rather stupid, child.

Schooling a horse needs infinite patience. First make it understand what you want; then this is learnt by constant repetition over a period of time, until the action becomes an instinctive reflex response to a known stimulus. Always give the same word of command with the same tone of voice, and exactly the same aid in the same way for a given movement; otherwise the horse becomes confused. Give fairly short lessons; 30–40 minutes is ample. Reward instant obedience by voice and a tit-bit. A horse goes by the tone of voice; its vocabulary being very limited. It quickly differentiates between a warm, praising tone and a sharp, scolding one. Similarly, directly it obeys a flexion of the rein, give instantly with the hands, relieving pressure on the bit.

A horse is easily bored so do not always ride over the same route. While out, keep it interested; vary your routine by not always walking, trotting, or cantering at exactly the same pace. A horse's sense of direction is keen. If it does not want to go out it will stiffen its back and walk or trot unwillingly. Yet on the homeward journey it will start pulling, all eagerness to go. If lost, throw the reins on the horse's neck, letting it find its own way home. Van-horses on a round know exactly where to stop, and when the driver reappears will move on, unasked, to the next house.

Horses like regular routine and apparently have an instinctive time sense. If there is any alteration in their daily routine they will fuss and fidget.

The more human companionship a horse has, the more knowing and intelligent it becomes. A horse constantly with its owner shows more intelligence and responsiveness than one left neglected and uncared-for in a field. Fondle and talk to your horse constantly, and handle it as much as possible. Talk to it while grooming and sing to it while riding. Horses like the sound of a human voice. They are instinctively gregarious, becoming bored alone.

Some, especially mares, may kick when ridden in company. This may be jealousy or fear, and an instinctive defensive attitude. As it is incurable, tie a red ribbon on the tail and keep well away from other horses. Horses are very jealous, especially at feeding time or in their owner's presence. Two mares together are more likely to show jealousy than a mare and a gelding, or two geldings. Mares may become rather uncertain-tempered during the breeding period (February onwards), especially when in season.

Horses have definite likes and dislikes; e.g. pigs; they appear to dislike their smell. Most horses hate blood; it terrifies them. Many hate noise although they apparently like making a noise themselves, such as the motononous sound produced by kicking their stall partition. Jangling a bunch of keys will quieten and amuse a restive horse. Sudden noises apparently frighten more than actual loudness. An unexpected gunshot will startle a horse. Yet it can be trained to stand or lie motionless while its rider shoots from or over it.

The unknown, anything not understood, easily frightens a

horse, while familiarity breeds contempt. A pony will shy at a tree-trunk, yet pass the noisiest tractor!

Having very acute hearing, a horse will hear sounds inaudible to us. Quite possibly, like a dog, it can hear sounds beyond the limit of human audibility.

The rider's psychology

Man shares fear in common with all animals. It is a natural reaction derived from the instinct of self-preservation. Wild animals show fear and timidity because they face as many dangers today as they always have done. With horses and domestic animals, which are more or less protected from danger, fear and timidity are inherited racial instincts from bygone days when they were wild.

With man, fear is a natural reaction dating back to primitive prehistoric humanity, which had good reason to fear when life was a daily battle for existence, and life depended on jungle law – the survival of the fittest.

Civilized man has lost many senses still possessed by wild animals; others like smell, hearing, and sight have become dulled. Many primitive instincts still survive; the blood lust which makes people enjoy blood-sports – a survival of the struggle for existence, when it was every man for himself. Much of the elemental savage still lingers; civilization is only a skin-deep veneer!

Also fear of the unknown: man still fears what he does not understand. Ignorance produced superstition, while religion evolved from fear because man needed something to reassure him, something to cling to. Mankind has always tended to venerate what it could not understand: sun and moon worship; deification of natural phenomena.

Through the ages man has gradually overcome fear, with increasing knowledge. He still has fear today but for different causes; the character of fear has changed. Man still has some elemental fears (e.g. fear of darkness, of confined places, claustrophobia, etc.), but primitive terrors have largely been replaced by more artificial, subtle ones.

A healthy person may experience fear temporarily, but shakes it off and eventually forgets it. He may be badly frightened

E

through some danger; or temporarily suffer from shock and feel afraid, but he gradually forgets the experience and the fear of it disappears.

When fear becomes an obsession it becomes a persistent phobia, eventually causing nervous breakdown and mental illness, because the sufferer loses his resistance powers and ability to shake off his particular fear. Modern civilization has filled the mental hospitals with people who cannot meet some situation, owing to fear of something real or imaginary.

Civilization produces new strains and stresses, caused by high-speed living under constant high mental and physical pressure; so it has brought many new sources of fear: the H-bomb, another war, unemployment, financial insecurity, etc.

Fear and the rider

Riding is beneficial because it brings mental release from modern civilization's strains and stresses.

A beginner's fear and nervousness are understandable and pardonable, especially if unaccustomed to horses. Fear at his first lesson, the first time he approaches, handles, or rides a horse, is perfectly understandable. Even a pony appears large, strong, and unpredictable the first time one comes at close quarters. On the first ride one feels so high up, the saddle seems so hard and slippery, and the reins so inadequate for controlling it! The rider's sensations spring from the instinct of self-preservation and fear of the unknown. How to approach and handle a horse is a mystery to a beginner; he does not know what to say to it. He has no idea what it will do or what to expect. He feels insecure, and, understandably, fears falling off. But he need not fear: a horse is normally a gentle, timid creature, probably quite as afraid of him as he is of it! And it is actually quite difficult to fall off.

People accustomed all their lives to horses have, unfortunately, probably forgotten their first reactions and feelings. A child probably finds it easier than an adult beginner.

Antidote to fear

'Perfect love casteth out fear.' This psychological truth applies to the rider. When attempting anything new, the beginner must meet and overcome his instinctive fear. Love of horses creates sympathy, leading in turn to insight and understanding. A horse very quickly senses that someone loves and understands it and this creates a bond between horse and rider. Hence some appear born horsemen, with the knack of handling the most difficult horses: others apparently have little or no aptitude. Women are often better than men at handling a restive horse, being more gentle and sympathetic.

Knowledge and confidence

A really enthusiastic horse-lover will want to know as much as possible about them. Increasing knowledge brings increasing confidence.

A rider must have complete confidence – in himself, his 'hands', 'seat', and his pony. Even the most experienced rider may have a few momentary qualms before mounting a strange, restive horse. But he has confidence born of knowledge, and this soon overcomes any fear.

Confidence and courage

Courage grows with increasing knowledge and confidence. He assesses risks, weighing up the chances of success coolly and calmly because he knows how to get the best from himself and his horse.

Our worst fears are imaginary, of things which may never happen! Confidence comes because a rider has faced all his fears from the beginning; experience has proved that they have not become realities; so growing confidence has brought increasing courage.

Fear of falling

Is one of the beginner's chief fears. He must learn that a fall is not so terrible! If he can balance a bicycle, which is much harder, without fear of falling, why should he be afraid of falling off his horse? He must face the fact that he will inevitably come off sooner or later if he is going to ride regularly and often. But if he learns how to fall properly he will not hurt himself. The secret is to fall limply without attempting to recover one's balance, or to save oneself. If you do part company with your horse, take your feet out of the irons, tuck your head into your shoulder and try to roll up into a ball. Never put out a hand or arm. As you fall try to hold on to the reins if possible, to prevent your pony galloping off.

Never ride without some sort of headgear, preferably some form of hard hat. Shows under BSJA rules forbid riders to jump, and the Pony Club will not allow members to attend a mounted rally, without a hard hat. This is not fear or cowardice but plain common horse-sense!

The number of riding accidents is very small compared with road accidents involving cars, motor-cycles, cycles, or pedestrians!

If you do fall, remount immediately. It is the best way of keeping your nerve. Do not dwell on or talk about the incident, or let people fuss over you about it! And never let your imagination run riot as to what might have happened. Having thought over the incident to see whether it was your fault, forget it, after learning what lessons you can.

Instinct v. reason

From the start beginners must learn to overcome numerous instinctive reactions of self-preservation.

1 Tensing and stiffening through fear. When riding be supple; relax mentally and physically.

2 Learn to relax and fall limply. Practise falling on a mattress. Then ride a quiet pony barebacked in a field with soft falling and deliberately practise sliding off, falling limply. It is surprising what confidence a few deliberate falls will give.

3 Learn to keep calm. The natural instinct when anything goes wrong is to become excited and worked-up. An excitable rider makes an excitable, nervous pony.

4 Do not meet force with force. A horse being much stronger, the art of handling and riding one consists of matching its brute strength with superior intellect. If a horse starts pulling, or refuses to move while being led, do not start pulling in return.

Determination and perseverance

However much one loves horses, enthusiasm may grow a little thin once the novelty wears off. Determination and will-power must then step in so that one perseveres. The real test of keenness is whether one takes the rough with the smooth!

14 First Rides

Mounting

Before mounting always examine your pony to see that everything is correct, especially if someone else has tacked up; they may be careless or not very expert. See that the bridle is level, with the forelock over the browband and the latter just below the roots of the ears. See that cheek-straps are the proper length so that the bit or bits (double bridle) are level, properly positioned in the pony's mouth. Check that throat-lash and noseband are not too tight, with the noseband level in its proper position. Finally, see that all strap ends are pulled neatly through their keepers and runners.

Always tighten the girth before mounting. Otherwise when your foot is in the iron as you spring up to mount, the saddle will twist towards you, making your pony very uncomfortable. You will have to stop, tighten up, and restart, or you may suddenly find yourself upside down underneath, instead of on top, which is, at least, disconcerting for both! Irons run up short on leathers should be a warning that girths need tightening, but this does not always work out, so always check. Measure the length of stirrup-leathers by placing your finger-tips on the stirrup-bar with the iron under your armpit, standing at right angles to your pony.

Speak while approaching your pony and after checking give it a cheerful, friendly pat on the neck before mounting.

There are various different ways of mounting: (1) facing the tail; (2) a leg-up by somebody else; (3) vaulting on without touching the iron (jockey's way); (4) mounting block (the elderly gentleman's way, which disturbs the pony least).

(1) and (3) can be done from the near or off side. Practise until you can mount easily equally from either side; this can be extremely useful if you have to dismount while out.

1 Facing the tail

The orthodox way, mounting from the near side.

(a) Pick up the reins and whip in your left hand, with off-side rein slightly shorter than the near so that the pony cannot turn its head and nip as you mount. Throw the slack of the reins on to the off side. Do not hold the pony's head too tightly; many hate this and it only makes them fidget and want to move off. During one's first attempts, or with a young, rather green pony, it is advisable for someone to hold its head.

Having gathered up the reins, grasp the neck or mane just in front of the withers, standing facing the tail with your left shoulder next to the pony's. Hold the iron with your right hand, twisting it clockwise towards you. Then place your left toe well home in it, pointing downwards so as not to dig the pony's side with it.

(b) Hold the saddle at the pommel with your right hand. Do not hold the cantle as your hand will have to shift out of the way as your leg swings over. The orthodox way advocated by cavalry training and the BHS, is to hold the cantle.

(c) Spring up lightly off the left foot, straightening your left knee and swinging your right leg over without touching the pony's quarters. Sit down gently without a bump. Taking the reins in both hands to collect your pony, find the iron with your right foot without looking down. Do not bother about the iron until your pony is under control with your reins in both hands. One can ride without irons but one cannot ride an uncontrolled pony. Racehorses have a disconcerting habit of trying to canter off before one has even reached the saddle.

Learn to mount quickly. Practise until the three separate movements can be accomplished as one, in a flash.

Mounting from the off side is exactly the same, only with reins in the right hand, right shoulder next to the pony, and right toe

in the iron. Otherwise you will find yourself riding back to front!
Twist the iron anti-clockwise.

2 *Leg-up*

Face the pony's side with whip and reins in your left hand.
Grasp the neck or mane just in front of the withers (as before),
your right hand on the pommel, or waist, of the saddle. Hold
your left leg out behind you for your assistant to grip with both
hands just above the ankle. As he heaves upwards spring lightly
off your right leg, swinging it over the saddle. Practise from both
sides. On the off side offer the right leg, swinging the left over the
saddle.

3 *Vaulting on*

One of the best ways of mounting for the young, athletic rider
as it does not disturb the saddle. The ability to vault on barebacked is also very useful. Face the pony's shoulder, standing as
close as possible, with both elbows over just behind the withers.
Press downwards, bend your knees, and spring vigorously upwards. Simultaneously, lean forward, bending right over with
your head hanging down towards the ground on the other side.
When on the point of overbalancing and sliding over head downwards, swing your right leg over, meanwhile straightening your
back and sitting upright. Once you have the knack this can be
done instantaneously in one movement with a little practice.
Practise from both sides.

4 *Mounting block*

Needs no explanation. A good way without disturbing the saddle,
although considered the elderly gentleman's method.

Having mounted, always make your pony stand still for a
short time before giving the aid to move off. Finally adjust
length of stirrup-leathers.

Adjusting leathers

They are correct when the stirrup-iron tread is just below the
ankle bone, with your leg hanging down loosely. With the ball

of the foot in the iron, press your heel down, keeping the toe pointing slightly upwards.

Shortening

Keep your foot in the iron without pressure. Holding reins and whip in one hand, with the other take the leather, feeling the tongue of the buckle with your thumb and forefinger. Pull the tongue out of the hole and gently press down your foot. When the length is correct push the tongue into the hole; pull the leather down with the buckle up against the stirrup-bar.

Lengthening

After releasing the tongue from the hole, press hard against the iron so that the leather slides through to the required length. Tuck the end of the leather under, after shortening or lenghtening. Have both leathers equal in length.

Tightening girth

The rider's weight often loosens the girth. To tighten, remove your foot from the iron and push the leather behind your leg. Holding reins and whip in the opposite hand, put your leg forward with the turned-up leather flap held under your knee; tighten the girth with your free hand similarly to adjusting the stirrup-leather. Drop the flap and replace foot in the iron.

Mounting a restive pony

If it refuses to stand while mounting get it against a wall in a corner. To teach it to stand, let someone hold its head facing the corner and distract its attention with a tit-bit. Placing your left foot in the iron, spring up as if mounting, but instead descend again; repeat quickly several times. Praise and reward the pony if it stands quietly. Next, spring and remain leaning over the saddle for a few seconds: repeat several times, praising the pony if quiet. Finally, mount and dismount quickly several times. Repeat the lesson daily for short periods several times a day until learnt.

Always stand absolutely still for a few seconds after mounting; nothing makes mounting quickly more difficult than a pony moving off while mounting or immediately after. If difficult to mount because fresh or excited, while you are alone, place it alongside a wall, fence, hedge, or furze-bush – anything to prevent its quarters moving about.

Grasp the cheek-piece, with short reins pulling hard down on to the poll. Stand square, and with left foot in the iron, right hand on pommel, swing up as quickly as possible; collect reins quickly in both hands in case of trouble.

Dismounting

The only safe way is first to take both feet out of the irons. Never imitate cowboys on television who keep their near-side foot in the iron. If the pony was startled and dashed off you would be dragged and perhaps seriously injured. It is very dangerous.

1 Reins and whip in left hand, resting on pony's neck. Right hand on the pommel with fingers pointing downwards.

2 Removing both feet from the irons, rest your weight on your hands on the pony's wither. Swing your right leg over clear of its quarters while leaning forward slightly; vault off lightly, landing on your toes, knees bent, feet together, reins in your hand. Land facing the pony's head, ready to control it and walk forward if it moves on suddenly.

Practise also from the off side: reins and whip in right hand, left on the wither. Swing your left leg over, landing as before. Be able to dismount easily and quickly from either side. There are many ways of dismounting unexpectedly!

Hands

Good hands are essential and are only acquired when one has a really firm seat and rides quite independently of the reins. Thus they depend on good grip and balance. Reins should only communicate the rider's wishes to his pony. They are really a means of talking to it in a language it learns to understand through good schooling.

Good hands mean firm yet friendly contact with its mouth, learning to give and take with its movements. The bit rests on the bars of the mouth which soon become hard and insensitive if the rider uses the reins to keep his balance, or constantly tugs at them. Learn to feel your pony's mouth and reward instantly for obedience; signal by tightening the rein or reins slightly; directly the pony obeys relax tension, making your hands soft and quiet again. A good rider's hands are sensitive like a musician's.

Hands may have to be very firm if a pony plays up, but immediately it stops, yielding to the bit, they should become soft and polite again. Bad hands quickly make the most placid pony restive and disobedient, because it is trying to escape from the pain they cause its mouth; it will toss its head, throw it up into the air, walk sideways, and try every sort of evasion to escape from the bit.

Hold the reins lightly yet always in contact with its mouth. Never leave them slack and sagging.

Holding the reins

Snaffle bridle

Reins should be held in both hands, passing between the little and ring fingers, across the palm of the hand and over the index (or first) finger, the thumb holding the rein in place and the loop

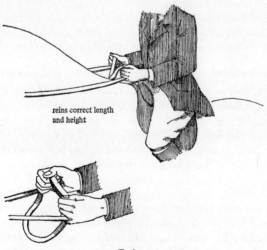

reins correct length
and height

Reins

of the rein lying on the horse's neck. Another method equally correct is to pass the reign *under* the little finger, across the palm and between the index finger and thumb; the former method is, however, more common nowadays and the style most frequently taught.

Mistakes: level flat knuckles; wrists bent inwards.

Position of arms: upper arm hangs down loosely and naturally to the side; elbows in. Bend your forearm naturally from the elbow so that your hands are about 2 inches above the withers, and about 4 inches apart. Forearm, hand, and rein should make a straight line with the cheek-ring of the bit.

If the reins are too short the hands will be too far forward with the forearm stretched out, upsetting one's balance and leg position. If too long, one's hands will be pulled in against one's stomach, so that either one's elbows stick out, or one leans back with one's legs too far forward, again losing balance and control.

Forming a bridge

With reins in each hand as before, bring both hands together, putting the left rein on the right. The slack of the reins hangs down on the off side. Jockeys often hold their reins like this; it is very useful as it forms a bridge, effectively preventing the hands sliding down the horse's neck if it suddenly lowers its head. It helps particularly when galloping or jumping.

Reins in one hand

Knowing how to hold the reins in one hand is useful, though one should normally always ride with both hands. The left is the usual bridle hand. Put the right rein across the left-hand palm on top of the left rein. To hold them right-handed, similarly transfer the left rein to the right hand. The slack hangs down on the same side as the reins are being held.

Double bridle

As one normally rides on the bridoon (snaffle) rein, with the curb only used for special purposes, the former passes under and is controlled by the little finger. Thread the curb rein between the little and ring finger. The bridoon lies across the palm, then

passing between the forefinger and thumb: holding it outside
the little finger gives much more control and contact with it.
Keep the curb rein slack and unused unless required. This is
the generally accepted way of holding double bridle reins; some
authorities advocate holding the bridoon between the little and
ring finger, with the curb between ring and middle fingers. It is
really a matter of personal choice, though the little finger apparently does give more control.

Reins in one hand

Left hand little finger again divides the reins with the bridoon
on the outside. Thread the two right reins between the ring and
middle finger, with the bridoon between the middle and forefinger (i.e. on the outside); hold the slack between forefinger and
thumb. The order is: bridoon, curb, curb, bridoon, slack. Use
the same arrangement when holding reins in the right hand,
working from the little finger towards the thumb.

Slack of reins

When holding single or double reins single-handed, let the slack
hang down on the near side when in the left hand, and on the off
when in the right.

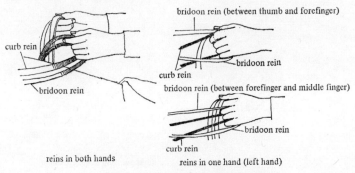

reins in both hands

bridoon rein (between thumb and forefinger)

curb rein

bridoon rein

bridoon rein (between forefinger and middle finger)

bridoon rein

curb rein

reins in one hand (left hand)

curb rein

bridoon rein

Holding the reins (double bridle)

Position of whip

Always carry the butt end pointing between the pony's ears, holding it in the right hand when holding the reins in both hands. When holding the reins left-handed carry the whip in the right, and vice-versa. When necessary, hold reins and whip together in either hand, leaving the other free for opening gates, etc. While riding, practise changing reins and whip into both or either hand, so that one can eventually change over quite automatically. On a long ride it is advisable to change as it prevents hands and arms tiring and becoming heavy on the pony's mouth.

Seat

Good hands are so dependent on a good seat that it is difficult to say which is most important, or which should be learnt first: probably a good seat. This is thigh and knee grip combined with balance. A large muscle (the riding muscle) running down the inside of the thigh is not otherwise much used, normally, and so needs developing. As beginners naturally tend to hang on to the pony's mouth through the reins to keep balanced, it is advisable to ask a competent friend to lead it, and to ride a lot at first without reins. Failing a helper, use a neck strap to hold when in

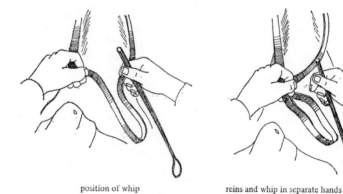

position of whip   reins and whip in separate hands

Position of whip

danger of becoming unbalanced. An ordinary martingale strap around the pony's neck will do.

Nothing gives confidence or a good seat more quickly than riding without reins in the initial stages. Once having gained confidence and learnt to grip and balance properly, on taking the reins one's whole attention can be given to learning the feel on a pony's mouth. Until one has an independent seat one's attention is divided between trying not to fall off ('keeping the joint *in* the plate') and handling the 'ribbons' without hanging on by them for dear life! This is chiefly psychological, until a beginner realizes he will not fall off.

Position in the saddle

Sit in the deepest part – the waist – of the saddle. Stretch your legs well downwards with thighs flat against the flap; wriggle down as far as possible into the saddle. The fork and seat-bones give a three-point, triangular suspension upon which one should sit. Leaning forward throws one only on to the fork, while by leaning back one rides only on the seat-bones. So sit upright, without stiffening or hollowing the back. Shoulders should be thrown back, not slouched forward, with head up, looking straight between the pony's ears. Let the upper arm hang down loosely from shoulder to elbow, with forearm, wrist, hand, and rein in a straight line to the pony's mouth.

From fork to knee, and including it, the thigh should lie flat, close to the saddle flap. Individual build has considerable influence: short-legged people with fat, rounded thighs find more difficulty in acquiring a good seat than those with long legs and flat thighs. Press the riding muscle against the saddle, keeping the thigh immovable from fork to knee. Keep the lower leg free and able to swing backwards and forwards from the knee, without moving thigh or seat off the saddle. This is very important as the lower leg gives the aids and creates impulsion; telling a horse what you want, making it go on, turn, or stop, by using either leg, or both together; kicking it on when necessary without losing one's seat. The back muscles are most important, providing all the strength and downward drive. Your helper should be unable to start to insert a finger between your knee and the saddle, or to shift your thigh off it. It should be possible to walk or trot with a penny between each knee and the saddle without dropping it. With practice this grip becomes habitual, quite unconscious and automatic. When the pony stands still or walks quietly, once grip is acquired, it is quite unnecessary to squeeze tightly the whole time; in fact it would be impossible because one's muscles would cease work through fatigue. But one's knees should always be touching the saddle ready to squeeze instantly should the pony do something unexpected.

Stirrup-leathers are already correctly adjusted for length, first roughly before mounting and then accurately from the saddle. With the foot in the iron, the knee should point downwards, with the lower leg slightly drawn back so that the stirrup-leather hangs vertically. Legs should neither be drawn back behind the girth nor poked forward; both upset balance and the body's upright position, and consequently the seat. When the leg is in its correct position it should be possible, on looking down, to see one's toe just below one's knee. Only place the ball of the foot in the iron, with the toe pointing slightly upwards and heel stretched well down. Never ride with the foot home in the iron up to the instep. Point the toe forward towards the horse's head. This means the feet are now parallel to the horse's flanks and so allows the rider to use the inside (rather than the back) of the legs as an aid.

When sitting correctly, fold your arms; letting your assistant walk the pony about while you maintain the right position in the saddle. Be supple, giving naturally to, and going with, your pony's movements. On no account stiffen your head, neck, or back, otherwise your whole body and your legs will stiffen. Resist the tendency to lean forward when the pony moves, and the impulse to grasp the pommel. Spend the first few rides being led at a walk with arms folded, until you feel supple and quite at ease. Riding is tiring at first as you are using many unaccustomed muscles in your body and legs – one reason why it is such healthy exercise! Therefore make the first rides short; start with thirty minutes, gradually lengthening them to an hour. Otherwise you will feel very stiff and sore the next day!

The aids

The means used to tell the pony what one wants. They are a way of communication, a language understood by both horse and rider. 'Schooling' really means teaching a horse to understand and obey this langauge, which has been known and gradually perfected throughout many centuries. Xenophon, the Greek author and soldier, wrote a book on riding and horsemanship in the fourth century BC and we still use many of his principles today.

Aids fall into two categories – natural and artificial.

Natural aids : voice; hands (through reins and bit, or bits); legs; body; in that order.

Artificial aids : martingale; whip; lungeing-rein; spurs.

The whip should be used purely as an aid; not for coercion or punishment. Only use it for punishment on the rarest of occasions and then only for correction if a pony does something really wicked! A horse should never fear the sight of a whip any more than it should fear the bit.

Voice

The kindest aid, already mentioned as a most important factor in controlling a horse, when discussing its psychology. Use it in the earliest stages of handling a foal, right through all stages as a colt, of breaking (first to a head-collar and then bridling), mouthing, saddling, and, finally, backing. Before backing, while being lunged, teach it to associate definite tones of voice with orders to halt, walk, trot, and canter. Always give these orders in the same way with the same intonation. As it associates each command with a particular tone it will learn to obey the voice alone. Clicking with the tongue does not really count in the same way when schooling. Later on when ridden, the voice is very helpful in teaching it rein and leg aids.

Hands

1 Guiding the pony.

2 Regulating and controlling the amount of energy created by one's legs and body. They should always be very sensitive, light, and responsive, always maintaining a light feel or contact with the pony's mouth; the only exception is when it is walking

completely relaxed on a loose rein. Hands must be able to act or give immediately: they act, producing slight tension on the reins, when one wishes to convey a signal, or relax the tension directly the signal is obeyed.

They either act both together, or each hand independently, according to the meaning of the given signal: the right or left hand each acts separately, as when telling the pony to turn right or left. If the rein is tightening to one side, the other should give slightly, but without losing contact. One cannot act, or give, with one rein without keeping contact with the other; otherwise the signal given is meaningless. Always keep the hands low.

Legs

When a horse moves correctly its hindquarters create impulsion; the rider's legs give the impulsion and also control the movement of the hindquarters. Summing up briefly: the rider's hands control the forehand and his legs the hindquarters. A pony sweating slightly between its hind legs is quite a good sign showing that it is being made to use its hindquarters energetically and correctly.

Legs and hands must act together. If the reins act, the legs must act simultaneously to enforce the required movement. Directly the signal is obeyed, hands and legs must cease movement, the rider sitting still until he wishes to give another order or stop any evasion by the pony.

Move the legs backwards from the knees, swinging nearly parallel to the pony's body. Never kick the lower leg sideways on to the pony's side as this takes the knee and thigh off the saddle, loosening the grip and upsetting the seat. The lower leg acts either at or just behind the girth, according to the movement required. A well-schooled pony should not need kicking along; it should respond instantly to the slightest pressure or movement of its rider's leg or legs. Keep them still, close to the pony, ready to act instantly. A well-trained pony should move forward, increase or decrease speed, and walk, trot, canter, or turn at the lightest touch. Keep the calf of the leg off the pony's side when not in use.

Like the hands, legs either act together or each independently. Thus in turning left, the left leg acts alone while the right must keep absolutely still, generally placed behind the girth to prevent the pony's quarters swinging outwards.

Body

Use of the body can be one of the most powerful aids to increase or decrease pace, and assist the legs to create impulsion; or its weight can be used when turning to make the pony change direction. It must act together with hands and legs. The back muscles, thrusting downwards, produce one of the rider's strongest aids.

The down-thrust of a straight back with muscles braced helps the rider's legs to extend the pony's action or to pull it up. If a hard-puller it is the braced back muscles, acting through the legs at the knees, which pull it up.

The back muscles compel the pony to lower its haunches and bring its hind legs more underneath, thus collecting it better and making it able to move in any required direction.

Body weight makes a pony move sideways on two tracks (e.g. shoulder-in) or turn, by shifting the rider's weight to one side or the other.

Martingale

A trained horse should lower and carry its head correctly in response to its rider's hands and legs. Using a martingale merely to force it to keep its head down is therefore a mistake. Directly it is ridden, without one its head comes up again with added vigour.

Use a martingale on a young, excitable horse which is liable to throw up its head and bolt. It should fit so that the horse does not feel it when carrying its head correctly, but only when it is flung up too high.

Whip

As already stressed, this is simply an aid. It is sometimes better to tap a lazy horse lightly behind the girths with a whip or stick than to kick continually; repeated kicks only deaden all feeling in a horse's sides so that eventually it stops responding to any leg-aid: it becomes 'dead on the leg'.

Spurs

Should only be worn for show on very special full-dress occasions, with the rowels either removed altogether or blunted. Never wear for hunting or show-jumping, or use them on a young pony. Even on very special occasions only an expert rider should wear them. A well-schooled pony should know and obey the leg-aids without any such severe aid. With sharpened rowels they are extremely cruel; unfortunately in bygone days it was all too common to see a horse with torn, bleeding sides being relentlessly spurred on over jumps or out hunting. Fortunately they are rarely seen now. One danger of using them (even without rowels) is that an inexperienced rider may inadvertently dig them into the pony every time he gives a leg-aid.

15 Lungeing and Exercises

The first step was gaining confidence and learning the correct position of body, arms, hands, and legs to acquire a firm, independent seat. After being led about for a few rides one should have gained some idea of grip and balance and be feeling fairly supple and at ease when the pony was walking quietly.

Lungeing

Next, one should get one's assistant to lunge the pony, this being one of the best ways of gaining an independent seat and learning to get right down into the saddle. Side reins are fastened to the saddle.

The cavesson is a separate noseband with separate headband, browband, and adjustable cheek-straps. The lungeing-rein is attached to a swivel right in front, in the middle. Fasten the cavesson noseband fairly tightly, tighter than an ordinary noseband; after fastening, pass the strap through the keeper, but not the runner. Have the side-rein slightly tighter on the side the pony is circling. Leave the bridle-reins knotted on the pony's neck.

With stirrup-leathers at the correct length, mount without picking up the reins, placing your feet in both irons. Having mounted, before being lunged, check that the leathers are correct and of equal length; adjust if necessary. Sit with thighs and knees pressing against the saddle. To gain confidence at first, hold the pommel, or a neck strap, but try to keep on by balance and grip; *not* by holding the pommel! Look between the pony's ears, keeping your body supple from the waist upwards. Keep your lower leg from knee to foot away from the saddle flap. Let your leg hang straight from the knee downwards so that your stirrup-leathers hang perpendicularly to the ground. Having acquired confidence and grip with thighs and knees, fold your arms.

Lungeing should only be done with a knowledgeable helper, as being lunged by an inexperienced person can do more harm than good.

Before mounting, your pony should have been lunged for a few minutes without a rider, to let it settle down and go quietly. Only use a pony accustomed to being lunged.

Your helper stands in the middle holding the other end of the lungeing-rein; using his voice and a whip with a long lash he sends the pony round him in a large circle. It must be quiet and obedient as at first you will ride with arms folded (without reins); after several rides practise without reins or stirrups.

Walk at first, later, as grip and balance improve and you gain confidence, trot, and finally canter. Having no reins, give your whole attention to your seat and the correct position of your legs. Do not always lunge in the same direction as it makes the pony move unevenly. Lunge equally to the right and left.

Having practised walking, trotting, and cantering with stirrups, when you are beginning to go with your pony and feel the rhythm of each pace, practise without stirrups: fold the leathers across the saddle in front of you. Begin at a walk, progressing by easy stages to a trot and canter. Do not hurry these early stages of your riding. To have added confidence, fit a neck strap to hold if necessary.

When riding without stirrups, sit deep in the saddle, stretching your legs down as far as possible. Keep your head upright, elbows into your sides with arms folded, or hands resting lightly on your thighs. Sit upright, keeping your whole body supple. Point your toes upwards.

Exercises

Very valuable: a beginner should practise them at every ride. Even an experienced rider should do them to keep supple and his muscles in trim. Practise either being led or lunged, or when alone, provided your pony is quiet and well schooled.

When being led first practise at the halt, then at a walk. Then practise while being lunged, first with then without stirrups. Do not do these exercises for too long at first; some are particularly tiring and you must not risk straining your muscles.

While practising an exercise keep your legs in their correct position as they will tend to move back behind or level with the girth, which is wrong.

When being led, practise all exercises without reins: knot, and rest them on the pony's neck.

1 Turning ankles

Remove each foot from the iron and rotate several times first outwards, then inwards. Then rotate both ankles together. Practise at halt, then walking. Keep thigh and knee on the saddle with legs held correctly.

2 Lean forward, touching pony's neck

Bend forward as low as possible, first on the near, then on the off side. With thighs and knees gripping, do not move your legs backwards or forwards out of position. Valuable for suppling and grip. Practise with, then without, stirrups at halt, walk, and trot.

3 Turning in saddle

Raise both arms outwards at shoulder level. Swing round and look behind you as far as possible from the waist. Keep seat, thigh, and legs still. Valuable for suppling. Practise at halt, walk, and trot: with, without, stirrups.

4 Arm swinging

Swing right arm several times, backwards then forwards: repeat with left arm. Keep seat, thighs, and legs still. For grip and balance. Practise at halt, walk, and trot: with, without, stirrups.

5 Body swinging

Hands on hips. From the waist swing forwards, then backwards, as far as possible. Keep a straight back throughout. Keep thigh and knee grip, legs immovable. For suppling waist, strengthening back and stomach muscles, thigh and knee grip. At halt, walk; with, without, stirrups.

6 Bend, touch toe

Swing right arm forwards and downwards from above your head; touch your right toe. Then swing up again above head. Repeat with left arm. Keep seat in saddle; grip with thighs and knees without swinging lower leg backwards. For strengthening grip. Practise with, without, stirrups, at halt, walk, trot.

7 Bend, touch opposite toe

Harder than 6. Perform in same way, but touch opposite toe. Try to remain seated. Grip with thighs and knees, keeping legs correctly placed. Practise as with previous exercises.

8 Bend, touch both toes simultaneously

Raise both arms above head. Swing forwards and downwards, touching both toes. Keep seat as near saddle as possible. Grip (thighs, knees). Keep legs correctly placed.

9 Lying back on pony's quarters

Severe exercise, imposing considerable strain on stomach muscles. Do not overdo it. Only practise when pony is being held. If practising alone make sure that your pony will stand still. Bend backwards until head and shoulders rest on pony's croup. Keeping head and back in a straight line while lying back and sitting up: do not poke your head forwards. Remain lying back relaxed for a few moments before sitting up. Grip (thighs, knees) Do not let legs move forward. Strengthens grip, back, and stomach muscles. Practise only at halt; with, without, stirrups.

10 Standing in stirrups

Knee grip; balance; keeping legs correctly placed, without going back. An essential preliminary exercise for learning to trot, canter, and jump.

Grip with knees; pushing upwards, stand without leaning forward or letting legs go back. Feel as if the power from the down-thrust of your back muscles were coming out of your knees.

Do not rise too high off the saddle. Have leathers the correct length; this exercise is impossible if they are too short. Either fold arms, stretch them out sideways to balance, or put your hands on your hips when first practising.

Practise at halt, walk, trot, and canter. Eventually you should be able to canter round the 'school', or field while standing. Practise without reins when led or lunged: use reins at walk or trot if riding alone. Do not use reins to hold on to or balance. Rest your hands on your pony's withers.

11 'Round the world'

An agility and balance exercise much enjoyed by children: also teaches confidence. Usually known by this nickname. Have pony held while practising. Swing left leg over pony's neck; sit sideways on off side. Swing right leg over; sit facing tail. Swing left leg over; sit sideways on near side. Swing right leg over pony's neck; sit upright. Do this in one continuous movement. Practise in the opposite direction, starting with right leg. Also practise bareback.

12 Swinging legs

Remove both feet from irons in turn, swinging each freely backwards and forwards from the knee. Do not move body or seat, thighs or knees. Practise at halt and walk.

13 Sitting trot

Formerly called trot *à la Française*: ordinary (rising) trot was called trot *à l'Anglaise*. Practise sitting trot without stirrups: valuable for developing a good seat. Practise without reins, while led or lunged. Keep legs in their correct position with heels down gripping firmly with thighs and knees. Do not grip with the back of the calf. Only practise at first for short periods as it is very tiring.

14 Pivot trunk at canter

An advanced exercise. Only practise when you have complete confidence and a good seat. Practise when lunged, first with, then without, stirrups.

Pivot body as far as possible round from the waist, first to the left, then to the right. Stretch out your arms to balance. Keep your seat in the saddle; grip with thighs and knees, keeping legs correctly placed. Have a neck strap. Be supple, moving rhythmically with your pony. Valuable for balance and a strong seat.

Bareback riding

Having had some experience riding bareback strengthens grip and seat. One has much closer contact with the pony than with a saddle, and can therefore feel its movement better. When first mounting bareback, get a leg-up from a helper. Learn eventually to vault on jockey-fashion (see page 136). Being able to vault on and ride back bareback is useful, having caught one's pony. Riding bareback is very tiring, so begin with short periods.

At first have the pony led, walking, until you feel confident and are accustomed to the feel of riding without a saddle. Use a neck strap. Knot your reins, riding with arms folded. Sit where the saddle normally fits, stretching your legs well down. Grip as usual with thighs and knees, not with your calf. Flex your ankles, with heels stretched down, toes up.

When accustomed to your pony's feel and movement walking, let your helper lead it at a trot. Do a sitting trot, sitting well down: do not attempt a rising trot until you have a really strong grip. Trotting barebacked is tiring and uncomfortable so do it only for short periods at first. You will jolt and bounce all over the place at first, but sit down, grip with your knees and try to move rhythmically with your pony. Keep your whole body supple without stiffening.

Practise exercises already given (touching toes on the same and opposite sides, etc.). One cannot do this bareback unless one's legs are in the normal riding position (heels down, toes up). Also practise turning from the waist, and alternate arm swinging. Practise each exercise at the halt, walking, and finally trotting. Also practise lying back at the halt; this is easier and more comfortable than with a saddle.

When secure and comfortable bareback, being led, walking, and trotting, practise being lunged. Eventually practise cantering bareback: then try exercise 14 (pivoting trunk at the canter).

Having learnt to jump with a saddle, practise low jumps bare-backed. This is the final stage when you can ride bareback, alone, using your reins as aids, without hanging on by them.

Blanket riding

Fold a blanket into four to make a comfortable pad; fasten where the saddle goes with a surcingle, a web, leather, or nylon strap, used like a girth.

Some advocate it as better and more comfortable than riding bareback. It is useful to avoid dirtying a clean saddle, for riding to the blacksmith, or exercising on a wet, muddy day. Blanket riding does not give the same close contact as bareback riding, but is good practice, improving one's seat. As when riding bare-back, sit well down as close as possible, with legs stretched well down, heels down, toes up. Practise sitting and rising trot; also cantering. Girth up the surcingle tightly enough to prevent the blanket slipping. See that the surcingle fits in the girth-groove and not too far back under the belly, otherwise it slips forward and loosens.

When you have learnt to vault on unaided, blanket riding has the advantage that a helper is unnecessary.

16 The Paces of a Horse

Natural paces

Walking, trotting, cantering, and galloping are all natural paces; others developed from these like the extended walk are artificial and the horse must learn them.

When schooling a young horse it is essential to preserve the purity of its natural gait at each pace. Note the grace and freedom of a horse's stride, with long, level, even beats, when walking naturally in its paddock. It is naturally collected when trotting free. When cantering its correct leg leads naturally, according to the direction it is moving, and when changing direction it changes legs quite naturally. The rider must persuade the horse to preserve that natural grace and free action when being ridden, and must hinder its movements as little as possible. Hence first lessons on a lungeing-rein, without a rider, are vitally important.

The walk

The aids: push down and slightly forward with back and seat muscles, squeeze with thighs and knees and ease the reins, letting the hands move slightly forward. A well-schooled pony walks forward immediately; if it does not, kick with both heels behind the girths, saying, 'Wa-alk', slowly. If badly trained or very lazy, it may need very lightly tapping with the whip behind the girths, purely as an aid, accompanied by the voice. Do not squeeze with the calves of the legs. Directly it obeys sit still, with long reins and only very light contact with its mouth.

Teach a pony to walk on with long, free strides. If it slackens pace or tries to stop tighten the reins, using the little fingers and bending the wrists slightly inwards (use the action of squeezing a sponge); simultaneously use the heels behind the girths.

Halting from a walk

Push down and slightly forward with back muscles and seat, squeezing with the knees. His seat pushes slightly forward, the rider feeling as if the thrust of his back muscles were coming out of his knees. At the same time increase contact with the pony's mouth by tensing the fingers (squeezing a sponge). Feeling resistance to its forward movement it should quietly halt, standing correctly with front legs together, haunches well under, and hind legs together. Never let a pony halt 'uncollected', with one front leg in front of the other and back legs sprawling out behind. Never try to halt a pony by pulling back the arms and/or raising the hands. If so, its head goes up; it will not come up to its bit or stand collected with its haunches under it, but will stop with front legs sprawling and hind legs stuck out behind.

Never pull at a pony; it only resists by pulling in return. The harder one pulls, the more it will pull; being the stronger it will win every time in a trial of strength! This applies to all paces. One of the rider's greatest sins is pulling at his pony's mouth. It is a natural, instinctive reaction which he should overcome from the beginning; it soon makes a pony a confirmed puller and gives it a hard mouth.

Many riders complain that their pony pulls, when often it is their own fault. It is only trying to escape from the pain in its mouth. Tugging backwards at the reins with the arms is very different from resisting with the hands, which is a passive resistance against the pony's activity.

Kinds of walk: 1 free (natural) walk; 2 ordinary walk; 3 collected walk; 4 extended walk; 5 disunited walk; 6 amble.

1 Free walk

Pony walks on a loose rein with head and neck completely free, giving it a chance to rest and relax its muscles by lowering its head and stretching its neck forward. Keep only the lightest possible contact with its mouth. Use after schooling.

2 Ordinary walk

Natural walk in 4-time. Movement always begins with the hind leg, the sequence being near-hind, near-fore, off-hind, off-fore. It is a moderate pace, free, even, regular, and unrestricted. Make the pony come up to its bit and use its quarters energetically, using back muscles and seat to produce impulsion. It should walk calmly yet briskly with even steps, evenly spaced with four distinct beats. Reins should have a light, steady contact with its mouth.

3 Collected walk

Ride pony up to its bit, with raised, arched neck, so that its head is nearly vertical. Haunches should be well under so that the hind legs move forward well under its body. Its legs are raised higher and are more bent at the joints; although there is more movement, it walks a little slower, each stride covering less ground. Again in 4-time, with legs used in the same order.

4 Extended walk

A fast walk covering as much ground as possible at each stride, as quickly as possible. The pony should walk calmly and un-excitedly, with the ordinary succession of beats and even, regular steps. Hold the hands slightly forward, giving a longer rein without losing contact, so that the pony can stretch out its head and neck. It should be so collected that it can alter pace direction or speed instantly at a given order. Hind feet move forward beyond the tracks of the fore feet.

5 Disunited walk

Means an uncollected, improperly controlled pony and should never be allowed. The beats become uneven, irregular and con-fused.

6 The amble

Was much used by travellers in olden times; mentioned by Chaucer in *Canterbury Tales*. It was especially used by ladies and today is cultivated in the American horse. The lateral legs move together, giving a very comfortable gait for the rider.

The trot

1 *Rising trot* – most generally used. The rider 'posts', rising in his stirrups as one diagonal moves forward and sitting down as the opposite diagonal moves forward. It is used for the ordinary and extended trot.

2 *Sitting trot* – the rider sits in the saddle the whole time, going with his horse. It is the most comfortable when riding bareback. Used for the collected and slow trot.

Kinds of trot : 1 ordinary; 2 collected; 3 extended.

1 Ordinary trot

One of the horse's natural paces and generally used by a rider. Hind legs should move straight, following exactly in the tracks of the forelegs, with very even steps. Keep the pony collected and balanced, moving freely with haunches very active and well underneath. It should move in a straight line from head to tail and must not turn its forehand sideways. Reins should only have slight contact.

2 Collected trot

The slowest of the three, slower than the ordinary trot. It is an artificial pace, in which the hind legs move energetically, with haunches well underneath. Neck should be raised so that the shoulders can move freely. The pony should move lightly and actively with somewhat short steps.

3 Extended trot

Not necessarily faster than ordinary trot, but with a longer stride. Impulsion from the hindquarters should make the shoulders move energetically. Neck more oustretched than in the ordinary trot.

The trot is in 2-time, each pair of diagonals moving alternately: off-fore and near-hind (right diagonal); near-fore and off-hind (left diagonal). All four feet are momentarily off the ground.

Rising trot

Sit in the saddle as one diagonal comes forward. The pony's forward movement pushes its rider upwards; he remains out of the saddle as the other diagonal comes forward and reaches the ground. The rider should lean slightly forward from his hips, keeping his head and body in a straight line; his knees and stirrup-irons take his weight. He can start trotting on either diagonal. If he sits as the right diagonal touches the ground he is trotting on the right diagonal. If he sits as the left diagonal reaches the ground he is trotting on the left diagonal.

Practise trotting on either diagonal, making a habit of changing them frequently on a ride. Always riding on the same diagonal makes a pony stiff and uncomfortable to ride on the neglected one. Change by sitting in the saddle for one stride.

To find out on which diagonal you are riding notice which foreleg touches the ground as you sit. Eventually you should be able to tell by feel, without looking to see on which diagonal you are riding.

Sitting trot

Very tiring at first as one does not move out of the saddle. Until one learns to grip and can go with the pony's rhythm, giving to its movements, one bounces up and down and finds balancing difficult, especially riding bareback.

The sitting trot is useful, being the beginning of several movements used in more advanced riding. The beats are more marked. Do not use it on young horses with back muscles not yet fully developed, but only on fully grown ones.

Aids for trotting

Move your hands forward and give slightly with the reins while bracing your back muscles and seat, and squeezing with knees and thighs. Directly the pony obeys by trotting, sit perfectly quietly, with your legs still: have only a light contact with the reins. Kick a lazy, sluggish pony behind the girths with your heels, while squeezing your knees; if necessary, reinforce leg-aids by touching lightly with the whip behind the girths, or just behind your leg. Never flap the reins about or tug them backwards.

Keep your pony moving on, repeating the same aids if it slows up unasked. Try to anticipate what it intends doing by feel, and so do not wait until it actually slows up before reapplying the aids.

Halting from trot

Use the same aids as when halting from a walk. You should equally not reduce pace from a trot by pulling back with your arms and/or by raising your hands; never lean backwards when reducing pace.

Do not lean too far forward when trotting; keep your head and back supple, in a straight line; do not poke your head forward or have rounded shoulders.

The canter

A pace in 3-time. Either the near or off foreleg can lead. When the near foreleg leads the order of leg movements is: off-hind, right diagonal, near-fore. When the off-fore leads the order is: near-hind, left diagonal, off-fore.

When cantering the seat should not leave the saddle; sit well down, still and upright, without leaning forward. Let your body sway slightly in time and rhythmically with the pony's movements. Horse and rider should swing along appearing as if one. Do not round your back so that your shoulders go forward; keep elbows and toes in.

Always keep your pony collected and moving at a moderate speed. Never let it get control and start quickening its pace. Cantering excites some horses, especially when moving in a straight line; if not kept collected and well under control they break into a fast canter and then a gallop, or may try to buck. Cantering in a circle helps to keep a steady, even pace.

Kinds of canter : 1 ordinary; 2 collected; 3 extended.

1 Ordinary canter

Another natural pace. The horse should move freely at moderate speed, keeping in a straight line from head to tail, with its body balanced. Its speed is approximately 5–6 mph.

F

2 Collected canter (or school canter)

Active haunches kept well under, shoulders free with plenty of movement. This pace is used for schooling and in the show-ring. A horse should be able to go from a walk straight into a collected canter.

3 Extended canter

Faster than the ordinary canter, the horse stretching its head and neck our further. While lengthening stride it should remain calm and move lightly.

The aids

As a horse may become excitable when cantering, always keep it collected. Do not let it increase speed, otherwise it will start galloping. It should lead with either foreleg according to the direction of movement, the off-fore going to the right and near going left. When moving straight forward its off-fore should lead. To make a horse lead with the near-fore, draw your right foot back behind the girth, slightly tense the left rein, simultaneously using strong leg-pressure, helped by your back and seat. This applies to cantering straight or to the left. To start cantering to the right, apply your left heel behind the girth, slightly tighten the right rein, using strong back, seat, and leg-aids. Sit in the saddle while starting to canter.

Slowing up

From a canter to a trot: push downwards with back and seat; squeeze with your knees. Resist slightly with your hands. Never lean back or pull backwards with the reins.

Cantering false

The horse leads with the wrong leg; leading with the near-fore when it should lead with the off-fore, cantering to the right, or vice-versa. This is dangerous when turning or cantering in a circle as it may cross its legs and fall.

Disunited canter

Instead of using fore and hind legs on the same side the horse canters with the hind leg on the opposite side to the leading foreleg. Sometimes called a 'butcher boy's' canter.

Changing legs

A horse can be made to change legs and will do so naturally when cantering free without a rider.

When riding, either bring it back to a trot for a few steps – the fewer the better – and then start cantering on the other leg, or make it change legs in mid-air, while cantering (called a flying change). The latter is advanced schooling, only possible when the rider can canter well, on a well-schooled pony.

The feel should indicate which leg is leading, without looking to see. The rider should turn slightly towards the leading leg, with his thigh on that side turned slightly more inwards towards the saddle, and his hip slightly more forward.

Galloping

An extension from the canter; a horse's fastest natural pace. 4-time, the order of leg movements being: near-hind, off-hind, near-fore, off-fore.

Only gallop when thoroughly experienced and safe in the saddle, with complete control. There is always the danger of a horse getting excited and out of control, taking the bit between its teeth, and bolting. There are few more frightening experiences than being on a horse out of control, bolting at full gallop. Furthermore, too much galloping breaks its wind quicker than anything, while hard ground quickly ruins its legs. One gallop a week is enough for any horse.

The rider shortens his reins, with his hands well forward and low down on the horse's neck, beyond the withers. Lean forward, sitting well down in the saddle, for a slow gallop. At full gallop, lean forward in the stirrup-irons, seat off the saddle, gripping with the knees and keeping knees and ankles supple, so that one goes with the horse's movement. One must not stiffen knees or ankles.

Aids for galloping

Put your horse into an extended canter. Shorten the reins, lean forward, seat off the saddle, urging on the horse with your legs until it breaks from a canter (3-time), into a gallop (4-time). Keep it collected at a steady pace, so that it does not become excited and out of hand.

Slowing-up

Sit in the saddle, bringing your hands back to their normal position. Resist with your hands, bracing your back and seat while squeezing your knees until the pace slows from a gallop to a canter, or, by continuing resistance, to a trot.

Galloping 'hell for leather' is only necessary out hunting, with hounds running, racing, or playing polo; and then only in short bursts. Only an ignorant, inconsiderate rider gallops unnecessarily; if he comes to grief he has asked for it, and thoroughly deserves the consequences! Unfortunately the horse usually suffers as well as the rider.

17 Elementary Training (Dressage)

Purpose

This might be summarized briefly as making a horse more obedient and move more lightly and gracefully. The meaning of dressage (a French word) is best expressed by the French definition, 'agreeable'. The horse becomes a better ride because training makes it handy and more obedient to its rider, while developing its muscles and suppling it, thereby improving its performance at all paces. Broadly speaking, it includes all training, from beginning to end. Every rider should therefore understand and be able to school his horse in elementary dressage movements.

Whatever movement one wishes to make, the three essentials are balance, collection, and impulsion. One must balance one's horse through the proper use of body-weight and seat, and collect it, going forward freely into its bit, through correct combined use of one's hands, back, seat, and leg-aids. As already explained (page 33), impulsion is created by and comes from, the horse's hindquarters.

Balance

A horse balances by stretching out its head and neck, as can be seen by watching one move freely without a rider. Unhampered by a rider it balances itself naturally when galloping or jumping, by stretching out its head. This explains why a rider must put his hands forward, low on its neck, when jumping, to give it free, unhindered use of its neck and head, without interfering with its mouth. The rider's weight unbalances the horse so that it must readjust itself, especially if his seat and weight are too far back near the loins, on the horse's weakest part, instead of being well forward, just behind its withers and shoulders on its strongest part. So the rider must help the horse to readjust itself (a) by sitting with his weight correctly placed, and (b) by collecting it.

Collection

This is a matter of interdependence between hands and leg-aids, holding the horse between them. The rider 'talks' to the horse, conveying his wishes through the combined medium of hands and legs, which together speak a language the horse must learn to understand, and then obey freely.

To make it obey willingly, it is essential for it not to fear the bit, but have confidence in the bridle, and in its rider, and his hands. If it fears pain from the bit, or from clumsy use of its rider's hands, obviously a horse will not go freely up to, and forward into, its bit. Instead of holding the bit lightly in its mouth, it will move 'behind its bit', or lean upon it, or try all sorts of evasions, like tossing its head up in the air, poking its nose forward, putting its head down or sideways pulling, etc., to escape from the bit.

If the rider sits deep into his horse, on the correct part of its back, with thighs and legs well stretched down, he can immediately feel any evasions before they actually occur, by stiffening of its neck and spine. When moving forward freely, up to its bit, its spine and neck will feel supple. A good rider reads his horse's thoughts, and prevents any evasions before they occur, by anticipating them; which is what he should do.

Through the bit, the rider, by flexing the reins with his hands, can raise, lower, or bring back his horse's head, while simultaneously pushing it forward into its bridle with his back, seat, and leg-aids. Beginners make the great mistake of pulling their horse's head back, thinking thereby that they will make it move forward up to its bit. The actual effect is exactly opposite. Hands should give forward while back, seat, and legs push the horse forward, with its hocks and haunches well under, driven forward by the impulsion and energy created by its hindquarters – the source of all movement.

Moving forward thus, the horse then contacts the rider's hands through the variable pressure, or resistance, of the reins. It is really the horse that resists, not the rider. Directly it gives obediently his hands should become passive and motionless, only keeping the lightest of contacts with its mouth. Thus his hands continually interact and play on the horse's mouth, 'talking' to it as delicately as a musician's hands on his instrument.

If reins alone are used to make a horse bend or flex, by pulling with the hands, without the leg-aids' forward impulse, it will get behind its bit, because, having been forced to bend its head and give with its jaw, it has more or less lost the feel of the bit, and will be uncontrolled and difficult to collect.

Impulsion

The rider's back, seat, and leg-aids impart energy to the horse's hindquarters, which should move freely. When using them correctly the effect is to drive its haunches and hocks underneath it thus really shortening its length from its fore to its hind legs and pushing its quarters up. When collected it is therefore ready to obey its rider's wishes instantly, extending (lengthening) its stride without necessarily quickening its speed, or shortening stride again without necessarily slowing up; all this must be done without the beats becoming uneven or irregular: so it is ready to alter its pace (walk to trot or canter; canter to gallop) or turn right or left, and so forth. That is, a collected horse gives itself willingly to its rider, ready and willing generously to obey his wishes. And all this is initiated by the hindquarters.

The turn

The simplest movement to execute, it should be practised walking, trotting, and finally cantering. Go large, turning on a wide circle, not sharply.

Lateral aid

As explained (page 33), a horse's body should move in a straight line from head to tail, when turning, its hindquarters move round, the forehand following; not vice-versa. Hence, when turning, never pull its head round with the reins, but push its hindquarters round with the leg. The rider's shoulders and hips should be parallel with those of his horse, sitting upright and looking in the direction he wishes to go. His leg, on the side he wants to turn, acts behind the girth to give impulsion, his hand on that side acting simultaneously with his leg, having slightly more contact (tension) on the rein. His hand on the opposite side goes forward, giving slightly so that the rein has no tension, while his leg keeps perfectly still at the girth. His hand should act as if squeezing a sponge; it must not pull the rein backwards.

For a right turn, flex with the right rein, using the right leg. The left hand moves forward, relaxing tension on the rein; the left leg is inactive behind the girth. Legs must be used quite independently. The body leans slightly throwing its weight on to the side of the turn.

Turning left, apply left leg at the girth, with the right behind it. simultaneously, flex with the left rein, relaxing contact with the right.

While turning, the horse's stride should remain level and its beats even.

Diagonal aid

The opposite rein and leg act together. To turn to the right use right rein with left leg acting behind the girth. To turn left use left rein and right leg. Keep the leg not acting at the girth away from the horse's side.

The circle

Simply a continuation of the turn. Practise walking, trotting, and cantering. At each pace the horse should move calmly, with regular beats and level, even strides, its haunches well under. The circle should be large.

Figure of eight

Valuable for suppling a horse. Practise walking, trotting, and cantering. Both circles should be large and equal in diameter. If too small, the horse may turn its neck and head because the rider is pulling it round with the reins.

The rider completes a right or left circle, putting his weight over to the side he is turning. Leg and rein are then reversed to circle the opposite way, completing the figure eight and putting his weight over in the new direction.

Turn on the forehand

Easier than the turn on the haunches: practise it as an exercise. For ordinary riding use the turn on the haunches.

When turning on the forehand a horse moves its hindquarters round, pivoting on one of its forelegs according to the direction of the turn, while the other foreleg crosses over it.

To teach it how to turn, stand correctly on all four legs alongside, but not too close to, a wall or fence, turning its head in the required direction, just enough to see its eye. Draw back your leg behind the girths on the same side, to push its quarters round the opposite way, with your other leg at the girths to prevent it moving backwards.

To turn right, turn its head slightly to the right, with its right eye just visible. Draw the right leg behind the girths, pushing its quarter round left, with the left leg at the girths. The horse turns on the right (off-fore) leg, which either pivots or is lifted up and replaced in the same place. The off-hind leg crosses over in front of the near-hind. The horse must not step backwards or become unbalanced and step forwards, the latter fault being worse. Its head must remain still as it turns. For a left turn reverse leg and rein aids. Practise turning only through a right angle.

Turn on the haunches

Turn the horse's forehand on its hindquarters, using a hind leg as a pivot to the direction. Collect it before starting the turn.

The inside rein leads in the direction of the turn with the opposite, outside rein pressing against its neck in support. Pressure on the outside rein is outwards, not backwards. Apply the outside leg behind the girth to prevent the hindquarters swinging out. Keep the inside leg, on the side of the turn, close at the girth. The rider's weight is slightly back and inwards. The horse must not step backwards, raise its head, or poke out its nose.

To turn right, use the right (inside) rein to lead round the forehand (head, neck, and shoulders). Do not pull the horse's head or make its neck bend round; the entire forehand must move. Simultaneously bring the left rein across to the right, pressing against its neck to support the right rein, making its neck and shoulders turn with its head. Meanwhile the rider's left leg, acting strongly behind the girth, stops the horse's hind-quarters swinging left: the rider's body leans slightly right and backwards, throwing his weight on its hindquarters to the right. The right (off) hind leg turns, either rising and falling in the same place, or pivoting. Only turn through a right angle.

To turn left, reverse hand and leg-aids.

Turn on the haunches at the halt or moving. When turning from a halt, collect the horse; make it stand correctly on all fours.

Turning on the move is difficult; only practise it when the horse can turn correctly standing still. Beats must be even with both hind legs walking without pivoting. Start at a collected walk.

Neck reining

One can also turn on the haunches with the reins in one hand, using indirect reining and lateral aids.

Instead of the inside reign leading the forehand round, the outside rein presses against the horse's neck, with the outside leg acting. The rider's weight again shifts backwards and inwards. Move the hand holding the reins forwards as well as sideways.

Right turn: reins in left hand, bringing it forwards and across, the left rein pressing against the horse's neck. Use the left leg. Move your weight backwards, to the right.

Left turn: reverse hand and leg-aids, with reins in the right hand.

Indirect reining can be used with diagonal aids; the outside rein presses against the horse's neck while the inside leg acts with strong pressure.

Rein back

Collect your pony, making it stand squarely on all four legs. Use some object directly ahead as a marker. In a 'school' this will be one of the letters marking the various points to which it moves.

Use even pressure with both knees, leaning slightly forward from the waist, with a straight head and back. Feel your pony's mouth gently, with a slight backward tension on the reins. Your legs urge your pony forward while hands and reins resist the forward movement; it therefore starts moving backwards. Directly it yields and begins stepping backwards, relax tension on the reins. Your legs continue their pressure to keep the pony moving straight backwards. Keep your eyes on the marker ahead, and stop directly the pony starts turning its quarters sideways. After relaxing your hands, reapply tension on the reins; the effect is like vibrating the hands simultaneously with your legs. Your pony should walk back in 4-time with level, even steps. Six or seven steps are enough as it is a great strain on its hindquarters and muscles.

More advanced work

Normally a horse should move in a straight line. When it does this at all paces calmly, with level, even steps, work on two tracks can be started. These exercises supple a horse as it must bend its spine. Instead of its hind legs following in the tracks of its fore-legs, it must move diagonally on two separate distinct tracks.

A horse does not normally move on two tracks, unless for an occasional sideways bound, as when it shies. Such work uses muscles otherwise comparatively unused; being tiring it should not be overdone at first. Only start it after obtaining full control of the hindquarters and the horse's willing co-operation, having made it supple by riding circles and figures of eight at various pace from a walk to a slow canter.

Shoulder-in

Excellent for suppling a horse's spine, making it bend its forehand from head to shoulder, following a curve with the rider's leg as the centre. It moves forward diagonally, its forelegs following a different track from its hind legs. Practise in a school or, if unavailable, parallel with a wall or fence.

Right shoulder-in

Ride in a circle until its circumference meets the wall or fence

The outside (right) rein bends its neck outwards, also controlling and limiting its direction. The left rein gives the flexion. The forehand turns outwards, with the rider's right leg as the centre: the left leg gives the aid for forward movement. The horse moves forward diagonally on two tracks, its forehand bent outwards in the opposite direction to the movement and its hindquarters nearest the wall or fence.

Left shoulder-in

The left rein is now outside, bending the horse's head outwards (left), and controlling and limiting its direction. The right rein flexes. The forehand turns outward, centring on the rider's left leg; his right creates the forward impulsion. The head faces outwards (left), with the hindquarters nearest the wall.

The shoulder-in is the only two-track movement in which the horse bends away from its direction of movement.

Shoulder-in on the circle

Moving on two tracks in a circle. A difficult exercise, only to be attempted after much practice of the shoulder-in on a straight track, when horse and rider are both thoroughly proficient. The forehand revolves round an inner circle, and the quarters round an outer concentric circle, at an angle of 30°–40° with the tangent. It can only be performed at a walk.

Quarters-in (head to the wall)

Diagonal movement on two tracks with the horse's head to the wall and its quarters outwards. Unlike the shoulder-in the horse bends in the direction of movement, not away from it.

More difficult than the shoulder-in because it is less natural; correct use of reins is harder. The same muscles and joints are used but quite differently. It is a good preparatory exercise for the half-pass.

Circle left until at the point where the horse leaves the circle, the rider pushes it away sideways along the tangent. The right leg pushes to the left, the reins also leading to the left; the left rein flexes the horse to the left, looking in the direction it is moving.

At first a horse finds flexing in the direction of movement

difficult; at first it may try to straighten its neck, or even to bend
it the opposite way. When it leaves the circle, to move at a
tangent on two tracks, keep the left rein tension unaltered; lessen
right rein tension by lengthening it slightly. Do not increase left
rein tension, and do not pull it back. As the rider leaves the circle
he should look and press his horse, to the left with his right leg.
Left hand and rein move slightly away from the horse's shoulder;
his right hand and rein move slightly closer to it, the right rein
pressing lightly against the neck. Slightly lengthening the right
rein encourages the horse to flex leftwards.

Quarters-out

In quarters-out the horse moves with its tail, instead of its head,
towards the wall. It again bends in the direction of movement
and the aids are alike. The relative position to the wall is the only
difference.

If possible, practise all more advanced work in a proper riding-
school, but if unavailable try it alongside a wall or fence.

Quarters-in on the circle

Move in a fairly big circle on two tracks, with hind legs on the
inner and forehand on the larger, outer circle. Do not move at
too acute an angle.

Quarters-out on the circle

Again a fairly large circle on two tracks, but with its head now
on the inner and its hindquarters on the larger, outer circle.

Full pass

Use for moving sideways when there is insufficient room to turn.
The horse walks sideways, crossing over both hind and fore feet,
its spine flexed from head to tail.

Full pass to the right

Make the horse look right by very slightly tensing the right rein,
supported by the left rein on its neck. Resist with both reins
just enough to prevent it moving forward. Simultaneously press
with the left leg to push the horse sideways to the right. Its body

remains perfectly straight, its near-fore and near-hind legs passing in front of its off-fore and off-hind.

Full pass to the left

Very slightly tense the left rein to make the horse look left, supported by the right rein on its neck, both reins resisting any forward movement. Simultaneously press the right leg, pushing the horse sideways to the left. Off-fore and off-hind cross over in front of near-fore and near-hind.

Half-pass

Only front or back feet cross over. The horse moves forward diagonally across the school, while keeping parallel to the side.

Half-pass to the right

Slight tension on right rein makes the horse look right; right hand held higher than the left. Simultaneously press with the left leg, heel behind the girth. Both legs maintain the horse's forward movement.

Changing leading-leg at canter

Needs a well-trained horse and proficient rider who can ride a good collected canter.

Incline the horse's head slightly towards the side opposite the leg required to lead. Then shift your weight, using leg and heel on the same side. This momentarily unbalances the horse on its leading-leg, swinging it on to the other leg during the brief moment when all four feet are off the ground. Correct timing is the secret; it needs much practice.

Knowing how to change is necessary because cantering in a circle with the wrong leg leading may make the horse fall through crossing its front legs. The near-fore leads on the left circle and the off-fore on the right.

Changing leg, right to left circle

Incline the horse's head to the right. Shift your weight to the left, using left leg and heel.

Changing leg, left to right circle

Reverse aids; horse's head to the left. Rider's weight shifts right, using right leg, with heel behind the girths.

Attempt advanced work at first under expert supervision and tuition. Even a well-schooled pony can be ruined so quickly if its rider does not really know what he is doing.

More advanced work is only mentioned so that the rider knows of its existence. There is much still more advanced work which only the most expert riders – the few – can attempt. Most average riders are content with having a good seat and hands, collecting and riding their horses correctly at the walk, trot, and canter, being able to rein back, shoulder-in, turn on the forehand and haunches and jump normal, medium-sized obstacles. Only the fortunate few especially gifted riders, with time, who can afford to buy the best horse and have the best available tuition at a famous school, can hope to reach the heights.

The same difference occurs between the average good pianist and the great virtuoso. In both cases achievement takes years of hard work. Riding is as much an art as music. They are rather akin; both requiring a sense of timing and rhythm and hands with a delicate touch. A really good rider plays on his horse with hands and legs, as a musician plays on his instrument! His hands and legs talk to his horse, which talks back through its mouth and spine, producing the sensation which the rider feels from them: e.g. if the horse stiffens, resisting with its jaw, the rider feels it through both hands and seat as a stiffening of its spine. A rider with good hands and seat, sitting well into his horse, can feel every reaction; by experience and applying a little horse-psychology, he can anticipate its next move. This is the foundation of all riding, from the most elementary to the most advanced.

18 Hacking

Road safety

Even in the country hacking inevitably involves some road-work. For safety, certain rules must always be remembered, especially with the volume and speed of modern traffic:

1 Ride on the left, as close in to the edge as possible. Never wander all over the road.

2 Always keep your pony collected, under control.

3 Ride on the grass verge if present, but first ascertain if this is legal. Some rural councils forbid it.

4 When dismounted always lead a horse on the left side, walking with the traffic. When leading, walk on the outside, keeping the pony on the insde. Train a pony to lead from the near or off side.

5 Never trot downhill on a road. Never canter or gallop on a hard road. Never trot for long on a hard surface. Trotting a short distance on a level road or up a slight incline is harmless, if not slippery. Trotting up a slight slope does a pony's muscles good, preferably off a hard road. Dismount when descending a steep hill, especially if slippery.

6 If the road is slippery, always dismount and lead slowly.

7 Dismount ascending a steep hill. It also stretches your own legs.

8 Turn your pony's head towards an approaching vehicle. If travelling fast, grip firmly with your legs, holding the reins in both hands, prepared for any emergency.

9 When being overtaken turn the pony's head outwards, so

The Welsh Cob, a
good driving pony.

The Welsh Mountain,
one of the world's
prettiest ponies.

The Dartmoor, a
good child's pony.

Lungeing – legs a little too far back from the knee.

Lungeing – acquiring an independent seat. Note the side reins.

Leading a horse in hand.

Jumping – note the hands and seat. Head free and weight off horse's hindquarters.

Seat – a good example of the general purpose riding seat.

The author on his Fell pony, Lassie.

that it cannot suddenly swing its quarters outwards into the overtaking vehicle. Always walk; if necessary halt, especially when overtaken by a fast, noisy vehicle. Keep as close in to the side as possible. If the pony shies, do not let its hindquarters swing outwards; swing its head outwards, pushing its hindquarters in to the left.

10 Always thank the driver who slows down for you. Courtesy costs nothing; lack of it gives riders a bad reputation with other road users. If a vehicle does not slow down, collect your pony and stand still.

11 Always walk round blind corners.

12 Look both ways before moving off, turning, or halting.

13 Always give the correct traffic signal before altering direction or stopping.

14 Always halt at a cross-road.

15 Never 'slop' along on a loose rein. Always have your pony collected and under control.

16 Obey police, traffic lights, and traffic-control signals.

17 Wait for pedestrians at zebra crossings.

18 Give pedestrians plenty of room, and do not splash them. If too close to your pony may unexpectedly shy and swerve into them. Some people are nervous of horses.

19 Look behind and ahead before passing any vehicle parked by the roadside. Before pulling out to pass give the correct hand-signal in good time. Halt if a car is nearing.

20 Never ride on a pavement, or on mown grass in front of houses in a built-up area.

21 If it shies, turn your pony's head away from the object. Do not look at it yourself.

Road signals

Know the *Highway Code* and all correct hand-signals. Give them clearly with your whole arm. Signal in plenty of time beforehand. Hold reins and whip in the other hand when signalling.

1 *Turn Right :* right arm out straight at right angle to body.

2 *Turn Left :* left arm out straight, at right angle.

3 *Please Overtake :* sweep right arm forward with semi-circular movement.

4 *I am Slowing Down or Stopping:* lower right arm from shoulder level, palm downwards.

5 *Please Slow Down:* lower right arm to side from half-way down, palm downwards.

6 *Please Stop:* right arm held out shoulder high, forearm pointing upwards at right angles. Palm facing the front.

Riding in company

1 Single file, especially on a narrow road. Never ride three abreast, even on a wide road.

2 Keep two horses' lengths between each horse. Riding too close behind another horse is asking to get kicked.

3 Never suddenly trot up quickly from behind another horse. If the one in front takes fright it may kick out.

4 Never ride too close alongside another pony. Leave at least a pony's width between.

5 Do not go too near another horse that is restive or playing up; leave it ample room.

6 Before starting, arrange who drops back to form single file if necessary. The outside rider should drop back.

7 Do not shout, fool about, or show off.

8 A large party should divide into columns of four or five, with at least 50 yards between each group. A good rider with a reliable horse should lead.

9 Put children, beginners and/or small ponies in the middle of a file.

10 Leading and rear riders give signals, clearly, in plenty of time. The rear rider takes the signal from the leader.

11 Leader rides at the slowest pony's pace. Keep an even pace to avoid rear riders trotting or cantering to catch up.

12 Put nervous or traffic-shy horses in mid-column, on the inside when two abreast, with a reliable pony next to the nervous one.

13 Never start crossing a road until everyone is near enough to cross together.

14 Never separate or straggle. All riders must keep on the same side of the road. If anyone stops or dismounts the rest should wait until they have remounted.

Night riding or leading

1 Take extra care. Keep close in to the left; also in fog or mist.

2 When leading, walk on the outside, next to the traffic.

3 Carry a lamp showing white in front and red at the rear. A stirrup lamp attached on the off side is now obtainable.

4 Tie something white, fairly large, to your right arm or stirrup. Better still, wear a strip of reflecting material, obtainable from most garages, round the ankles or heels.

5 The leader of a party should carry a white lamp, the rear rider a red one.

Slippery roads

Dismount and lead, Never pull. Walk slowly, reins hooked over your arm. Never turn and look at your pony.

Snow

Smear thick motor grease on pony's frogs and soles, to prevent snow forming a solid frozen mass in the hooves. On a long ride repeat several times. Fit snow studs.

Insurance

Have a third party insurance policy. If a horse shies, backs into, or kicks a vehicle or pedestrian, inflicting damage or injury, the rider is legally responsible. Similarly, the owner is responsible if his pony breaks loose. Also insure against injury while travelling. Some insurance companies specialize in insuring horses and have a comprehensive policy covering even foaling risks to mares.

Country lore

1 Never leave litter about – one can now be fined. Especially never leave glass bottles or tins.

2 Never throw down glowing cigarette-ends, matches, or pipe-ash, especially in summer or autumn. Scatter picnic-fire ashes before leaving.

3 Do not ride on private land without permission. If there is a warning sign and you deliberately trespass, you can be prosecuted and fined. If one inadvertently trespasses the owner has to prove damage.

4 Keep to bridle-paths. There is a legal difference between bridle- and foot-paths. Riders cannot use the latter. A bridle-path is a public highway, even when crossing private land. It becomes a right-of-way if used without objection for over 20 years. To keep his claim on land over which a bridle- or foot-path runs, the landowner must close it once annually, usually on Good Friday. Ordnance Survey maps show all bridle- and public foot-paths.

5 Shut all gates. Do not damage fences or trees. Never jump fences, gates, or hedges.

6 Never ride in a hay or ploughed field, or across growing crops. Ride the headlands close to boundary hedges, never straight across a field.

7 Never ride among grazing cattle, horses, or sheep.

8 Watch for holes, concealed ditches, or drains when riding along grass verges, or across fields; especially dangerous when cantering or galloping.

A few careless, thoughtless people can give all riders a bad reputation, making them unpopular with landowners and farmers, and making things unpleasant for the innocent as well.

After a long ride, dismount. Walk the last mile. Run-up the irons, loosening the girth.

19 Travelling

Preparing for a journey

Groom thoroughly. Protect legs with rest bandages; knee-caps (forelegs); put on a tail-bandage. Rug-up in cold weather to protect from cold and chills caught through perspiring; nervous horses sweat through fear. In summer use a light rug for cleanliness and protection against chills.

When rugged-up use a tail-guard, fastened over the tail-bandage to the arch of the roller, on the surcingle keeping the rug in position. Always use a tail-bandage. Plait the mane.

Put a hood or blinkers on a nervous, temperamental horse.

Water and feed before starting and en route, at least every three hours on a long journey. Take a full haynet, some oats or bran, and a pail.

Whenever possible travel personally with your pony. Your presence will soothe and calm a nervous horse.

Rail transport

A horse can either travel loose or with partitions forming a stall, when railway regulations require it to wear a head-collar, tied to a ring at head level.

Opinion is divided as to whether a horse travels best loose or partitioned off. Some maintain that standing loose is dangerous; it may fall and injure itself struggling to regain its feet in a swaying, jolting box; or if frightened it may injure itself by kicking. Give it a really thick wheat-straw bed to provide a firm foothold, to prevent slipping or overbalancing. It also deadens noise, thus lessening the risk of fright.

Conversely, if partitioned off and tied to a ring, if the pony slips it has less chance of regaining its feet, having no room to move; in falling, the jerk on the head-collar may break its neck, or it may strangle or choke.

The only safe way is to travel personally in the groom's compartment, which has a small window and a door for entering the box in an emergency. One can also water and feed.

Always insure your pony. The railway automatically insures it for a certain amount. Insure for as much as possible over and above the pony's actual value. It makes the carriers more careful!

Road transport

Some ponies enter nonchalantly and quietly; others panic, refusing even to go near the box. Trying to force a frightened pony into a box is useless; it only bucks, rears, plunges, or kicks, becoming progressively more terrified and unmanageable, and all hell breaks loose.

Keep absolutely calm. The ramp must not be too steep, and well covered with straw. The top of the ramp into the box should give ample head room.

Never force the horse up directly it comes out and sees the ramp. Allow it time to inspect the box thoroughly. Walk once or twice round the vehicle, approaching nearer each time. Then lead it to the ramp, letting it inspect it thoroughly. Let it place one or both forefeet on the ramp and then descend again. Let it eat some oats or bran off the ramp.

Many horses refuse if the box is dark inside; let it face the sun, or put a light inside.

A nervous horse will often follow one that enters calmly.

Cover the box thickly with straw; hang up a full haynet. Carrying a pail of oats or bran ascend the ramp slowly and quietly, focussing interest on the food. Hold the leading rope and try to persuade it to follow. Let it eat a mouthful of food; then take the pail up a few more yards, trying to entice the pony to follow up to the top.

Once initial fear of being boxed is overcome there is usually no further trouble.

These methods may take a little longer, but that is surely

better than ending with a thoroughly frightened pony, which may always refuse to be boxed in future. Once in the box reward it immediately with a small feed. Try to understand the pony's psychology and point of view. Making it realize there is nothing to fear is half the battle. Always tie with a quick-release knot.

20 Showing

Preparation

Shows and gymkhanas usually begin at Easter, but entering without previous schooling and training of pony and rider is useless. Train throughout the winter; all riding, even hacking, should be continuous schooling. Always try to improve a pony in some way on every ride. Slopping along aimlessly on a loose rein, letting your pony shuffle along anyhow, is very bad for pony and rider. Improving your pony improves your own riding. Keep it interested, up to the bit and collected. After energetic schooling let it walk for a short time on a loose rein, to stretch its neck and ease its muscles.

Schooling teaches a pony to be handy, turn quickly, lead from either side, follow easily, and trot while led. Teach it to stand while mounted and dismounted barebacked. Practise vaulting on to a barebacked moving pony. Practise walking, trotting, and cantering without irons. Practise trotting – sitting and rising – barebacked.

Schooling includes obeying the aids quickly; trotting or cantering in a large circle, saddled or barebacked; halting correctly up to the bit, with both fore and hind legs together, standing absolutely still. A fidgety pony gives judges a bad impression, however good otherwise. Teach it to rein back with level, even steps, ready instantly to walk forward or back; to turn on the forehand or haunches, walk well on a loose rein, and at a free or collected walk or trot. If expert enough also teach it the shoulder-in, half and full pass and to change legs cantering. Do not sicken the pony with too much at a lesson.

Also practise jumping; use quite low jumps to avoid over-facing pony or rider. Variety is more important than height: low walls, brushwood, spread jumps, 'in and out', small gates; low tables, narrow ditches, and tree trunks.

Bending and potato race: pony must bend equally well on either near or off side; practise trotting and cantering in and out between poles, and for the potato race, throwing stones into a bucket – not easy on an excited pony.

During the last few weeks invite mounted friends to practise, accustoming your pony to others and doing things in company without getting excited.

Ask show secretaries to send schedules on publication: decide on events, practising specifically for these. Or consult the Show numbers of *Horse and Hound* for a list of the forthcoming shows and gymkhanas around Great Britain.

Practise opening and shutting gates for the handy hunter class, if eligible and scheduled.

Spend final weeks before showing giving special attention to the pony's coat, mane, and tail. Thin and trim very thick, shaggy manes and tails, removing a few hairs at each grooming. Do not pull a mane or tail unless you know how, otherwise you will ruin it; it is an expert's job. Never use scissors on either, especially hairs near the root of the tail; if they cut they become coarse and bristly, and stick out.

Pulling and trimming a mane and tail depends on a pony's type and breed: Thoroughbreds and show ponies look better with fairly thin, shaped tails and well-kept plaited manes. Some prefer them to have a hogged mane. Native breeds naturally have long, fairly thick manes and tails.

Thick-set, clumsy legs look thinner if hair at the fetlocks is carefully trimmed with a comb and scissors; work upwards. Show ponies look better with closely clipped fetlocks. Some Native ponies and Arabs should have fine silky hair ('feathers') at the fetlocks.

Coat, mane, and tail need plenty of thorough grooming and strapping with a whisp, to tone up muscles and skin and encourage the oil glands at hair roots to function freely. Good grooming produces a wonderful natural shine on a healthy coat.

Opinions differ on clipping. Some say that clipping after January, just before the winter coat is shed, ruins the summer coat; others that it makes no difference. After moulting, a lovely, sleek, glossy summer coat grows naturally, which thorough daily strapping and grooming keeps in lovely condition. While moulting, removed dead loose hairs with a rubber curry comb; they irritate if left.

Use a tail-bandage to preserve the shape of a trimmed tail. If damp it shrinks, becoming too tight, stopping the circulation and making the tail sore; probably causing white hairs. Only leave it on for a few hours. Bandage daily when quartering before exercise and remove afterwards before strapping.

Train the mane over the off side. Damp an unruly mane before brushing; never damp in cold weather. Or use a mane board, clipped the whole length; its weight pulls the mane down. Some recommend wet clay, brushed out when dry.

The day before the show

Clean all tack thoroughly, taking it to pieces. Riding kit must be immaculate with well-cleaned breeches or jodhpurs.

Have tack, clothes, and everything required for the show ready overnight. Required at the show: grooming kit, French chalk (for any white markings), stable-rubbers, hoof-pick, needle and thread (for plaited mane), hoof-oil, vaseline, exercise bandages, rug or cotton sheet to keep pony clean, saddle, bridle, head-collar, tail-bandage and guard, knee-caps for travelling by box. If possible take a spare bridle or pair of reins; also strirup-leathers. A small bag of oats and bran, hay, two buckets (food and water).

If possible, stable your pony the night before and groom thoroughly. Plait the mane last thing at night to save time next morning. Normally do not leave plaits in overnight as it splits the hair. After grooming give a final polish with a few drops of Bay Rum, without getting any in the pony's eyes. Apply hoof-oil and polish hooves.

Use a light rug or sheet overnight with a roller to prevent soiling when the pony lies down. Give a deep, clean straw bed.

The day of the show

Rise early. In old clothes, water, feed, and muck out, putting down clean bedding. Remove night rug; brush out any night stains. Pick out feet and re-polish hooves. Put on day-rug. If being boxed let pony travel in it and wear tail-guard and knee-caps. Leave tied up with a haynet, while you breakfast and change.

Aim at arriving at good two hours before your first event, allowing time to park and find a shady spot to tether your pony, fetch water, and collect your number(s). Some shows provide horse lines for competitors with allotted positions.

If excited or fresh ride your pony in for at least half an hour.

Having tethered your pony, water and feed. It should not eat or drink for an hour before an event, especially jumping.

When riding-in never gallop near spectators or other ponies. After an event rest your pony. Water and feed before you have lunch.

In a large class keep away from other horses in the collecting-ring to avoid being kicked, or your own pony kicking in excitement.

Showing

In a Hack class you will have to walk, trot, canter, and demonstrate obedience and handiness. Do not attempt anything complicated; a few simple movements, practised and well done, are better.

On entering the ring ride up to and salute the judges. While riding round do not let another competitor ride between you and the judges. Keep your pony moving freely, up to its bit. If called into the centre, make your pony stand well. Play gently with its bit, keeping it alert, yet quiet.

Unsaddle quickly if asked, asking a waiting friend to hold it, or placing it neatly on the ground behind your pony where it cannot be kicked or trodden on. One then usually walks the pony past the judges, returning trotting. Lead from the near side and turn the pony away from you. Never go between it and the judges. Then having resaddled, a judge may ride the pony.

If your pony is not even placed, take it sportingly. Never bemoan your bad luck, blame your pony, or abuse the judges or show secretary. Enter for the fun and experience, not simply for winning. If lucky enough to win a rosette, thank the judges politely – and thank your pony! If it plays up in the ring never show temper, hit it, or saw at its mouth. Spectators hate it and will dislike you.

Show jumping

Try to inspect the jumps beforehand on foot, especially a cross-country course. Practising over the jumps is forbidden, but you can show them to your pony. If possible, make a small jump in a quiet corner and go over once or twice to loosen up your pony, but do not tire it.

Memorize the order of jumps. Jumping in the wrong order disqualifies unless the competition allows a free choice. Jumps are usually numbered and jumped in order. If your pony plays up or refuses, do not show temper or use your whip.

Jumping is usually under British Show Jumping Association (B S J A) rules. Classes are: Novice, Grade C, B or A and Open. Horses and ponies are graded according to ability and height.

There are various types of competition which include open jumping over a set course with or without a time limit, touch and out, against the clock, accumulator, puissance, etc. With large classes a standard is often set to save time, a horse being eliminated after gaining a certain number of faults, or a time limit is set.

The penalty for knocking down a fence or lowering its height (but not in the case of knocking out a lower pole without disturbing the higher pole) is 4 faults; a refusal warrants 3 faults (three refusals mean the eliminations of the competitor); and fall of horse or rider is 8 faults. No penalties are incurred by rapping a fence without knocking it down.

Musical sacks

Mounted 'musical chairs'. Ride round the outside of the arena. Moving into the centre, or not cantering disqualifies except where the rules are modified for beginners. When the music stops dismount and lead – do not ride – your pony to the nearest sack. Directly it restarts, remount quickly.

Bending race

Needs a soft-mouthed pony, supple, handy in turning, and fast. The rider needs good hands, seat, and strong, independent leg-aids.

Potato race

Needs a fast, easily controlled pony, ridden one-handed, which stops quickly. Good hands and seat and strong leg-aids required, with a straight eye for judging distance and direction when dropping potatoes into the bucket.

Scrambles

Especially popular up north. Really races. Avoid them if you value your pony's mouth and legs, and your own safety. Going full gallop, cornering sharply round a comparatively small arena on hard ground, puts tremendous strain on a pony's legs. It is dangerous as a pony may skid and fall, its rider getting trampled on or kicked by other ponies, and seriously injured or even killed.

There are numerous other types of events, varying in different districts.

Classes

Arranged by heights: 12·2 hh. and under (children's ponies; leading-rein class); up to 13·2 hh.; up to 14·2 hh.; over 14·2 hh. (open classes); also show hacks; ladies' hacks; handy hunters; novice classes (horse/ponies which have never won a first, have only won up to a certain value, or previously unshown); Championship classes, etc. Musical sacks, potato race, obstacle race, etc., are usually open (ponies of all sizes). Also classes for specified breeds: Arabs, Mountain and Moorland, Native British, New Forest, Welsh Mountain or Cob, etc. Also the annual Ponies of Britain Show. Whips are forbidden in gymkhana or dressage events.

Feeding

Important when preparing to show. Bring the pony in about a month beforehand, gradually getting it on to hard feed. Begin with a small corn ration (small pony): 1 lb. 14·2 hh.: up to 3 lb.

daily), increasing gradually according to amount of work, and to individual temperament. Reduce bran and hay in proportion.

A worm powder as a precaution may be advisable if the pony looks at all thin or listless. If suspicious send samples of droppings for a worm-count.

After showing

Get your pony home as quickly as possible after your last event. Trying to unload and attend to a tired pony after dark is no fun, especially if tired yourself!

Directly your pony is in shake straw under it and whistle to encourage it to stale. Give a lukewarm drink – not too much. Inspect feet and legs for strain or swelling. Remove tail-guard and bandages; groom thoroughly; put on rest bandages. Give a good feed of corn and/or bran, or warm bran mash. Rug-up; give a thick straw bed. Leave water and hay for the night.

Dress

For small country shows

Ordinary hacking kit; jodhpurs or breeches; pullover, collar and tie, hacking jacket, jodhpur or top boots, string gloves, bowler hat or hard riding cap.

For large shows

More formal wear: white breeches, top boots, black hunting jacket, white stock, hunting waistcoat, huntsman's cap or bowler.

For children

Jodhpurs, stout shoes or jodhpur boots, pullover, collar and tie, hacking jacket or black coat; hard velvet hunting cap or bowler.

21 Jumping

How a horse jumps

As the hinquarters provide all impulsion a horse must jump off its hocks. Therefore when jumping the rider must sit forward to take the weight off its loins and leave its hindquarters completely free. It balances itself by stretching out its head and neck, so leave these absolutely free as well. The rider must never pull his horse's mouth or its head back with the reins.

Great speed is unnecessary for jumping. When training, show-jumpers are made to jump off their hocks from a trot, over obstacles up to three feet in height and five feet in width. Also, very little space is needed in which to jump. The hindquarters should be so powerful that fairly low obstacles can be jumped almost vertically, almost from a standstill. A horse must be collected and balanced when taking off, and must time its jump accurately.

Action when jumping

1 Collection at take-off.

2 Spring with forward and upward impulsion through hock action, the hindquarters providing the energy.

3 The horse then stretches itself to clear the jump, balanced by outstretched head and neck.

4 Landing; the front legs take the concussion and its full weight; momentarily unbalanced, this is when a peck or fall may occur, so the rider must leave his horse completely free, doing as little as possible so that his weight does not add to the impact of landing or unbalance it.

6 The horse collects itself, ready to move on again after jumping. The rider now takes charge again.

When taking off the horse resembles a coiled spring, ready to be released at the next stage when the hocks act.

To help as much as possible, the rider, must learn the correct body, seat, and leg position, his hands interfering as little as possible in order not to pull the horse's head back, or unbalance it with the reins.

First stages

Learn to stand in the irons by gripping with knees and thighs. Legs from the knees, and stirrup-leathers, should be vertical; feel as if on springs, from knees to ankles. Balance without hanging on by the reins. Bend forward from the hips, keeping back and head in a straight line. Never lean forward or raise your seat too far out of the saddle.

Practise standing in your irons at a walk until you can go round the school, or a level field, without sitting or balancing yourself with the reins. While a friend leads the pony at a walk, knot the reins and ride standing, with arms folded. Then practise this by yourself. Learn to squeeze your pony on and guide with leg and rein, while standing.

It is tiring until your leg muscles are trained, so increase the number of steps taken standing, gradually. Sit in between, relaxing for a few paces. Begin sitting two steps, and standing four. Then stand four steps and sit four. Increase the number of steps taken standing, to six, then eight, etc., sitting for four in between. Eventually stand the whole time.

Next, stand while trotting. Begin standing four to six steps, sitting for four, then standing again. Gradually increase the number taken standing, while decreasing the number taken sitting. Very tiring at first, so gradually increase the number of standing steps. Do not hurry this preliminary training.

Use a neck strap to avoid holding on by the reins and pulling your pony's mouth. Knot the reins and have it led at a trot. When you feel secure, fold your arms instead of holding the neck strap; simply have it for emergencies. Ask your friend to turn right and left and try to use the appropriate leg-aids.

Having successfully trotted right round the school or field with arms folded, while being led, practise alone, holding the reins. Do the same thing, working up from a few paces until you can trot right round, using leg- and rein-aids independently to guide. Practise turning right and left.

When you can trot right round, standing, canter and try to stand, gradually increasing the distance during which you stand. When cantering move your arms forward to shorten the reins, dropping your hands on each side of the pony's neck, just in front of and below its withers. This gives the position for jumping. Keep your legs straight down from the knee, with your leathers hanging vertically; do not let your legs go back or forward else you will lose your seat and balance. The positions for jumping and galloping are very similar.

Points to note

1 Take your weight off the pony's hindquarters, standing in your stirrups with your seat off the saddle.

2 The pony's head and neck must be free to balance itself, letting your arms go forward, with hands low on its neck. This leaves it free and unimpeded.

In the old-fashioned seat when the rider leaned back while jumping, his weight was thrown on to the pony's weakest part, its loins, hampering the free movement of its hindquarters. If his legs went forwards, and they almost inevitably did, he became unbalanced and liable to pull his pony's mouth on landing; thereby not only jabbing its mouth but also unbalancing it by preventing it stretching out its neck. If it pecked on landing the rider was more likely to come over its head, because he was unbalanced and his seat was insecure.

First jumps

Having mastered standing in your irons, and the correct jumping position, ride the pony at a walk and trot over a pole on the ground, and finally cantering, while in the jumping position. Then raise the pole just high enough to prevent the pony stepping over and repeat the process.

While approaching the pole, collect your pony, assume the

G

jumping position, and when about four feet away kick it to make it take off. When first jumping, use the neck strap (a rein or martingale strap) to give yourself confidence and something to hold should you lose grip and balance, instead of clutching the reins and jabbing your pony's mouth. Bad riding and jabbing their mouths has put many ponies completely off jumping. This is most likely when taking off or landing, when the rider is most liable to lose his balance and nerve and try to hang on by the reins. Sit still and leave it to your pony, especially when learning to jump.

Many people advise shortening stirrup-leathers a couple of holes. Others advocate jumping with them at their normal length, especially when beginning. This makes it easier to acquire a firm seat and good leg-grips: the danger lies in shortening them too much, bringing the knees up too high, away from their normal position where they exert the strongest pressure.

Timing

Correct timing is the secret of jumping. Do not let the pony approach too fast; try to place it at the right place to take off; leave it alone while actually jumping. The correct take-off position is about the same distance away as the height of the jump. It often helps to lay a pole on the ground at the correct distance from the jump for the take-off, making the pony jump from just in front of it. If it jumps too late and therefore too close, it gets too near under the jump, thus having to 'cat jump' almost vertically off all four legs, instead of taking off from its hindquarters with its haunches well under it. Sitting a pony at all, let alone correctly, is very difficult when it cat-jumps. If it jumps too soon it will probably jump into and knock down the fence.

Successful jumping depends on thorough schooling before-hand for collection, balance, and obedience to the aids so that it walks, trots, or canters immediately when asked. Learn and practise on an experienced, free jumper, with good manners.

A pony can take a jump surprisingly slowly. When training, show-jumpers have to take low obstacles, up to approximately 2 ft 6 in. from a trot.

Never attempt jumps beyond your pony's or your own capabilities, either too high or too wide, before you are both ready for them.

Later stages

When pony and rider are both thoroughly at home over small jumps, having developed mutual understanding and confidence, it helps to place them about six jumps in succession, 10 to 12 feet apart, jumping them without stopping. If the pony is excitable and inclined to rush them, do not have them in a straight line, but in a circle. Jumping successive jumps in a line tends to excite it, whereas jumping in a circle helps to quieten it.

Do not exceed 12–18 inches high at first. Then raise them gradually increasing the width of spread jumps: do not exceed 2 ft 6 in. to 3 ft high or 5 ft wide for practising.

When pony and rider jump confidently up to 18 in. high, reins should be knotted and left lying on the pony's neck; practise with arms folded, or holding its mane, keeping the neck straps for any emergencies!

Next practise small jumps without reins or stirrups. At first use the neck strap to gain confidence; practise on soft ground so that a fall does not matter. Falling may be undignified but you will not hurt yourself if you free your feet from the irons, curl up with your head into your shoulder and just fall limply. Wear a hard hat. A baby and a drunken man do not hurt themselves because they fall limply without attempting to save themselves.

Never go on for too long over the same jump and do not sicken your pony by jumping for too long at a time; most ponies love jumping naturally but can easily be sickened of it. Never let the pony end practice with a refusal; being its last mental impression, next time it will probably start by refusing. Try to end with a good jump. A pony jumps more freely when facing towards home.

Styles in jumping

Do not imitate styles seen at shows. Some rather weird ones are seen at small country gymkhanas. Equally, do not try to copy the great show-jumpers seen at big international shows. They are artists and immensely experienced riders who have developed their own individual styles. Knowing their own horse they may have developed some individual style which they have found from experience suits it best. But that does not mean that they are good for a beginner to copy. Develop the seat and position already explained to place your weight forward on the horse's strongest part, leaving its hindquarters free and its head and neck free to balance itself.

Cavelletti

Very useful, forming practice jumps of varying heights by rolling them over, or as spread jumps of varying widths. They are two pieces of wood 3 feet in length nailed together to form a St Andrew's cross. A 9-foot pole is then nailed in position between the two crosses resting in the uppermost 'V'. By turning the jump over its height varies between 10, 15 and 19 inches.

Practice jumps

The more varied in height and character the better. Use *cavaletti* in different ways, one alongside another, forming spread jumps, or one on top of another to increase the height.

Also, use tree trunks of different diameters, post and rails. fencing, brushwood, triple bar (spread jump) small gates, low walls or large stones or bricks, or wood painted to represent bricks: the more varied the better. Train your pony to jump any reasonable obstacle confidently. Variety is more valuable than increased height and/or width for training practice. Other types: grid, parallel bars, oxer, jump with wings, In and Out. For the last the two fences should be about 22 feet apart (two strides of a canter). If possible include a ditch and a water jump.

Refusing

Never allow a deliberate refusal. Preferably push the pony on over or through a small jump which knocks down easily rather than turn back.

A pony may refuse for several reasons: misjudging the distance and mistiming its jump, which is not very serious. There is usually some deeper reason for consistent refusals, as most ponies jump naturally and enjoy it.

Causes of consistent refusals

1 General weakness, weak back or hocks; out of condition. A long-backed horse is often weak in its loins and a poor jumper. The saying is that a long-backed horse never won the Grand National! The best jumpers are usually short backed and sturdy, with generous hindquarters. One running up light behind and herring-gutted usually has weak hindquarters.

2 Memory of pain from previously having its mouth jabbed when jumping. Having a long memory, a bad jab in the mouth may put a pony off jumping for a long time, if not for good. The only cure is a long rest and then re-education by a course of free jumping in a Weedon Lane, followed by being jumped by an expert rider who does not pull its mouth about, to restore its confidence.

3 Loss of nerve through previous falls. A bad fall can put a pony off jumping as it dislikes falling, and dislikes a rider who constantly falls. It spoils it, shaking its confidence and making it refuse.

4 A badly fitting bit or saddle. If it suddenly starts refusing the bit may be getting worn, or have sharp edges, especially at the joint of a 'broken' bit. The saddle may press down on the withers because the arch of the tree is widening; if so try a sheepskin numnah underneath the saddle for jumping. Or the panel stuffing may be hard or out of shape.

5 Sore feet or legs. Look for signs of corns; or sprained tendons, especially in the forelegs, which take the full force of any jar when landing. Rest; bathe with cold water: play a hose on its legs for about 20 minutes daily in summer (the best cure). Never jump on hard or slippery ground, or for too long at a time. Or, a splint; an injured frog or sole of the foot; or the blacksmith may have driven the nails too close when last shod.

6 Over-facing; attempting obstacles which are too high, wide, or difficult for its ability or particular stage of schooling or development. It becomes disheartened if continually faced with

obstacles it cannot jump. Restore confidence by using low, easy jumps for a period. Never over-face it. Practise over fairly low jumps – nothing over 3 feet – aiming at variety, not height or width.

7 The pony is sick of jumping. Ponies going the rounds of shows and gymkhanas frequently get sick of it and start growing careless and/or refusing. Rest is the cure. Show-jumpers may even have to miss a whole season and have a year's rest. Instead, they can be hacked and/or taught dressage.

8 It frequently is the rider's fault, presenting the pony badly at the jump or allowing it to rush at the obstacle too fast and uncollected. He may have made it jump too soon or too late. Or he has pulled its mouth and shortened its stride as it approached. He may have the reins too short instead of freeing the pony's head and allowing it to stretch out its head and neck, thus un-balancing it. It is always a bad sign if a horse fights for its head while approaching a jump.

Faults in jumping

1 Elbows out; reins loose without any contact with the pony's mouth.

2 Legs going back; knees off saddle and toes pointing downwards.

3 Standing too high in the stirrups; no grip on saddle with thighs and knees.

4 Rider thrown out of saddle and unbalanced as pony jumps; he therefore hangs on to the reins trying to save himself.

5 Back bent, instead of leaning forward from the hips, in a straight line from head to hips.

6 Leaning too far forward with legs forced back.

7 Hands and reins held too high. The rider cannot balance; he only stays on by hanging on by the reins.

8 'Calling a cab': right hand and arm thrown up into the air as pony jumps, with toes pointing downwards.

9 Sitting in saddle looking back, instead of standing in stirrups looking ahead. Probably causing a fall if the pony pecked on landing.

A pony jumps well when it:

1 approaches the obstacle confidently;

2 obeys its rider's wishes by approaching at a steady pace;

3 takes off the correct distance away, so that it clears the obstacle with the least possible effort;

4 jumps with head well forward, neck and spine supple;

5 lands quietly, ready to continue at whatever pace its rider wishes.

A pony jumps badly when it:

1 approaches nervously or excitedly and too quickly;

2 refuses;

3 runs out;

4 pulls up short, cat jumping or bucking over;

5 rushes the obstacle, head in the air, not looking where it is going.

22 Refractory Horses

Causes of bad behaviour

Many disconcerting habits are originally caused by bad handling and/or bad riding. Slopping along with loose reins, 'sitting like a sack of potatoes' and allowing the pony its own way not only ruins it but also lays up trouble for the rider.

Bad habits can start in the first stages of handling a foal, or when breaking and schooling a colt.

By nature horses are gentle and usually anxious to please, giving themselves generously to anyone they completely trust. Only a few are bad-tempered, vicious, or fundamentally evil, just as only comparatively few people are born criminals.

Most bad behaviour and bad manners in the stable, or when ridden, have some fundamental causes, such as fear or pain. The more highly bred and highly couraged horses are, the more nervous, highly strung, and sensitive they are, Their natural re-action to fear is to kick in self-defence, or escape from the cause as quickly as possible – hence bolting. Being sensitive, rough, noisy, boisterous handling, and pain, cause bad habits like rearing. Sudden fright may cause bolting or rearing; pain – a badly fitting bridle, bit, or saddle – may make it buck. Bad riding, using spurs or whip, sawing it its mouth, etc., can produce similar results.

Therefore always be calm and gentle when handling a horse, from the earliest stages. Experience must give it complete confidence in its groom and rider.

It was said (page 82) that one way to curb biting and kicking

was to be with the horse as much as possible, feeding and handling it gently. Kicking usually starts through fear rather than vice.

Jibbing

Stopping suddenly and refusing to move for no apparent reason.
Using the legs and whip only makes the pony more stubborn.

To stop a pony jibbing: (a) Allow it to stand still for a short
time. Expecting opposition it will be surprised at finding none.
It will soon become bored standing perfectly still, and will then
move forward; but do not let it. Make it stand still or even rein-
back a few steps; then make it walk forward briskly. A few
repetitions of this treatment will probably cure it. (b) Make it
circle several times, using very strong rein and leg-aids. It dislikes
these bewildering circling movements. (c) Reining back sometimes
cures it.

If it does not habitually jib, a sudden stop may be a pony's
way of indicating something abnormal. It may have seen or
heard something which you have not. The saddle or bridle may
be causing pain or discomfort. Also examine its teeth and feet.

It may stop simply to relieve itself or stale. If so, let it, taking
the weight of its loins and hindquarters by standing in the
stirrups. It will move on voluntarily when ready.

Shying

Due to fear of something unfamiliar and therefore frightening, or
of something imperfectly seen. On the other hand, the pony may
simply be short sighted. Noise also causes shying, as ponies
hate it especially when unexpected.

One may unwittingly make one's pony shy! Seeing something
which the rider thinks may frighten it, he involuntarily stiffens,
tightening knees and reins. Feeling this the pony imagines its
rider is afraid and that it therefore has something to fear. If he
had sat perfectly still and unconcerned it would probably have
passed the object without any fuss!

Scolding or punishment is useless; it only confuses and
frightens it more. Persuade it to go up to and thoroughly examine
its cause of fear. Once reassured it will walk quietly past. Then
return and make it pass the object several times.

A shying pony tries to whip round and turn its head away; it either wants to kick or bolt. Hence it always turns its head away from the object at which it shies.

Always slow down for a noisy, fast-moving vehicle, turning its head towards it.

Bolting

Follows logically after shying. It is usually simply due to blind panic, and a horse may bolt suddenly without shying or swinging round. Severe pain may also cause bolting.

A very nervous, highly strung animal, given to bolting suddenly, is dangerous to its rider and other people. So get rid of it! A bolting horse is temporarily insane and not amenable to reason. Few experiences are more frightening than riding a runaway horse! This is the one occasion when one must have no consideration for its mouth, which is one's only means of stopping it.

If your pony bolts on the road try to ride it into a hedge or field. Get it off the road if possible! Leaning back and pulling the reins is useless; the harder one pulls the more the pony pulls. Get right down into the saddle in galloping position with knees gripping tightly and hands low and forward. Give with your hands, then suddenly pull back as hard as possible with both reins. Continue doing this. Keep the reins very short.

Ride up a hill or circle the pony in a field, trying gradually to decrease the size of the circle. Or by sawing its mouth, pulling the bit sharply across from one side to the other; then in the opposite direction. Alternatively, put your left hand low and your right hand up. Then hard and quickly pull your left hand up and your right hand down, diagonally across the pony's mouth. Repeat immediately with opposite hands. Do not worry about hurting! These remedies can be tried quickly in turn if one keeps one's head.

If your pony bolts where there is plenty of room and no immediate danger, let it gallop until it tires. When it slows down and tries to stop, make it continue galloping until it lathers and is ready to drop. Find the heaviest going possible! Riding it to a standstill may cure it permanently. This is one occasion when you must be really tough!

Galloping on though sheer high spirits is not bolting, though a beginner might think so. With mere high spirits find a long safe stretch and entering into the spirit of it, gallop some of the nonsense out of your pony!

Bucking

A playful, high-spirited buck or two, and real bucking are entirely different. When really bucking seriously, a pony's head goes down between its forelegs, its back arches almost double, while both hind legs kick up and backwards. Its one aim is to rid itself of anyone or anything on its back.

Pain from its bit, or a badly fitting saddle, may make even a schooled pony buck. Too tight leg or rein pressure, kicking it too hard, or hitting it too hard with the whip may make a horse buck through resentment.

Discourage even playful bucking with a sharp reprimand lest it becomes habitual and real bucking. If it tries to buck, keep its head up, grip extra tightly with your knees and sit up, leaning and throwing your weight back on to the pony's weakest part, its loins. This also prevents it flinging up its heels. Hold the reins very short and tight.

Trying to sit a bucking pony is very tiring and uncomfortable.

When lungeing, a playful buck or two before settling down to work are quite harmless.

Rearing

Get rid of a horse that rears frequently. It is really dangerous. Stallions are more likely to rear than mares or geldings.

Causes: bad handling as a colt when breaking, due to impatience in the initial stages of leading it in a head-collar. If dragged forward it naturally tends to back away and rear. It may have been hit on the head; fear of a blow may cause it.

A badly fitting bridle, pain from the bit, wolf-teeth, or sharp teeth which need filing, or a badly fitting saddle may all cause rearing. So examine every possible cause before condemning a rearing pony. Sometimes fright causes it.

Grip the saddle tightly, with lower legs and ankles curved

round the horse's sides and belly. Throw your weight as far forward as possible, grasping its neck. Drop the reins if necessary; never pull them back towards you or you may pull the pony over backwards on top of you! That is the great danger.

Or lean forwards as far as possible, holding the cheek-straps low down near the snaffle cheek-rings, and try to pull its head down. If possible, try to pull it sideways – never backwards – making it overbalance and lower its forelegs.

No real cure exists for a habitual rearer. Very expert riders claim they can cure it by deliberately pulling it over backwards. This is extremely dangerous as they may not jump clear and be rolled on; or it may break its back, or do itself serious spinal or internal injury.

A tight martingale may help. A pony may rear if the curb chain is too tight, or the bit too severe.

Kicking

Already discussed – pages 84–5.

Rolling

A disconcerting habit, occasionally found; and dangerous if one is unprepared and does not jump clear quickly enough.

Ponies usually give some warning by pawing the ground with a foreleg, putting both forelegs out and stretching, or by fidgeting. They sometimes try to roll when crossing or drinking from a stream, especially in summer. If your pony is contemplating rolling, remove both feet from the irons, pull its head up, and distract its attention by trotting quickly or circling. Scold it, giving it a smart tap with the whip while kicking it on. Lean and pull back to prevent its head going down and its forelegs bending at the knees. If it does succeed in rolling, pull the reins over its head; try to pull it up before it actually rolls over on to the saddle. Rolling is more likely in spring or autumn when the pony is moulting; its skin may itch, and loose hairs irritate. So thorough grooming may prevent it.

It may also roll if one dismounts and loosens the girth; so if resting awhile remove the saddle. Knot the reins short so that its legs cannot beome tangled in them.

Napping

A self-willed horse tries to get its own way, opposing its rider's will. It may move in the opposite direction to which one wants to go, or refuse to leave home. Racehorses and horses in a riding stable often refuse to go out alone.

Never give in to a nappy horse, even if winning the battle takes an hour! Never dismount. A horse regards it as a victory and a confession of weakness by the rider.

23 First Aid. Simple Treatment of Ailments

Owners should be able to render simple first aid, recognize symptoms of illness, diagnose minor ailments, and apply treatment so that they may alleviate their pony's sufferings, give the vet intelligent help and recognize when he should be called.

If in doubt call the vet. Prompt treatment prevents unnecessary suffering and may save the pony's life.

Horses have an uncanny knack of getting into trouble and hurting themselves despite all precautions. In case of serious accidents one should know what to do until the vet arrives.

Always keep the nearest vet's address and telephone number at hand for emergencies.

A healthy horse

Appearance

Ears alert, pricked forward; bright, clear, alert eyes; head held up and carried alertly; skin loose; bright, glossy coat; tail carried gaily.

Behaviour

Wide awake; full of life, taking an intelligent interest in its surroundings; cheery and full of good spirits. Moves freely, carrying itself proudly with a light, springy step. It answers you with a cheerful whinny and amuses itself by trotting, cantering, or galloping round its paddock for exercise, giving an occasional buck and flinging up its heels through sheer high-spirited *joie de vivre.* When ridden it moves freely, carries itself proudly and happily, giving itself generously to its rider's wishes. Its appetite is large.

A sick horse

Fortunately a properly cared-for horse, living out, seldom gets ill. A sick horse is fairly obvious and easily recognized. It does not suffer illness gladly but quickly looks miserable and dejected.

Appearance

Dull eyes; drooping head, ears, and tail, listless and lifeless, looking all 'tucked up', usually resting one hind leg. Flanks heave; breathing heavy and irregular. No appetite. Stands about. Skin feels tight (hide bound). Coat dull, staring, and lifeless. If it sweats or drinks more than usual it may be feverish.

Temperature

Normal

100·2° to 100·5° Fahrenheit. Normal human temperature: 98·4°.

Suspecting a temperature

Listless; no appetite; coat dull and 'starey', standing away from body. Skin feels hot and dry. Abnormal thirst. Irregular, abnormally quick breathing. Normal respiration: 8–12 times per minute.

Taking temperature

Short-rack to prevent kicking or biting. Vaseline the thermometer bulb and tube to facilitate insertion. Shake the mercury down to 95°F. Lift the tail, inserting about three-quarters of the thermometer tube into the anus. Lower the tail; hold it down, leaving the thermometer in for 2–5 minutes, according to its make. A helper should hold up an unmanageable horse's foreleg to distract its attention and prevent it kicking. If this fails, using a twitch may be necessary. Alternatively, insert the thermometer with two fingers in one side of the cheek.

Pulse

Normal rates

Heavy horse: 30 per minute. Thoroughbred 60 per minute, or more. Pregnant mares: over 40. Foal: approximately 65 per minute.

Taking the pulse

At the angle of the lower jaw where the sub-maxillary artery passes close to the bone and is easily compressed with a finger.

Giving medicine

Powder or liquid: mixed with food. Provided medicine has neither taste nor smell it is eaten unsuspectingly. Drenching: for liquid medicine which cannot be mixed with food.

How to drench

Wear old clothes! Drenching can be very messy especially if attempted single-handed. It really needs two people. Use a drenching bottle or horn; or an ordinary long-necked bottle wrapped in leather or cloth in case it breaks. Never use a glass bottle without some sort of covering.

Pass a loop of leather strap, thick soft cord, or a hemp halter into the horse's mouth just behind the incisor teeth. Loop the end over one prong of an upright pitchfork, with corks stuck on both points to prevent accidents. Assistant raises fork by the handle, pushing up the horse's head. Stand on something of appropriate height, insert the bottle into the side of the mouth, allowing drench to trickle slowly down the throat. Do not raise the head too high. If the liquid flows too quickly the horse may choke. If it does lower its head, then restart. If it refuses to swallow pinch its nostrils to stop it breathing for a few seconds: if that fails put your hand into its mouth and pull out its tongue. Never rub its throat. It can retain liquid in its mouth for a long time without swallowing. Some horses are very cunning over this. Be very quiet and patient. If the drench accidentally goes down its windpipe into the lungs, it may cause pneumonia.

Pills, balls

Preferable, as much easier to administer than liquid medicines. The correct dose can be given without wasting half: a good deal is often spilt when drenching.

Pills: round; usually fairly small. Can be effectively hidden in bread, apple, or carrot.

Balls: usually cylindrical; about 2 inches long and 1 inch across. Weight: 1 oz, sometimes round.

Giving a Ball: short-rack and open the horse's mouth gently by inserting thumb and forefinger behind the front teeth; push the ball well back in its mouth, down its throat if possible. Then hold its lips closed.

Alternatively gently rub the groove of its lower jaw to make it yawn, slipping the ball quickly down its throat. Make it swallow by rubbing its throat. See that it does not spit out the ball, or hold it in its mouth. It may eject it several times before finally swallowing. Some horses are very cunning, holding it in their mouth for a considerable time. If troublesome ask a helper to lift a foreleg.

Infection

Infectious complaints are rare. Isolate the patient immediately. Coughs and colds are infectious. Stabled horses are more liable to them than those living out. Burn all bedding; scrub stable floor, yard, and walls with strong disinfectant, leaving doors and windows open to air the stable thoroughly. Fumigate or wash rugs and blankets with strong disinfectant soap, drying them outside. Treat brushes, stable rubbers, sponges, etc., similarly.

Do not go from an infected to a healthy horse; wear rubber boots and walk through a bath of strong disinfectant first, and wash hands and arms up to the elbows with disinfectant.

Contagion

Isolate immediately, disinfecting everything thoroughly. Do not go near a healthy horse. Never bring stable equipment or clothing used for a sick horse near a fit one. Contagious diseases, more serious than infectious ones, can be caught by contact. These are anthrax, glanders, colds, coughs. The authorities must be notified of the first two.

Sulphur is one of the best fumigants; perchloride of mercury is a very powerful disinfectant (4 parts per 1000 will kill bacteria); it is highly poisonous, so use very carefully.

Foot and mouth disease does not affect horses, but do not ride in an infected area; being contagious you can carry it to an unaffected area.

First aid

Keep a locked first-aid box in the stable or tack-room. Contents: pair of blunt-nosed surgical scissors; sharp scalpel; fairly long, large-eyed needles; thread; bandages, assorted widths, 4 inches downwards; large carton of lint; ditto, gauze dressing; cotton-wool; disinfectant (Dettol, permanganate of potash, etc.); tin of antiseptic oitnment (Ayreton's; Boots' Pink Healing Ointment); Witch Hazel or Listerine, etc.; wide adhesive plaster; assorted-sized safety pins. Keep everything airtight and dust-proof, really surgically clean.

Punctures, clean cuts, contusions : as soon as possible clip away surrounding hair and wash with soap and water or a hose. Apply weak disinfectant solution (e.g. TCP). Jeyes or Carbolic are too strong and may blister the skin. Dry boracic powder or Sulphanilamide are excellent after thorough cleansing.

Punctures

More dangerous than cuts or open wounds if deep. They are harder to clean thoroughly and heal more slowly. If not thoroughly cleaned they may become septic, matter collecting underneath while healing from the top. The opening may need enlarging, always downwards, for proper drainage and proper cleansing, right down to the bottom. Splinters, etc., may be present, especially if the sole is punctured by a nail, broken glass, barbed wire, etc. They may be deeply embedded and very difficult to find or extract, remaining in for a long time, causing suppuration and preventing healing. Small splinters may work their way out in most unexpected places.

Punctured wounds more often cause tetanus (lock-jaw) than

other kinds. If doubtful have an anti-tetanus injection given as soon as possible. Tetanus bacteria can remain in the soil for a long time; some districts are badly infected.

Clean cuts

Clean incisions thoroughly, cut away surrounding hair and apply an antiseptic dressing. Cover with lint or gauze-covered cotton-wool if possible; bandage lightly to allow for subsequent swelling. If bandaging is impossible fasten with adhesive tape. Have anti-tetanus injection given.

A deep and/or long cut should be stitched. Stitches must be fairly loose or swelling may tear them out. The lower end is not drawn together too closely to allow drainage.

Lacerations

Barbed wire can cause horrible tears. Clean thoroughly, replacing torn, hanging skin in position, to knit together by first intention. If it does not, the old skin will die and come away gradually as new skin grows and can be cut away. Leaving it gives protection. After disinfecting, bind it up in the blood. Ask the vet to give penicillin and anti-tetanus injections.

After-treatment consists of forming healthy granulations. Do not allow the surface of a discharging would to heal over. Dress it daily and then use Sulphanilamide powder.

Bleeding

From a vein; from an artery. Venous bleeding may cause considerable loss of blood; it looks alarming but is not serious and eventually stops as the blood congeals. Clots form naturally, therefore try to slow down the bleeding. Use a tourniquet if possible; if not press the ball of the thumb as tightly as possible against the skin.

Profuse venous bleeding, within limits, washes out any dirt and cleanses the would. Unless some foreign body is suspected, bandage while bleeding, until proper cleansing and dressing are possible; clotted blood protects from the air.

Arterial bleeding requires immediate attention to prevent possible bleeding to death. If an artery is severed draw the edges of the wound together, bandaging very tightly. Also bandage a pad very tightly above the wound to stop bleeding.

A strong piece of stick, pencil, pen, or even a 6-inch nail can make an emergency tourniquet, twisted with a large handkerchief very tightly above the wound. An emergency tourniquet used out hunting is a large round, smooth pebble twisted up in a handkerchief, folded cornerways, and loosely rolled into a long rope. Do not keep a tourniquet on for too long.

Venous blood is darker coloured, oozes or trickles fairly slowly, but continuously; rather thick, congealing fairly quickly.

Arterial blood is bright red; gushes out in spurts, pumped out by the heart-beats, thinner, flows more easily, taking longer to congeal.

Excessive loss of blood is weakening. If a tourniquet or bandage cannot be applied, press the ball of the thumb very hard right into the flesh on the artery, just above the wound. Call the vet immediately.

Clip or tie each end of a severed, exposed artery with a ligature; leave the ends long enough to hang out of the wound for subsequent removal.

Prevent the horse moving until bleeding stops, sitting on its head if necessary.

Contusions

Apply hot, or alternate hot and cold, fomentations to bruised, unbroken skin. After fomentation apply lead or other cooling lotion or an evaporating lotion. Bandage over a pad soaked in liniment, covered with waterproof or oiled sheeting; keep on all night. Repeat at least thrice daily; more often if possible. Bandaging too tightly stops the circulation.

Sprains

Tendons and muscles. Causes: jumping; over-galloping on hard or heavy going, etc.

Hose at least thrice daily. Trickle cold water over the sprain for about 15 minutes. Never hose in cold weather, or in a cold wind unless sheltered.

Alternatively foment; afterwards apply Elliman's Horse Embrocation; rub in until the skin is nearly dry, or use Radiol. Rub a leg upwards or with a circular movement, never downwards.

A pad soaked in lead lotion, bandaged on all night, is good. Also helpful: a poultice of really hot Kaolin paste, to draw out inflammation. Apply a rest bandage at night.

Only use turpentine, or anything which blisters, under the vet's instructions. 'Workalin' ('working blister') may be used, as a horse need not stop working.

Symptoms: swelling and heat in pastern, fetlock, forearm, shoulder, hock, gaskin, stifle or hip-joint, causes lameness.

To detect, compare the unsound and opposite sound limb. If puffy the skin only fills out slowly when pressed down hard with the thumb. The swollen part is tender to touch. Detect heat by resting the hand on the sprained joint and transferring it quickly to the sound limb. Sound legs feel cool.

Lameness

Causes

Slight rheumatism ('Monday morning leg'); noticeable when first exercised, wearing off as the joints warm up and become supple.

Detection

The paces and stride become uneven, the pony going lame in front or behind. Especially noticeable when trotting, either when led or ridden. Lameness in a hind leg makes its quarters drop on that side. It nods its head if lame in front, as the injured limb touches the ground. Lameness in both fore and hind legs is difficult to detect unless very bad as it goes level.

The seat of lameness (foreleg): may be anywhere from the sole up to the shoulder; (hind leg) up to hip and thigh. Work methodically upwards from the sole, checking each joint in turn.

It is sometimes difficult to detect whether lameness is in front or behind, on the near or off side, or in which leg. Have the horse walked or trotted away from and towards you. Hind leg; hindquarters dip towards the lame side. Foreleg: it nods its head towards the lame side to avoid putting any weight on that leg.

Also have the horse trotted up- and downhill. Foreleg lameness is more noticeable trotting downhill, and hind leg uphill.

A horse frequently rests a lame leg; this is not infallible as many stand resting a hind leg.

Foot

Examine the sole for any punctures; it may have been pricked, or a nail driven too near the 'white line' when shod ('bind'). Check that the shoe is properly in position and firm, with no risen clenches. Look for anything wedged between the frog and the bar. Look if the frog is healthy and uninjured and that the shoe fits correctly. Examine for a possible corn; whether the horn requires trimming, especially the toe; the bulbs of the heels for cuts or soreness; also for cracked heels, especially in wet, frosty weather.

Pastern

Heat or swelling, especially at the back. Navicular disease (navicular bone) can cause serious trouble, originating from concussion and causing both ulceration and permanent lameness. The frog shrinks and shrivels. Immediate treatment, blistering, and rest may cure it; otherwise it is incurable, steadily growing worse. If de-nerved it may go sound, but without any feeling in its foot. A de-nerved horse may be hacked quietly but is unsafe for hunting or jumping.

Fetlock

Heat or swelling caused by a sprained tendon, pulled muscle, or concussion when jumping – foreleg especially – which momentarily takes the whole weight.

Foreleg

Knee : heat or swelling. Bend leg at the knee, noticing any signs of pain, wincing, or trying to draw away the leg. Examine for cuts. *Shoulder :* test for pain and/or stiffness by stretching leg forwards and bending it backwards from the shoulder. Rheumatism or sprain are possible causes. Pain causes refusal to have the leg moved.

Hind legs

Hock : heat, swelling. Causes: thoropin, curb, bone or bog spavin; lying on insufficient bedding when stabled. Fit hock boots at night.

Thoropin : soft enlargement between the bone and point of hock. Swelling moves from the inside to the outside when pressed. Treatment: blistering (under vet's supervision); at least three months' rest at grass, wearing a rubber truss.

Curb : sprained ligaments behind hock joint. Heat; swelling. Cause: jumping a young horse before its bones, etc., are strong enough to stand the strain. Curable but may recur. Foment; cooling lotion; hose in warm weather; rest for 2–3 months or longer.

Spavin : bone spavin; cause: severe jar. Curable; may recur. Blister and rest (2–3 months).

Bog spavin : soft enlargement instead of a bony deposit. Usual cause: concussion. Bandage or use specially designed apparatus to give continuous pressure. Blistering is more effective; repeat a month later; then rest at least 2–3 months. Firing often succeeds when other treatments fail.

Hip

Stiff joint; rheumatism. Probably early morning lameness, working off with exercise. Hot fomentations; massage (liniment; embrocation; green oils). Lack of exercise causes stiffening so do not rest. Stable in winter, warmly rugged-up. Never leave damp; dry immediately. Knocking the hip may injure it. Hence the care needed when entering or leaving stable. Bathe broken skin (warm water); apply antiseptic ointment or Sulphanilamide powder.

Leg injuries

Faulty conformation, may cause injuries, cantering or galloping.

Brushing

Cause: toes turned out from fetlock, especially when tired. One leg strikes the opposite, walking or trotting. Protect with felt brushing boots, tied round fetlock; use feather-edged shoes, thicker and narrower on inside quarter and heel, well bevelled under the foot. Wash (dilute disinfectant); apply antiseptic ointment or Sulphanilamide.

Over-reach

Hind foot strikes foreleg. *High over-reach:* above fetlock. *Low over-reach:* side of coronet or back of heels. Cause: pulling up suddenly and unexpectedly. Bandage after bathing (dilute antiseptic) and apply antiseptic dressing. A fairly thick cotton-wool pad prevents undue pressure on the injured skin. Bandage fairly loosely to prevent swelling.

Tread

Self-inflicted or caused by another horse: generally on outside of coronet or above hind-leg fetlock. Severe tread can be serious, severing a tendon or severely lacerating and bruising the coronet. A downward-glancing blow usually produces a hanging piece of skin.

Treat for as over-reach. Replace torn skin in its proper position; if hanging by a very narrow shred, cut it off. Bandage upwards.

Speedy cut

Cause, bad conformation (crooked legs). A blow, inside the leg just below the knee, inflicted by the opposite inside toe when galloping. May cut skin; bruising is more serious. Leg swollen and very painful. Remedy: shoe opposite foot as closely as possible inside the toe and quarter, rasping away some of the wall if necessary. Round the lower edge of the web of shoe. Apply hot fomentation, followed by a cold bandage.

Saddle galls

Causes: too narrow arch of tree, pinching just below the withers; panel lining worn too thin or lumpy, rubbing the ribs; arch too wide, the saddle pressing too low, rubbing withers or spine as far back as the cantle; saddle too loosely girthed; rider sliding his seat and shifting his weight about; too much bareback riding.

Severity varies from slight scalding to a worn patch of hair or a raw place, which can be quite deep and discharge; troublesome, taking a long time to heal. Unbroken skin: rest until hair re-grows; harden back with saturated warm salt and water, methylated or surgical spirit, but never use on raw skin! Wash and dress broken skin thrice daily. Keep flies away. Cover with lint and gauze fastened with adhesive tape, cutting away surrounding hair. When healed, harden with salt-water solution or spirit. Newly grown hair may form a white patch.

Girth gall

Hard, dirty, folded-leather girths are the most likely cause; also bad grooming; a dirty, muddy girth; girth slipping because too loose, or cutting into skin because too tight.

Passing the girth through car or motor-cycle inner tubing to take the friction may prevent galling. Treat as for a saddle gall.

Chin-groove gall

Curb chain too tightly fastened.

If the arch of the tree is too wide use a wither pad under the saddle. It must lie smoothly, uncreased, pushed well up into the arch. For galls on spine or ribs use a felt numnah with a hole cut over the sore place to remove pressure. It must lie smoothly and unwrinkled.

Fractures

Bones inside the forearm, thigh, and cannon bone easily crack from a severe blow, being only covered with skin. Usually swells, subsiding after a few days if not seriously cracked. Severe bruising or a badly cracked bone causes a flat, hard, persistent swelling and acute lameness. Being covered by very tough skin, badly cracked bones may not sever completely, but reunite given rest.

Sling if possible to take weight off the leg. Broad webbing passes underneath in the girth groove; ropes fastened at both ends pass through a pulley over a strong beam, hoisting the horse until its feet just touch the floor without taking any weight. Lying down strains the fractured bones too much when rising.

Bandage if possible over a long splint with thick cotton-wool.

Bandaging too tightly aggravates any swelling. Keep slung until swelling subsides. Wash broken skin with antiseptic.

A horse, especially if young, need not be destroyed if it fractures a leg. Much depends where the fracture occurs. If the leg can be bandaged and the horse kept slung without any weight on its leg, it will probably completely recover. Rest is essential. Rebandage daily. If a sling is unavailable short-rack to prevent it lying down.

Ailments

Anthrax

Usually occurs in the tropics: rare in England. Attacks all animals, including man. Contagious: carried by food and water. Generally fatal, coming rapidly to a head.

Symptoms: high fever; loss of appetite; blood discharge from nose, sometimes from bowels. Swellings in various parts of body, rapidly increasing in size. Nose and eye membranes become purple and spotted. Throat may rapidly swell, feeling soft and doughy. Swollen belly and chest, with griping, colic-like pains. Blood-like or rusty discharge trickles from nostrils. Death within 24–48 hours. Cremate body or bury deep in quicklime. Fence off site of grave with a warning notice.

Isolate. Call vet immediately to inject other horses with anthrax serum. Notify authorities.

Burn all bedding. Burn or thoroughly disinfect everything else in contact with the patient. Fumigate, then limewash stable, leaving all doors and windows open.

Bots

Gad-fly larvae; a menace in summer, affecting horse's legs and underside with minute yellow eggs, either laid on it or picked up from the grass. Eggs enter stomach through licking its legs; larvae hatch, adhering to the stomach's lining, remaining all winter. The following summer they are expelled with the droppings. Pick off by hand, or scrape with a blunt knife. Call the vet if larvae are suspected in the stomach.

Cracked heels

Especially liable on wet, muddy ground, in frosty weather or cold winds, even without frost.

Symptoms: lameness: tenderness when picking-out feet.

Treatment: Vaseline, fat, goose-grease, or clean motor grease, applied thickly, well rubbed in daily in wet or frosty weather.

Colic

Can be dangerous, even fatal, causing a ruptured stomach or twisted gut.

Causes:

1 Watering after a heavy meal.

2 A large drink of cold water when hot and sweating, or when tired. A small, preferably tepid, drink is harmless if the horse walks about afterwards for about ten minutes. Not allowing a drink until it has cooled is safer.

3 Hard exercise too soon after a heavy meal. Also allow at least an hour between feeding and exercising.

4 A chill, through standing about when hot. Rub down thoroughly. Never turn out when hot or sweating.

5 Bolting food. Mix chaff with food, or put fairly large pebbles in the manger.

6 Over-eating: give small quantities frequently. A horse may over-eat when first turned out. Only turn out for about an hour at first, gradually increasing the time daily.

7 Poor-quality food: musty hay; oats; sour bran. Dirty trough.

8 Stable vices: crib-biting; wind-sucking.

Symptoms: *Spasmodic* – spasmodic pain; intervals of relief. Horse repeatedly looks round and snatches at its flanks; kicks at its belly; stamps; paws the ground; straddles as if trying to stale; crouches at the loins while walking. Violent if pain is severe; lies or throws itself down on the ground and rolls. Bright red eye-lining; dry mouth; rapid pulse; hurried, distressed breathing. Acute pain causes sweating in patches, or all over. Normal temperature.

Treatment: keep walking; must not lie down or roll, or it may twist its gut or rupture its stomach, already distended with gas.

Keep warm; give 3–4 oz whisky in tepid water. Give an enema; half a bucket of warm soapy water. Grease syringe nozzle well before inserting into rectum; afterwards hold down the tail so that liquid remains sufficiently long in bowel. Have a vet's colic drink in medicine cupboard for emergencies, containing nitric ether (stimulant) and tincture of opium (opiate). If a severe attack does not respond quickly call vet to give an injection.

Flatulent colic

Cause: fermented food; resulting gases distend the bowels. Inflated, unnaturally rounded belly. Continuous, not severe, pain. Horse not violent but rather drowsy; uneasy; fidgets and scrapes; wanders slowly round as if wanting to lie down but afraid to do so. Fast pulse; normal temperature. Usually very constipated.

Treatment: do not let horse lie down. Apply hot fomentations to belly. Work bowels; give a large enema every 30 minutes. If no relief after two hours give a physic ball.

Other remedies: 2 teaspoonfuls ginger; whisky or brandy, 4 oz. in tepid water; 1–2 oz. turpentine in 1 pint oil, or 2 beaten eggs and 1 pint milk.

Call vet. if prolonged or severe. Give warm bran mashes after attack ends. Vet will advise about diet.

Colds

Highly infectious; isolate immediately. Keep stable rubbers, sponges, grooming kit separate. May lead to influenza or pneumonia. Stable if living out; keep warm but allow abundant fresh air; a warm, fuggy atmosphere breeds germs. Use rest bandages. Symptoms: discharging nostrils and eyes; rapid breathing; rapid pulse. Temperature may rise slightly. Listless; off its food; looks tucked up and thoroughly sorry for itself. Thirsty if feverish.

Treatment: sponge nostrils and eyes, using weak permanganate of potash. Burn swabs immediately. Keep warm: bowels open and regular; give warm bran mash. Lead horse for 15–20 minutes' gentle walking exercise. Do not take out in a cold wind; rub down thoroughly on returning and rug-up. Careful nursing essential. Do not work for 3–4 days after the cold has gone and normal appetite and spirits reappear. Inhale Friar's Balsam in boiling water; or Eucalyptus. Pour the boiling water on hay in a sack.

Coughs

Stabled horses seem more prone, chiefly in spring and autumn, it running through the whole stable.

Causes: irritation of lung, air tubes or larynx; broken wind, cough may accompany pneumonia and pleurisy; stomach cough.

Symptoms: difficult, painful swallowing, impossible when severe; food eaten returns through nostrils. Short, painful cough if throat lining is inflamed, hot and dry; much phlegm causes a more prolonged, hoarse cough. Broken wind: easily recognizable, rather short, dry, deep-sounding cough.

Treatment: contagious, keep food and water utensils, cloths and grooming kit separate. Avoid hard, dry food. Apply flannel soaked in boiling water, wrung out, to throat; cover with waterproof material to conserve heat; renew when cool. Loosen a hard, dry cough by steaming (Eucalyptus; Friar's Balsam): smear cough electuary on the tongue. Balls may be coughed back to stick in the nose; liquid medicines may choke. Rub throat with a liniment, warm camphorated oil, or something like Vick. Avoid dry, dusty food; indigestion can cause broken wind; hay and bran should be damped.

Glanders

Known to Hippocrates over 2000 years ago. Contagious to men and animals. Rare in England. Incurable. If suspected call vet immediately: victim must be destroyed. Notify authorities.

Symptoms: slight sticky discharge: usually only one nostril; hard lumps on jaw on same side as discharge. Small sores with same discharge, on nostrils and skin; sores do not heal. Called Fareg when these ulcers occur on legs; small, angry looking with ragged edges, on insides of legs; sometimes on face and neck.

Influenza

Contagious: can follow colds, affecting an entire stable.

Symptoms: very swollen eye; called Pink Eye because its lining becomes bright pink. Affected air passages and chest cause eye and nasal discharge; lung inflammation can follow. Appetite: lacking or capricious.

Forms:

1 Simple (catarrhal).

2 Pulmonary (thoracic).

3 Abdominal (enteric).

4 Rheumatic Usually follows catarrhal influenza: limbs may swell, with occasional diarrhoea.

Treatment: horse becomes very thin and weak. Try to make it eat; rebuild its strength. Nurse very carefully. Wear rugs and rest bandages, thickly padded (cotton wool) for warmth. Avoid draughts. Long convalescence to regain flesh and recover strength before working.

Poll evil

Abscess on poll.

Cause: a blow on head. Very shy about letting head and ears be touched. Behaviour becomes uncertain and abnormal.

Curable: consult vet regarding treatment.

Sore eyes

Running eyes; discharge from sore eyes. Usually in summer, caused by flies. Stable by day, grazing at night, or provide a shelter and escape from flies during heat of the day. And wear an eyeshade; leave forelock long for eye protection.

Treatment: bathe with weak, tepid boracic or potassium permanganate; use separate cotton-wool pad for each eye. After bathing, at least twice daily, apply Golden eye ointment.

Eczema

Causes: dirt; neglect: incorrect diet, especially insufficient green food in winter. Groom regularly.

Types:

1 *Greasy heels :* attacks heels and skin behind fetlocks, especially

a heavy horse's. Skin looks wet, becoming inflamed: may thicken considerably.

Treatment: wash and dry; apply an astringent lotion. Frequently difficult to cure if severe. Consult a vet.

2 *Mallenders:* attacks skin; foreleg behind knee joint. *Sallenders:* attacks in front hock.

Glands oiling the skin, keeping it soft where bending knee or hock might cause friction, become inflamed through irritation by mud or dust.

Treatment: wash; dry thoroughly. Apply antiseptic, astringent lotion; Vaseline, Zinc Ointment; Ayreton's Antiseptic Ointment.

3 *Mud Fever:* attacks skin: abdomen and hind legs. Cause: mud not thoroughly removed; not drying thoroughly when mud is washed off, i.e. carelessness and neglect. Dry, caked mud and discharge form a firm, scabby coating.

In winter never wash off mud; when dry, brush off thoroughly.

Treatment: as Greasy heels.

4 *Impetigo (pustular eczema):* highly contagious and infectious; isolate.

Treatment: give laxative or enema. Change diet; give abundant green meat and carrots. Wash thoroughly: carbolic soap, warm water. Poultice. Apply antiseptic ointment. Put $\frac{1}{2}$ oz. potassium nitrate and potassium bicarbonate in drinking water.

Laminitis

Fleshy leaves or growing part of horn covering coffin bone, underneath the wall of foot, becomes inflamed.

Causes: too much lush grazing, especially when first turned out. Ponies are especially susceptible. Sudden over-exertion; concussion; sudden overwork after resting, when overfed.

Symptoms: severe lameness, usually in both forefeet. Pony stands still, afraid to pick up a foot as pressure on the other greatly increases pain. Puts heel down first. Fetlock blood-vessels throb. Feverish; no appetite.

Treatment: food: bran mash; green food. Give a physic ball. Re-shoe: thick wide-seated bar shoes. Cold swabs on hooves or stand feet in water for about an hour, or in a loose-box with 3–4 inches of wet mud. A few minutes' exercise several times daily. Deep straw bedding at night to induce lying down comfortably, to rest feet. After recovery continue the broad-seated shoes for some time. Return gradually to work.

Fever in the feet can cause permanent lameness. Consult vet.

Naviculitis

Inflamed navicular bone and surrounding structure, usually in forefeet. Contracted heels; shrunken frog. Produces permanent lameness. Affected foot pointed, a little forward when resting; heel only just touches ground. In the first stages lameness not always persistent; wears off during exercise. Incurable if neglected, steadily growing worse until keeping the pony alive is cruel. Consult vet immediately suspected.

Rheumatism

Cause: extreme temperatures; a very cold night after a very hot day produces one form of muscular rheumatism; horse is stiff all over ('cold struck'). Early morning stiffness when first exercised. Treatment: warmth, especially at joints. Liniment, embrocation or green oils thoroughly rubbed into joints. Keep bowels open and soft. Strapping, brisk brushing and hand rubbing all help. Moderate exercise in warm sun.

Sunstroke

Horses are liable. Affects the atlas and spine. Never turn out in hot sun without shelter.
Treatment: a cool, dark place. Cold water on head and spine. Keep very quiet. Give a laxative after recovery. Diet: soft food. Rest for several days.

Horses wear sun-hats in Spain and Portugal.

Staggers

A horse falls suddenly; cannot rise again.
Causes: possible pressure by some part of tack or harness on the large neck blood-vessels, producing brain congestion; strenuous work in hot sun. Similar to sunstroke.
Treatment: as sunstroke.

Sand crack

Hoof-wall splits; inside quarter of forefeet; sometimes hind-foot toe; crack very deep, extending from coronet downwards, penetrating wall to the fleshy leaves beneath.

Painful; split closes on to the sensitive inside parts; may bleed. Acute lameness.

Treatment: blister: 1 in 8 red mercuric iodide; apply to the coronary band above the crack. Clip hair off coronet above crack; brand a horizontal line 1 inch long and $\frac{1}{4}$ inch deep through crack's upper end.

Rasp away surface where crack ends to relieve pressure.

Seedy toe

Inner and outer horn forming the foot wall separates at toe, forming a hollow filled with powdery, greasy substance.

Treatment: a competent blacksmith should file away the separated outer horn. Clean; apply Stockholm tar, blister coronet to accelerate horn growth; or use Cornucrescene.

Thrush

Cause: neglect, dirt, and wet. A foul-smelling discharge from the cleft of an inflamed frog. Cutting the frog may cause it.

Treatment: clean cleft thoroughly with strong disinfectant. Plug Stockholm tar or dry boric-powder dressing in with tow to stop discharge. A good dressing: 1 part alum; 1 part common salt (or zinc sulphate); 4 parts Stockholm tar.

Worms

Horse loses condition, grows thin, though appetite apparently increases. Hidebound (tight skin); ribs show. Thirsty, lifeless, starey coat. Serious if neglected; can cause death.

Worms in droppings if present.

1 *Round Worm:* white; stiff; approximate thickness of a pencil; very long.

Treatment: starve, keeping without water for 24 hours. Then drench: 2 tablespoons turpentine, 1 pint linseed oil. If severe call in vet to use a stomach pump.

H

2 *Red Worm:* the worst of all parasites attacking horses: bloodsuckers, eating into intestines. Neglect causes death. Reddish colour; approx. 2 inch long. Usually detected in droppings.

An infected horse may take 4–5 months to recover.

Treatment: Pheothiosone powder; in water as a drench, or mixed with food. Careful nursing; abundant best-quality food. Plough the paddock and thoroughly cleanse with quicklime. Leave ploughed during winter; resow next spring. On recovery have a worm-count to ensure complete freedom.

3 *Whip Worm:* very thin, approximately $1\frac{3}{4}$ inches long. Found in the rectum; larva of a fly which lays its eggs there. Irritation causes constant tail-rubbing.

Treatment: give an enema: a handful of salts in a gallon of tepid water. Do not put droppings on the manure heap.

Wind galls

Enlarged joint oil-glands at sides of and above fetlock, forming painless, soft, round, compressible swellings; may become inflamed if knocked. Cause: very strenuous work. Do not usually produce lameness.

Treatment: bandage pressure temporarily reduces them, preventing them getting worse. Blistering the fetlock and 2–3 weeks' rest causes complete disappearance. Never prick or open them.

Fomenting: soak a cloth in almost boiling water; wring nearly dry and apply to affected part. Conserve heat with a thick, dry covering. Renew every 20–30 minutes.

Tubbing: alternative to poulticing. Use a tall wooden bucket, add antiseptic to water. Preferable to poulticing as heat can be regulated and maintained.

Hosing: short-rack in yard near tap. Do not use too much pressure, and direct accurately on to the injury.

Poulticing: 1 to draw matter from a suppurating wound; 2 softens part where applied; 3 relieves pain. Use bran, linseed meal, kaolin; bread poultice is messy and quickly turns sour. Keep wet.

Apply very hot: retain heat with a thick woollen-cloth covering. Remove bran or linseed poultices after 12 hours; they turn sour, and in an open wound breed bacteria.

When poulticing a leg (e.g. knee-joint) make a bag from a clean sack or old, clean, woollen stocking: fill with poultice, draw up the leg and tie. Cover with thick flannel to retain heat; bandage lightly.

Bibliography

Wide reading about a subject which interests one is always wise; this applies specially to riding and caring for horses. One book cannot possibly contain all the numerous ways of doing things, and the many things to know about looking after horses.

Although Horsemastership and Horsemanship (including Riding) are essentially practical subjects one can learn so much by reading as many different books as possible. The subject of dealing with horses is practically inexhaustible; therein lies its fascination. Riding alone has so many branches: Dressage, Hacking, *Haut école* (High School), Hunting, Show-Jumping, etc.; books exist on them all. To obtain a comprehensive list write to J. A. Allen and Co., 'The Horseman's Bookshop', 1 Lower Grosvenor Place, Buckingham Palace Road, London SW1, for their catalogue. This contains a list of over 600 books on every aspect of horsemanship.

Even secondhand books are expensive, but the County Library is usually most helpful and willing to procure any book without any charge. Books are borrowed usually for a fortnight and are renewable as often as required, provided nobody else wants them, thus giving ample time to study them thoroughly.

Periodicals

Horse and Hound (Michael Clayton – ed.) IPC Magazines Ltd, Kings Reach Tower, Stamford Street, London SE1.

Riding (Elwyn Hartley Edwards – ed.) IPC Magazines Ltd, Kings Reach Tower, Stamford Street, London SE1.

Light Horse and Pony Magazines (Michael Williams – ed.) D. J. Murphy (Publishers), 19 Charing Cross Road, London WC2.

Pacemaker and The Horseman (Michael Harris – ed.) Pacemaker Publications, 25 Kings Road, London SW3.

Stable Management, 1 Tahoma Lodge, Lubbock Road, Chislehurst, Kent.

Sporting Life, Mirror Group of Newspapers, Holborn Circus, London EC1.

Societies concerned with the horse

Ada Cole Memorial Stables, 2 Gleneagle Road, London SW16.

Association of British Riding Schools: The Secretary, Chesham House, 56 Green End Road, Sawtry, Huntingdon.

British Equine Veterinary Association: P. S. Hastie, MRCVS, Overton, Maids Moreton, Buckingham.

British Field Sports Society: 26 Caxton Street, London SW1H 0RG.

British Horse Society, The National Equestrian Centre, Kenilworth, Warwickshire.

British Show Jumping Association: Lt-Cdr W. B. Jefferis, RN (Retd), The National Equestrian Centre, Kenilworth, Warwickshire. Tel. Coventry 20783/4.

British Show Pony Society: Capt. R. Grellis, Smale Farm, Wisborough Green, Sussex.

British Veterinary Association: 7 Mansfield Street, Portland Place, London W1.

Donkey Sanctuary, V. Philpin, Esq., Springfield, Posters Lane, Woodley, Berkshire.

Fédération Équestre Internationale: Chevalier H. de Menten de Horne, Avenue Hamoir 38, Brussels 18, Belgium.

Home of Rest for Horses, Speen Farm, Speen, Aylesbury, Bucks.

Hunters Improvement Society: G. W. Evans, National Westminster Bank Chambers, 8 Market Square, Westerham, Kent. Tel. Westerham 63867.

International League for the Protection of Horses, 67A, Camden High Street, London NW1.

International Pony Breeders' Association: Prof. Mitchell, Royal Dick Veterinary College, Edinburgh.

National Foaling Bank, Meretown Stud, Newport, Salop.

National Master Farriers' and Blacksmiths' Association: 674 Lofthouse Gate, Wakefield, West Yorks.

People's Dispensary for Sick Animals, PDSA House, 21–37 South Street, Dorking, Surrey.

Ponies of Britain Club: Brookside Farm, Ascot, Berks.

Riding for the Disabled Association: Miss C. M. L. Haynes, Avenue R, National Agricultural Centre, Kenilworth, Warwicks. Tel. Coventry 56107.

Royal College of Veterinary Surgeons: 32 Belgrave Square, London SW1.

Royal Society for the Prevention of Cruelty to Animals, Horsham, Surrey.

The Society of Master Saddlers: 9 St Thomas Street, London SE1.

Thoroughbred Breeders' Association: S. G. Sheppard, 42 Portman Square, London W1. Tel. 01–487 4586.

Weatherby & Sons, 41 Portman Square, London W1. Tel. 01–486 4921.

Worshipful Company of Farriers: F. E. Birch, Esq., 3 Hamilton Road, Cockfosters, Barnet, Herts., EH4 9EU.

Worshipful Company of Loriners: 3 St Helens Place, London EC3.

Worshipful Company of Saddlers: Gutter Lane, London EC4.

Appendix

Everyday terms used by horsemen

Aged (pronounced as one syllable): over 8 years old.

Aids : all ways by which a rider 'talks' to his horse, making it understand his wishes.

Aids artificial : martingale, reins, spurs, whip.

Aids natural : hands, legs, voice, seat/body.

Amble : a pace, at which the legs move laterally; near-fore and hind legs together, followed by off-fore and hind legs. A favourite pace for travellers, especially ladies, in the Middle Ages. Mentioned by Chaucer (one of the *Canterbury Tales*). Cultivated today in some types of American horses; a most comfortable gait, especially for long distances.

Balance : a properly schooled and trained horse is balanced, carrying its own and its rider's weight so that it uses its limbs and moves to the best advantage in all circumstances.

Ball : medicine in solid form; larger than a pill.

Bar : soft gum between incisor and molar teeth, *q.v.* Part of hoof, either side of frog, turning in at the heel.

Behind the bit : sluggish or lazy horses do not go up to their bridles but hang back. This habit (being behind the bit) is acquired through slovenly riding or being ridden by beginners.

Belly : abdomen: underpart beneath ribs.

Bishoping : a fradulent trick. Old horse-copers made a horse look younger than its age by filing down and shortening the front (incisor) teeth.

Bits : for controlling a horse; reins fasten to the cheek-rings of the bit(s). Three main types: Snaffle, Curb (Double Bridle), Pelham; with many varieties of each.

Curbs : Ward Union, Weymouth, Banbury, Chifney, 9th Lancer, etc.

Pelhams : Hanoverian, Mullen mouth (half-moon), etc.

Different types of bit vary in severity according to whether they are straight or jointed, twisted, rough or smooth, the height of the port, how they fit and their action on the mouth, and so on.

Snaffles : vulcanite, straight, jointed plain, jointed egg-butt, twisted, gag (very severe), etc.

Blaze : A broad, white marking down the face.

Body brush : has soft bristles to penetrate hair down to the skin; removes scurf. Useless for removing mud from the winter coat when living out.

Boring : horse leans the weight of its head and neck on the bit, lying heavily on its rider's hands. Usually occurs with a short, thick-necked horse, and/or a hard mouth; also due to fatigue. A horse that bores is difficult to control and most uncomfortable to ride.

Breast plate : prevents saddle slipping backwards: a neck strap fastened to front 'D's of saddle, and to the girth. Used for high withers and a dipped back.

Bridge : reins held in both hands in a special way, used by jockeys. Bridge prevents the hand slipping forward if the horse puts its head down. Especially useful galloping or jumping.

Bridle : straps attached to bit(s).

Bridoon : snaffle bit and reins of a double bridle. Reins are called Bridoon reins.

Broken wind : a lung affection, generally caused by over-galloping or hard exercise too soon after a long drink or a heavy meal. Broken-winded horses usually make a whistling, or in a bad case, roaring noise when exerted; exhaling is difficult.

Browband : part of bridle and head-collar.

Brushing : striking the inside of leg with the opposite toe. Bad conformation: foot turns outwards from the fetlock which bends inwards and backward. Other causes besides bad conformation: fatigue, poor condition, bad shoeing; if shoe is projecting; nails not properly clenched. Persistent brushing causes permanent enlargement on inside of fetlock joint.

Brushing (Yorkshire) boot : special boot to prevent brushing. Cut a piece of Kersey horse clothing about 12 inches long by 9 inches wide. Place round fetlock with the join in front, and tie round the centre with tape. Turn down the top, forming a double fold round fetlock.

Bull necked : short, thick-set neck.

Burnisher : formerly used for cleaning steel bits, stirrup-irons, curb chains, etc. Never use on nickel-plated or stainless steel. Made of a fine meshed square of chain sewn on to chamois leather.

Calf-kneed : bad conformation. Also called 'back at the knees' and 'stag knees'.

Calkin : projection on a shoe, formed by turning down at right angles to the outer end of one or both heels. Raises the heels; also gives extra grip when the horse's weight forces it into the ground.

Cannon : the leg from knee to fetlock. The bone is called the cannon bone.

Canter : a pace in 3-time.

Cantering disunited ('Butcher Boy canter'): when leading hind leg is on the opposite side to the leading foreleg.

Cantering false : also galloping false: leading with the wrong leg when turning or circling, e.g. circling right with the near (left) fore and hind legs leading, or left off (right) fore and hind legs leading. Dangerous as a horse may cross its legs and fall.

Cantle : back part of saddle, curving upwards.

Cast : a horse cannot rise again after getting down.

Cat-ham : hock is abnormally far back; thighs have a pronounced backward slope.

Cat-jump : jumping from too close underneath, almost standing still, and landing on all fours together.

Cavaletto : wooden cross-pieces so joined that a pole can be laid across at different heights by turning them over.

Cavesson : padded head-collar and noseband used for schooling young horses on the lunge rein.

Cheek-piece : strap on the bridle connecting the headband (crown piece or poll strap), with the strap which fastens the cheek-ring of the bit.

Cheek-ring : ring at each side of a snaffle bit.

Chestnut : (a) colour, varying from bright golden, through liver colour to a light, washy shade, which should be avoided. Varieties: Bright Chestnut, Golden Chestnut, Liver Chestnut, etc. Usually supposed to have a fiery temperament.

(b) a horny projection on the inside, just above the knee of foreleg, and just below hock of hind leg. May be the last vestiges of a toe in prehistoric times when the horse's ancestors had four toes.

Clench: the ends of nails fastening the shoe are twisted off by the farrier with the hammer claw, turned down and hammered into the wall of the foot.

Cob: a thick-set, stoutly built type of horse, capable of carrying considerable weight. Usually up to about 15 hh. A useful ride-or-drive type; generally hogged and docked before docking became illegal in Britain.

Cock-throttled: a thin, scrawny, chicken-like neck.

Coffin head: a large, heavy head in proportion to the horse's body. Often rather slow and stupid.

Collection: completely controlled and ridden up to its bit at any pace.

Colours: Bay; Bright Bay; Black; Brown; Chestnut; Bright Chestnut; Liver Chestnut, etc. *Cream or Dun:* white mane, tail, and skin. *Dun:* sandy coloured, black points; can be almost yellow; usually has a dorsal stripe. *Blue Dun:* coat a rather washy black all over, giving a bluish colour; black mane, tail, and skin. *Yellow Dun:* almost yellow; black points. *Grey:* dappled grey: round, dappled markings, usually on quarters and shoulder. *Fleabitten Grey:* dark grey, black hairs predominating. *Light Grey:* white hairs predominate over black. *Roan: Red (Sorrel)* or *Strawberry*; red, yellow, and white hairs intermingled. *Blue Roan:* Black, white, and yellow hairs intermingled. *Chestnut Roan:* chestnut, white, and yellow hairs intermingled; rather rare. *White:* usually an old grey horse. Greys and roans tend to become lighter with age. *Albino:* pinkish eye; pinkish, unpigmented skin; rare. *Piebald:* large, irregular-shaped black and white markings. *Skewbald:* large, irregular, brown and white markings. *Odd Coloured:* indefinite or peculiarly marked; any colour; horse or pony. *Palomino* (Golden Horse): golden, becoming more pronounced when warm after exercise: chalk white mane and tail. Named after Juan de Palomino: Cortez owned some in Mexico, giving Palomino one (1519). Were also called 'Ysabellas', after the famous Spanish Queen Ysabella who sponsored Columbus. *Appaloosa* (Spotted Horse): a definite breed, descended from and named after horses bred by Nez Perce Indians, Palouse country in Oregon, USA. Body covered with many varying sized chocolate spots. British Spotted Horse Society recognizes three different markings: *Leopard*: darker spots widely distributed over lighter background. *Blanket*: rump only spotted on white or light coloured background. *Snowflake*: white spots on darker background. *Austrian Pinzgauer*: well-known spotted draught-horse. *Danish Knabstrup*: originally had some Palomino blood. *Libyan Leopard Horse*: probably from Barbary. Also, *Bladgen* (Wales). *Colorado Ranger*. Spotted horses exist in Arabia, North and South Africa, Tibet. Some breeds favour certain colours more than others. Washy coloured horses or ponies of any breed are unpopular, though the old saying is, 'A good horse is never a bad colour.' Character and temperament are supposedly associated with colours: e.g. a bay with black points: usually considered hardy and placid; chestnut, fiery; grey, apt to be temperamental and rather a handful; black, used to be thought bad tempered, etc.

Colt : young male horse, aged 6 months to 3 years.

Condition : a horse's general physical fitness and well-being; state of muscles and skin. Just up from grass: in soft condition. Unwell: in poor condition. Racing and/or hunting fit: in hard condition. Improved general physique: gaining condition. When deteriorating: losing condition.

Conformation : a horse's shape and appearance. Good conformation: well shaped. Bad conformation: badly shaped.

Coronet (coronary band): junction of foot and leg. Living tissue from which the hoof (wall of foot) grows downwards.

Cow hocked : bad conformation. Crooked hind legs; hocks nearer together than feet.

Cradle : strapped round the neck to prevent horse putting its head down and biting a bandage, or licking a sore place. Separate wooden pieces fastened together top and bottom with thongs; long enough to encircle neck from just behind the poll nearly to the withers. A kind of straitjacket preventing horse's head or neck bending.

Crest : the neck's curve between poll and withers. A stallion by sex and nature has a pronounced crest. A horse gelded (neutered) too young does not develop a crest; this only develops at sexual maturity. Geldings are apt to lose their crest.

Croup : the broad, top part of hindquarters behind the back, above hips.

Crown piece : headband of bridle.

Crupper : a strap fastened to 'D's below the cantle, passing round hindquarters underneath the tail. Used with low withers and upright shoulder, to prevent saddle slipping too far forward.

Curb : second bit of a double bridle. Its action raises the horse's head, drawing it inwards. Also, an affection of the leg just inside the hock.

Curb chain : flat chain used on curb bit. Lies in chin-groove, fastening together the lower ends of the curb's two side-pieces.

Curry comb : used to remove dirt and hairs from brushes when grooming. Two kinds: (a) Metal, with parallel, serrated edges. Civilian pattern: wooden handle. Army type: web strap across back, enabling the groom to lean the back of his hand against the horse. Never use it on a horse. (b) Vulcanized rubber with a web strap. Used on the horse; invaluable, especially when moulting, for removing loose hairs; also effectively removes mud, sweat, dirt, scurf.

Daisy-cutter : a long, low action. When galloping, feet are close to the ground just brushing the grass.

Dandy brush : has stiff bristles; removes dried mud. Do not use for brushing out mane and tail as it pulls the hair.

Diagonal aid : leading with inside rein on the side to which one is turning, supported by outside, opposite rein and leg, with body weight shifted slightly back and inwards.

Dipped back : an exaggerated slope of withers into the back. Bad conformation; also with old age.

Dish-faced : facial contour is slightly concave. Found in Arabs and some native ponies.

Dishing : faulty action. Lower part of foreleg below knee is thrown outward when moving forward.

Dock : cutting the tail short through the bone. A cruel practice depriving a horse of its natural protection against flies, besides the pain of the actual operation; also depriving a horse of one of its greatest natural beauties. Now illegal in Great Britain, but still allowed in Eire. Before becoming illegal, cobs and hackneys were usually docked.

Doer : a horse's appetite and the effect on its condition. *Good Doer*: a hearty eater which gains condition. *Bad Doer*: a poor or finicky eater, which does not gain condition.

Donkey mark : the dark stripe running along a donkey's back. Found on mules, some breeds of ponies, and a few horses.

Dorsal stripe (or list): the stripe running along a Dun horse's back.

Drench : liquid medicine.

Dressage : the art of training a horse to absolute obedience to all aids and performance of certain specialized movements.

Dumb jockey : reins leading from bit to the saddle 'D's, or to a saddle-pad. Used when schooling on the lungeing-rein to accustom a young horse's mouth to the feel and pressure of reins.

Dumping : a serious shoeing fault. Rasping the hoof wall to make the toe look shorter and the foot smaller.

Eel mark (stripe): black mark along the back; found on Highland ponies.

Entire : stallion which has not been neutered.

Ergot : a small bony protuberance just above all four heels.

Ewe-neck : bad conformation: concave instead of convex at the crest, between the poll and withers.

Feather : long, silky hair on the fetlocks of some breeds (horse and pony); e.g. Shire and Clydesdale horses, Fell and Dale ponies, etc.

Feather-edged shoe : a special type to prevent brushing, with its inner edge narrowed from toe to heel; it also slopes inwards under the heel.

Fetlock : the joint between the cannon (shannon: hind legs) and pastern.

Fiddle-head : a large, ungainly, ugly-shaped head.

Fillet springs : fastenings of a New Zealand rug, passing between the hind legs. Also so-called and used on hindcorners of rugs and sheets, passing under tail. Used in racing since 17th century.

Filly : young female, aged from 6 months to 2 years.

Firing : strengthening tendons by burning. Pin-firing: done with a red-hot electric needle or acid firing.

Flap : thin, leather side-pieces covering the saddle panels, protecting the rider's legs.

Flexion : bit's action on a horse's mouth through the reins. There are direct and lateral flexions.

Foal : a new-born horse, either sex, up to 6 months old.

Forehand : all the horse's parts before the saddle.

Forelock : hair hanging down the forehead between the ears.

Forging : the noise a trotting horse makes by striking the hind shoe against the fore. Also called 'clicking'.

Frog : the leathery, triangular formation in the sole of the hoof. Takes the weight; acts as a shock-absorber and anti-skid device. Is elastic, expanding under pressure.

Full mouth : full set of permanent teeth.

Gag snaffle : the most severe type of snaffle bit.

Galvayne's groove : a dark, brown-coloured mark appearing on the corner incisor teeth at 10 years. See page 25.

Gelding : a male horse, neutered by removing its reproductive organs.

Girth : fastens the saddle on securely. Types: leather, web, string, nylon.

Girth groove : the slight groove between elbow and belly, underneath where the girth fits.

Goose rumped : the tail is set on very low down, with hindquarters sloping down steeply from croup to dock.

Greyhound gutted : running up light like a greyhound, with insufficient heart and lung room.

Gullet : (a) reaches from throat to stomach, on the left side, lower part of the neck. As it enters the chest it passes through the first two ribs between the lungs, over the heart, through the diaphragm (midriff), ending at the stomach. Tightly closed except when forced open by food passing down; (b) the groove running down the centre ‚underneath the saddle, to prevent it pressing on the spine.

Gummy legs : owing to general fullness or sprain of some particular part, legs look abnormally rounded.

Hack : a horse for ordinary general-purpose riding, in contrast with one used for some special purpose.

Hacking : riding for sheer pleasure of riding and being on a horse, contrasted with specialized riding.

Hackney : most showy of all harness horses; characteristic high action, well-arched neck, great trotting speed. For showing the natural action is developed giving an extravagant, exaggerated action.

(a) *Hackney horse :* height 15–15·2 hh., sometimes 16 hh. All colours; grey is rare. Hackneys have existed for over 200 years, being also ridden in the eighteenth century. The Hackney Stud Book started about sixty years ago, when the present type was first recognized. Their ancestors were probably the old trotting mares mated with Arabs.

(b) *Hackney pony :* not exceeding 14·2 hh. Has the same showy action. Commonest colours: bay, brown, chestnut. Native ponies were used in its development, Welsh mares predominating.

Hamstring : a strong tendon running down the back of hind leg to the point of the hock. In early cavalry warfare, fighters, especially infantrymen, tried to disable enemy horses by cutting their hamstrings called houghing.

Hand : unit of measurement for horses. 1 hand = 4 inches. Measured from the highest point of the withers to the ground.

Hand canter : a moderately slow, collected canter.

Hand gallop : a moderately slow, collected gallop, with the horse kept well in hand.

Haunches : the haunch bone forms the marked prominence above each hip. Should be well covered and rounded.

Haut école : the highest form of horsemanship, demanding perfect seat, hands, and control, with the horse's absolute obedience. *Dressage* is an off-shoot of *Haut école*. It is both a science and an art. It originated in Europe, with the Spanish Riding School now the great centre. The Viennese Spanish Riding School was the greatest exponent before World War II. The *Passage* and *Piaffe* are two examples of *Haut école* movements.

Head-collar (head stall) : for catching and leading in hand and for securing in the stable.

Herring-gutted: running up light like a greyhound, lacking heart and lung room. Synonymous with greyhound-gutted, *q.v.*

Hidebound: the skin of a sick horse feels tight.

High-blowing: a rattling noise or snort, made by an excited horse blowing through its nostrils with each breath. Is not a sign of broken wind.

High-tailing: a sign of high spirits. A horse trots or gallops round the field with springy steps, tail held high in the air.

Hindquarters: the part behind the saddle.

Hobdayed: an operation on the larynx as a cure for 'roaring'. Named after Professor Sir Frederick Hobday, CMG, FRCVS, Principal and Dean of the Royal Veterinary College, London, who popularized it.

Hock: the hind leg's hock joint corresponds to the human ankle.

Hogged: a mane which has been clipped short. Once hogged a mane frequently does not regrow satisfactorily and may take two years. Keep clipped about once a month. Do not hog manes of native breeds.

Hoof: the hard, horny part of a horse's foot.

Hoof-pick: for picking dirt, stones, etc., from a horse's hoof. It should be blunt-pointed. As it invariably gets lost if dropped in the straw, tying a cotton reel to its handle makes it more easily found.

Horse: a general term. Strictly speaking a male, contrasted with a mare (female). 'Horse' should only be used in that sense.

Horse length: equals 8 feet: the length of ground over which a horse stands.

Hound jog: a slow trot named from the pace used when accompanying hounds at exercise.

Hunter: any horse used for hunting. No special breed or type: usually a Thoroughbred; may have some Arab blood. Usually about 16 hh., though children's ponies, 13·2 hh. or less, can be excellent hunters.

Independent seat: a firm, safe seat due to grip and balance: the rider's hands do not pull the horse's mouth at any speed, or when jumping. Impossible without a firm independent seat.

Indirect rein: direct rein: a direct flexion with hand and leg acting together on same side. Indirect rein (neck-reining): the hand opposite the side one wants to turn is brought over across, pressing against the neck, without any flexion (without tightening) with the direct rein: e.g. a properly schooled horse turns left (to the near side), if one brings the off rein across its neck to the near side, pressing against it. Always use indirect reining when riding with reins in one hand, especially playing polo. Direct reining applies tension with the rein on the side one turns.

Jibbing : suddenly halting and refusing to move. See pages 201.

Jodhpurs : The popular undress for riding, instead of breeches and boots, introduced by the Jodhpur Lancers (India), *circa* 1880. Adopted by British officers for hacking: women in India always rode side-saddle until 1914. About 1920 women started wearing jodhpurs in India; they then became popular in England. Now becoming popular with men for informal hacking. Can be worn with stout walking shoes or special jodhpur boots. They should fit the calf of the leg tightly; the 'skirt' should not be too full. Elastic or zip-fastener ends makes putting on or removing them easier. Have 'cross', not side pockets as in ordinary slacks. Buckskin strappings on inner side of knee prevent chafing: self strappings on cheap jodhpurs are less good.

Lane : a long, narrow, fenced-in enclosure for teaching a horse and rider to jump. Used pre-1914 by the Indian cavalry and later at Weedon. The Indian Lane was fenced in by high mud walls, with identical jumps. Most horses thoroughly enjoy this free jumping. It teaches them to jump, gives confidence, and supples them. A horse made to dislike jumping by a bad rider can thus be re-schooled. Can also be ridden down, forming a progressive system of schooling horse and rider.

Leading-rein : (a) for schooling, teaching a young horse to lead in hand; (b) leading very young children, or beginners, who cannot be allowed to ride alone; (c) leading another horse when mounted. When leading a child, fasten the leading-rein to a cavesson noseband, like a lungeing rein, not to be the cheek-ring of the bit. When leading in hand, fasten leading-rein to 'D' on the near side of head-collar. When mounted, leading a ridden or unridden horse, always have it on the inside; have the leading-rein on its off side, fastened to a cavesson noseband, not to the bridle cheek-ring. The latter pulls the led horse's mouth, and can cause a nasty accident if it shies or plays up and the bit is dragged sideways through its mouth.

Lip strap : used with curb chain of double bridle.

Long reins : for schooling young horses. The trainer walks behind as if driving. German and Spanish schools favour this method in early training for *Haut école*.

Lungeing rein : a long rein fastened to a cavesson lungeing bridle, for schooling and exercising at all paces. The trainer stands in the centre holding a long-thonged lungeing whip. The horse circles one way and then the other. Never continually lunge in the same direction as it makes it stiff on one side. The aim is to teach it to move freely, use itself correctly at all paces, and to supple it. It is an essential initial stage in schooling a young horse. Also for remaking a horse with a mouth spoilt by bad riding. See also pages 149–55.

Manège : a riding school. Usually fenced in, of correct dimensions for teaching various branches of equitation; e.g. dressage, jumping, etc.

Mare: adult female horse, from 3 years old.

Mark of mouth : the tables (wearing surface) of permanent incisor teeth have a black mark. Food discoloration during mastication causes the blackness.

Markings : fully described on pages 29–31.

Martingales : types are fully described on pages 107–8.

Molar teeth : back teeth which masticate food.

Mouldy, musty hay : hay stacked while damp or subsequently wetted may become musty or even mouldy.

Mouthing : teaching a colt to accept the bit; there are special vulcanite mouthing and snaffle bits, with 'keys' attached.

Mowburnt hay : fermentation has overheated it in the stack, either slightly or severely.

Nagging : training (schooling) for hunting or hacking. Teaching behaviour with hounds and manners in and out of stable.

Nagsmen : one skilled in schooling young horses and in retraining bad-tempered or vicious ones.

Navicular bone : small boat-shaped or shuttle bone lying across the back of the central part of coffin bone, lying against the latter's narrow smooth surface.

Navicular disease : causes chronic lameness, nearly always in fore-feet, through an inflamed navicular bone and its surrounding structures.

Near side : left side. Horses are generally handled from near side.

Neck strap : give confidence to nervous or novice riders, providing something to hold should they lose grip or balance so that they do not hurt the horse's mouth by pulling the reins; also for teaching jumping for same reasons.

New Zealand rug : a specially designed waterproof rug for trace-clipped horses turned out in winter. Waterproof and windproof.

Niggle : a tiresome habit; walking with a short-stepping action; uncomfortable and tiring to ride. Sometimes accompanied by walking diagonally, crab-wise.

Nosebag : a canvas food bag fastened on to noseband, allowing a horse to eat while out. Generally used for harness horses (cart-horses; van-horses) or others out for long periods so that normal feeding times are impossible; cab-horses always had nosebags. usually given when stationary, and taken off before moving on again. Not used for riding horses which can generally graze when standing still, and are not all the time on roads.

Numnah : a saddle-shaped pad, made of felt or sheepskin, with wool outermost. Used under a saddle; prevents pressure or friction causing a scald or gall. Foam rubber numnahs now obtainable. Useful for jumping to prevent saddle pressure as the horse's back bends. A child's felt saddle is also called a numnah.

Off-side : the right-hand side.

Over bent : head is too bent at its poll; moves in an exaggeratedly collected way, often through too tight a curb. It was once fashionable for carriage horses to be curbed up too tightly, thus being deliberately over bent, with necks arched and heads pulled right into their chests. Horses suffered agonies, being unable to stretch their necks, especially pulling against the collar when going uphill. Fortunately this cruel practice no longer exists.

Over-reach : striking the inside of the foreleg heel with the inner rim of the hind-shoe toe. May cause a severe bruise or cut. A horse liable to over-reach should wear an indiarubber over-reach boot round the pastern.

Oyster feet : feet marked by ridges or rings of horn caused by unequal growth.

Passage : advanced dressage or *Haut école* (high school) movements. Lateral movement on two tracks, with horse moving diagonally, its neck and body parallel with the object it is moving towards or away from.

Pastern : the joint between the fetlock and coronet.

Pelham : a bit attempting to combine the functions of a double bridle with curb and a snaffle, in one bit. Has two reins like a double bridle. Some horses go better in a Pelham than in any other bit. Can be used with 'D's' and only one rein.

Pelhams : Hanoverian; Mullen (half-moon) etc.

Piaffe : another advanced dressage or *Haut école* movement.

Pirouette : advanced dressage or *Haut école* movement. The horse turns on its haunches with front legs in the air.

Plaiting : crossing, or appearing to cross, one front leg over the other; due to faulty conformation.

Plate : slang for saddle, used by horsemen. 'Keep the joint in the plate' is often said to beginners, meaning keep their seat on the saddle. Also slang for shoes, e.g. racing plates.

Point pocket : the points of the saddle-tree fit into pockets in front of the saddle, beneath the flaps.

Pointing : resting one forefoot in advance of the other.

Pommel : front arch of saddle.

Port : curved part of mouth piece of a bit. A bit's severity partly depends upon the height of the port which presses against the roof of the mouth.

Prick : result of bad shoeing. The blacksmith drives a nail into the growing, sensitive part of the hoof wall, too near the 'white line'.

Pulling : a horse takes the bit between its teeth, pulling against its rider's hands.

Quartering : light grooming, removing night stains, dust, or mud to make a horse presentable before exercising. 'Knocking on' is another term in stable parlance. Compare with strapping, thorough grooming after exercise.

Quidding : food drops from the mouth after attempting to chew it.

May signify trouble with teeth, sore mouth or throat, or injury or obstruction in mouth or throat.

Quittor : a festulous sore in the coronet, often caused by a prick. Pus works its way upwards through the coronary band.

Racing plates : very light aluminium, fullered, concave shoes put on specially for a race and removed again afterwards.

Razor back : spinal vertebrae are very prominent. Most uncomfortable to ride barebacked. Cause: bad conformation, poor condition, and overwork.

Ring bone : bony enlargement of pastern anywhere between coronet and fetlock. Can occur on all four legs. Less severe on forelegs than hind legs. Hobbling can cause them through irritation from the rope. May produce severe, continuous lameness.

Roach back : upward, instead of slight downward, curve of back and loins.

Roller : a broad web girth passing round the horse's body; keeps rugs in position when stabled. It prevents a rugged horse becoming cast when rolling.

Roman nose : the horse's face viewed sideways is increasingly convex towards the nostrils.

Roughed off : gradually acclimatizing a stabled horse to changed conditions before turning out to grass. Put it out daily for a gradually increasing period. Remove the shoes, substituting grass tips if not going to be used. Acclimatize for about two to three weeks.

Saddle : used for riding for at least a thousand years. The date of their first use is unknown, but we know that the Greeks rode barebacked. Earlier civilizations (Assyrian, Babylonian, Egyptian) used harness horses for chariots in war and peace. The Romans rode extensively, especially their army, using saddles. King Henry V's saddle now lies in Westminster Abbey.

Since first used saddles have been built on the same principle. Saddle shapes vary according to their purpose: 1 *Military saddle.* 2 *Hunting saddle.* 3 *Jumping saddle.* 4 *Racing saddle* ('plate'). 5 *Dressage saddle.* 6 *American Western (cowboy) saddle :* like Colonial saddle, has an even higher pommel and cantle than the old military saddle, for which both American and Colonial types developed. The high pommel and cantle with very deep seat is because cowboys and Colonials ride with a much longer leather

than is customary for ordinary English civilian riding; theirs
more resembles the old army seat from which they undoubtedly,
developed. They do a sitting trot.

Sand crack: horn of the foot wall splits at the inside quarter (forefeet) and sometimes at the back (hind feet). Crack begins at the
coronet, splitting downwards and penetrating in depth through
the wall into the underneath fleshy leaves.

Seedy toe: the inner and outer layers of horn forming the foot wall
separate, usually at the toe, forming a hollow filled with powdery,
greasy substance.

Short-coupled: short-backed.

Sickle hocks: bad conformation. Hocks bent at too great an angle,
like a greyhound's. Hocks shaped like a sickle. A sign of weakness
as they can never be properly under a horse.

Side bones: cartilages at sides of foot become ossified. Commonest
among heavy horses. Does not incapacitate for slow work, but
makes fast work impossible. May cause lameness after heavy work.

Skep: a wicker basket for collecting droppings in the stable.

Snaffles: vulcanite, straight, jointed plain, jointed egg-butt,
twisted, gag (very severe), etc.

Sold with a warranty: when sold as good hunter at Tattersalls
horses 'must be sound in wind and eyes, quiet to ride, have been
hunted, and be capable of being hunted'. Good hacks must be
sound in wind, limb, and eyes and not lame. A vendor's written
warranty, when given, should cover everything which concerns
the buyer. Expressions like 'ridden by a girl', 'driven in harness',
are not a warranty and mean little. Nor is 'believed sound' a
warranty as to soundness, but only an expression of opinion.

Spavin (bog): the hock's joint oil-bag distends at the joint's inner,
upper part; seldom causes lameness except when worked with
heavy loads in hilly country. When lame, swelling is tense and
hot and sometimes tender.

Spavin (bone): the small inner and lower hock bones grow together
into a solid mass, causing enlargement. When the bones have
knitted firmly together, bone spavin does not incapacitate or
cause lameness.

Stag knees (back at the knees: calf knees): joints, viewed sideways,
appear concave, not convex, down the front of the knee.

Staggers : a general term: any condition suddenly making a horse fall and be incapable of rising. Usual causes, brain congestion. Sunstroke; effects of hot sun and work. Horses are very prone to sunstroke; the vulnerable spot is on the neck, just behind the poll. Symptoms: reeling gait, generally falling, with hindquarters often quite paralysed; some horses are quiet after falling, others very violent, needing holding down.

Star-gazer : head held awkwardly; horse 'pokes its nose' with face upturned. Ewe-necked horses generally star-gaze. Cannot bridle or flex properly.

Stifle joint : the large joint behind the lower part of flank.

Stifle slipped : stifle-cap becomes dislocated. Causes: slipping; struggling to pull a heavy load; straining on heel-ropes. Most frequent when out of condition or very young horses. Leg is dragged behind, front of foot on the ground; cause – displaced bone. Sometimes young racehorses have it.

Stringhalt : one or both hind legs lifted abnormally high when moving. Incurable, becoming worse with age. An unsoundness which may cause lameness.

Surcingle : girth passing round horse's body. When saddled it passes over it, keeping it more firmly in position; prevents the saddle flaps moving. Also keeps rugs in position.

Tack : horsemen's general term for all saddlery, abbreviated from 'tackle' (harness).

Thorough pin : a soft enlargement between bones and point of hock. If pressed one side it bulges on the other as if a bolt or pin were going through.

Thrush : foul-smelling disease of the frog. Cause: dirt and neglect; feet not picked out regularly: want of pressure on the frog due to incorrect shoeing.

Tied in below the knee : measurement below knee, across cannon and tendons, is smaller than it is lower down. Should be greater.

Tobin's tube : a form of tube used as an air inlet for stable ventilation. Outer opening is low down outside stable wall. Tube passes through the wall upwards, with interior opening considerably higher than the exterior, considerably raising the air temperature before it reaches the horse.

Toe : front part of hoof.

Toe-clips: front shoes are usually fastened by toe-clips; hind shoes have clips each side.

Tread: a similar type of injury to an over-reach, but is inflicted by another horse. Generally occur on the outside of coronet, sometimes above the hind-leg fetlock. A severe tread can be a serious injury.

Tubed: an operation (tracheotomy) is performed on horses which breathe with difficulty. An artificial tube is inserted in its windpipe. A tubed horse is said to be hobdayed.

Tushes: small pointed teeth behind the corner incisors. Mares grow them occasionally and are said to become barren if they grow.

Twitch: a piece of cord fastened to a fairly short, stout piece of stick. It is place round a refractory horse's nostrils, being twisted tight to make it stand still. Its use is now illegal.

Unnerved: if a horse has navicular disease the foot nerves are sometimes removed to prevent pain. An unnerved horse is unsound and unsafe to ride.

Weak heels: often found in flat feet. The horn grows very slowly.

Weaving: a stable vice. Isolate the sufferer as others easily and quickly copy. Many wild animals, especially elephants, acquire this nervous habit, of continually rocking to and fro, sometimes lifting each forefoot in turn as their bodies sway to the opposite side. An incurable habit.

Wedge heels: calkins only fitted to a shoe's outer heel, the inner heel being narrowed and thickened, bringing it level. Toes of calkined shoes are similarly thickened for the same reason. A wedge heel lessens the chances of brushing.

Well ribbed up: a point of good conformation. A horse is well hooped, having well-rounded ribs with very little space between its last rib and hip.

Whistler: a slight noise made when breathing quickly during or after exercise, e.g. galloping. Cause: an infection of the larynx. When more pronounced it is called 'roaring'.

White line: where the hard outside horn of the wall joins the inner fleshy leaves (sensitive growing part) of hoof, is marked by a distinct white line; becomes very prominent after soaking the foot in water.

Wind galls: the joint oil-bags above and at the sides of fetlocks enlarge, appearing as small, soft, round painless swellings; easily compressed with a finger. Most hard-worked horses have them.

Windpipe : extends from larynx to lungs, along the lower edge of the neck. Can easily be felt as far down as the entrance to the chest.

Wind-sucking : a stable vice, *q.v.* Wind-sucking and crib-biting both cause colic and indigestion. A crib-biter wears away its upper and lower front teeth, sometimes to gum-level. Horses with these vices, when sold, must be so described.

Wings : barriers on either side of show-jumps to prevent a horse running out. Often made of hurdles interlaced with furze or wattles.

Wisp : for grooming. Hay or straw twisted into a rope, about 2 feet long. Is hit smartly in the direction of the hairs. A form of massage, stimulating the skin; helps circulation.

Withers : horses are always measured in hands from the highest part of the withers situated just below the end of the neck.

Wolf teeth : tiny rudimentary teeth sometimes growing between the first incisors.

Worms : infest the bowels, causing loss of condition. A horse can be very ill and even die.

Yawing : when a horse reaches outwards and downwards with its head. Use a cavesson noseband when a horse yaws and bores at its bridle. Alternatively, try a figure of 8 (Grackle) or a dropped noseband.

Yearling : colt or filly aged one year. A Thoroughbred's birthday is counted from 1 January. Other breeds and types from 1 April.

Yew : deadly poison to horses.

Yorkshire boot : fitting round fetlock to prevent brushing. An exercise bandage can be used.

Zebra markings : stripes on neck, limbs, withers, and/or quarters. Common on mules and donkeys; uncommon on horses.

Index